MW01289871

PRAISE FOR
THE PROTECTED

"The world can be a dangerous place. Whether you are a senior government official, business leader or celebrity, you need highly trained people to watch your back. When I was Director of Central Intelligence, I relied on Mike and his colleagues to keep me and my family safe around the world. In *The Protected*, Mike provides invaluable insights and intelligent perspectives into the world of personal protection."

~ **George Tenet**
Former Director, Central Intelligence Agency

"Mike has effectively framed the many complexities that are essential for any international close protection professional to know and for those needing protection to consider. Enlightening yet straightforward and entertaining, Mike's manner and style are as unique as his insights and experiences – from his days in the Air Force Security Forces to the CIA and beyond."

~ **Brigadier General Richard A. Coleman (Ret.)**
Former Director, U.S. Air Force Security Forces

"*The Protected* clearly illustrates both the rewards and risks that come with our growing reliance on technology to aid in protection. Mike's detailed and insightful look at cybersecurity makes this a must-read for those in the world of executive protection."

~ **Marie O'Neill Sciarrone**
Former Special Assistant to the President for Homeland Security;
Former Senior Director for Cybersecurity and Information Sharing Policy

"A thought-provoking look into the world of protecting VIPs. Trott has done a wonderful job in laying out what you need to think about in putting together a protection team for your family or company. *The Protected* shines a light on the good and bad of the business."

~ **Fred Burton**
New York Times Best-Selling Author;
Former Special Agent, U.S. State Department, Diplomatic Security

"A fascinating look into the rarefied world of personal protection. Mike's stories are as riveting as any work of fiction, but the fact that they are true makes them all the more compelling. It is of interest to anyone who is concerned about our national or economic security and the important role continuity of leadership plays in both realms. And, beyond that, it's just a darn good read!"

~ **Joan Dempsey**
Former Deputy Director of Central Intelligence
for Community Management

"Mike's intimate experience with international close protection is evident throughout *The Protected*. He provides numerous interconnected topics and perspectives to assist individual practitioners, organizations and special units with the responsibility of protecting others. His insights on those who provide this personal service is revealing and inspiring, which is why the friendship forged between our two special units has lasted for more than 30 years."

~ **Horst Mehlinger**
German Special Police,
Spezialeinsatzkommando (SEK), Chief Training Instructor (Ret.)

"*The Protected* is an excellent resource guide for those seeking to pursue a career in executive protection. Mike has uniquely blended operational accounts that provide practical lessons, help to reduce misconceptions, and improve operational effectiveness and safety."

~ **Jeffrey Miller**
Former Senior Vice President and Chief Security Officer for the NFL;
Commissioner, Pennsylvania State Police (Ret.)

"Mike's years of experience and knowledge of security drivers are are both evident in his book. The chapter on security driving effectively outlines the risks associated with executive transportation, and Mike defines those risks and offers suggestions on how they can be mitigated. In my opinion, *The Protected* is a must-read for all involved in secure transportation."

~ **Tony Scotti**
Executive Vice President, Vehicle Dynamics Institute;
Founder, International Security Driver Association

"*The Protected* provides an in-depth and relatable view of the many challenges concerning the ever-changing complexities of protecting individuals. Even though executive protection can be very complicated, Mike's insight, experience and clarity provide an excellent protective operational resource for the profession. His interesting reflections add a depth of perspective which also remind us of our own experiences."

~ **Bill Hackenson**
Supervisory Special Agent, U.S. Secret Service (Ret.)

"Mike is one of the most professional and experienced security operatives I've had the pleasure of working with throughout my career. *The Protected* will be considered an international 'must read' for many years to come regarding the complexities surrounding executive protection."

~ **Anders de la Motte**
International Best-Selling Author; Former Swedish Police Officer

"Mike combines his lifetime of experience as a protector with a perceptive understanding of the many simple to complex threats that challenge the safety and security of the protectee. With keen insight, Mike explains the delicate balance between safeguarding and personal service. *The Protected* is a great resource for anyone who is called to serve and protect."

~ **Kathy Leodler**
Special Agent, FBI (Ret.); CEO, Rampart Group

The PROTECTED

Corey,

Great meeting you.

All the best

MICHAEL W. TROTT

ARCHWAY
PUBLISHING

Archway Publishing books may be ordered through booksellers or by contacting:

Archway Publishing
1663 Liberty Drive
Bloomington, IN 47403
www.archwaypublishing.com
1 (888) 242-5904

ISBN: 978-1-4808-7099-4 (sc)
ISBN: 978-1-4808-7098-7 (hc)
ISBN: 978-1-4808-7100-7 (e)

Library of Congress Control Number: 2019931418

Printed in the United States.

Archway Publishing rev. date: 07/26/2019

I could not have come this far in my life and career without those who have loved and inspired me, patiently enduring extended absences, secrecy, long hours and many years of intense focus on my professional goals.

Mom & Dad

My son and my hero – Jonathan

My love, my wife – Cheryl

In memory of

U.S. Army Maj. Rocco M. Barnes

(April 9, 1958 – June 4, 2009)

Acknowledgments

Though writing a book can be an isolating process, I could not have completed this without the collaborative effort and honest feedback I received during this entire venture. I would like to thank the many gracious professionals, former colleagues, friends and international practitioners who took my phone calls, answered my emails and reviewed this manuscript, providing valuable feedback and perspectives that made this book better than what I ever could have created on my own.

I also would like to convey my special thanks and deepest appreciation to my editor, Steve Keller. He not only patiently supported my efforts but managed to ensure the manuscript maintained my voice and perspective throughout this long process – no small feat.

For the many of you who still serve in classified positions or work for high-profile principals and clients where you have requested anonymity, I will not mention you personally by name, but you know who you are, and you have my greatest gratitude. Thank you.

Where needed, I've taken extra steps to protect the identity and privacy of my former principals, companies and other operators with whom I've worked throughout my career (many of whom still serve in the shadows of our military and intelligence agencies). Where necessary and appropriate, I have changed or modified names and locations to ensure a proper level of anonymity and privacy. It is not my intention to disclose critical tradecraft, sources or methods that would cause harm to a principal, protective program or the mission of my former employer (the CIA). I would like to thank the CIA Publication Review Board for assisting me through the review and redaction process.

Agent Jerry Parr pushing President Reagan into his limousine during the 1981 assassination attempt. Of the gunshots, Parr said: "I'd been waiting for them all of my career, in a way."

A Special Tribute

In 1939, nine-year-old Jerry Parr saw the movie *Code of the Secret Service*, starring a young Ronald Reagan as Agent Brass Bancroft. Jerry decided on that day he would become a Secret Service Agent.

On March 30, 1981, President Ronald Reagan, White House Press Secretary James Brady, Secret Service Agent Timothy McCarthy and D.C. police officer Thomas Delahanty were shot by John Hinckley Jr. as they left the Washington Hilton Hotel in Washington, D.C.

Special Agent in Charge Jerry Parr quickly covered President Reagan and pushed him into his armored limousine. Agent Parr's critical physical assessment while in the vehicle determined the President was very possibly injured, and he redirected the limo to nearby George Washington University Hospital. The President underwent emergency surgery on a gunshot wound to the chest, where the doctors determined a bullet had stopped approximately one inch from his heart. Agent Parr's training and immediate actions were credited with saving the President's life.

After Jerry's retirement from the Secret Service in 1985, he continued serving our country with distinction as an instructor and subject-matter expert for various government and commercial protective courses. One of these courses was on protective operations for the CIA, which is where I first met Jerry in 1997. He continued making significant contributions to the field until his death.

A true professional – always humble, and always a gentleman.
Jerry S. Parr
September 16, 1930 – October 9, 2015

CONTENTS

Author's Note

As I was in the process of finishing this book, a friend and former colleague asked how long it had taken me to write it. Without hesitation, I smiled and said, "Thirty years."

One might think I'm just a slow writer, but this book on executive protection (EP) could only be written as the product of all the education, training, real-world experiences and, perhaps most importantly, the many lessons I've learned throughout my career (and am still learning). All of these elements have been significant in developing my knowledge and perspectives regarding this unique profession to which I have devoted most of my life.

Over the course of 30 years – from my days as a young airman in the U.S. Air Force (USAF), to the training I received from other military organizations, and on to becoming a special agent with the CIA – I have had the good fortune to work with respected mentors, talented operators and colleagues from around the globe while receiving advanced education and significant real-world experiences. These experiences were invaluable as I transitioned into the corporate and private sectors, providing close protection and EP management to various executives and ultra high net worth (UHNW) individuals and families.

I have often been asked by principals for my thoughts on what is required to establish or evaluate a protective security program. Some of these questions have also come from those considering a career in EP who wanted to know more about the profession. At the beginning of my own career, I tried to find this sort of resource myself – with limited success. In recent years, I recalled this challenge, and it has been part of my motivation for writing this book.

Surprisingly, even today there still aren't many works properly addressing this topic. I suspect that's because the field is so confidential and diverse, and the topic so complex – there really is no "one-size-fits-all" approach.

A goal for this book is to spark positive conversations within the ranks of our occupation by asking the difficult questions, including: "Are we doing our best to protect our principals?" and "Are we adequately addressing the rapid changes in our global environment that keep challenging us as new risk factors continue to emerge?"

Finally, I hope *The Protected* enlightens and entertains readers about a profession that normally takes a back seat to those we serve.

INTRODUCTION

EXECUTIVE PROTECTION (EP) ENCOMPASSES such a wide variety of people and their unique perspectives, concerns and capacities – all of which are important to understand. Each facet of this field will affect your own unique EP experience, and each person involved in your sphere will have to consider a variety of questions whose answers will invariably impact everyone else.

With this broad scope in mind, one of my objectives is to cover the essential elements of executive protection (EP) while also incorporating other topics worthy of consideration. To accomplish this, it is important I directly address all of the many individuals who are involved under the "EP umbrella" at various times throughout the book. For example, I may address principals directly on topics they need to consider, but I also want to be sure security professionals of all levels will find this information helpful as we explore the methodologies behind EP. While it may seem counterintuitive, sometimes the best programs aren't necessarily built from the top down – skilled practitioners can and do bring many layers of experience to educate principals who have never been exposed to executive protection.

Below, I've outlined the various groups of people most affected by or involved with the world of executive protection:

- **The Client**
  You are the first order of business – i.e., the "principal" or "protectee." You hire executive protection because your exposure, profile, position, financial success or family legacy has brought you to a point where you or someone else has decided

it's prudent to have consistent security coverage to anticipate risks and threats. Or perhaps you simply want to facilitate your complicated foreign travel and receive the comfort of knowing someone is watching out for you and can prepare for the worst as you enjoy the best. At times (because of your association), your family members and other close individuals can also require a level of personal protection.

- **The Practitioner**
  You have been called EP, bodyguard, close protection, security officer or agent, and many of you have been in protective operations for most of your career. You have either chosen this profession or, in some cases, it chose you. You have gained years of real-world experience protecting others in unique environments and conditions.

- **Chief Security Officer (CSO) / VP, Director or Manager of Security**
  You are either a generalist or subject-matter expert in a specific security discipline (e.g., IT, cyber, facility or supply-chain security) and you may or may not possess previous close protection experience. You may not have been formally trained in EP but are now required to arrange a level of protection for someone. As a CSO or security manager, you might find yourself in the center of a hurricane of demands as your organization has grown rapidly, increasing the profile of your CEO and other executives. Either deliberately or circumstantially, the need for an EP program has grown almost overnight, and you are in the pilot's seat.

- **The "Concerned"**
  You are a family attorney, corporate general counsel, estate manager, head of a private family office, financial advisor, or a family member or close friend. You may be placed in a position of responsibility and care for your client or loved one's safety, security and privacy, but you may not understand the

requirements and need help navigating the process in order to assist them in evaluating, hiring and building a level of EP that sensibly meets their security needs.

- **New Protection Specialist**
  The future of our time-honored profession depends on you, as you are just beginning your career (or perhaps are in transition from another career). You're looking to the senior practitioners for training, education and mentoring as you gain the exposure and experience necessary to one day become a true veteran of our profession.

With that introduction behind us, let me now give some insight as to where this book will take you.

Understandably, most EP-related works are written primarily for practitioners (rather than clients/principals or the general public) and include a lot about *how* to provide EP, often in a physical sense. Though I'll talk about these topics, it's not my intention to present a step-by-step guide to working in this field.

Instead, I'll focus more on what might influence a principal to consider personal protection – i.e., the *why* – and how that by extension affects the design and implementation of an EP program. Properly defining the *why* question is crucial because the answer shapes this important work from the start. Your reasons could be mandated, threat-based, event-driven or derive from a personal comfort factor. Whatever they are, the reasons behind starting such a program permeate through its establishment, management and daily functioning.

We'll begin this journey with an exploration of what executive protection looks like, who might need it, and the present and future threat environments. As we proceed, I will address establishing an EP program and who may fall under the protective umbrella, while keeping in mind the *why* behind each individual situation. What influences someone today might also be different next month or next year. You can be assured those reasons will continue to *evolve* – and it would be my hope they may even *dissolve* over time.

The middle of the book is more about the details of designing and running an effective program. This information is very important for clients/principals and other concerned people with a "need to know" as a program is developed. Everyone involved at this level needs to understand this process in order for a program to truly work.

For many, the persona of an expressionless agent behind dark glasses is the only image that comes to mind when they think of security details or bodyguards. Having often been asked to describe what motivates and drives a person to commit his or her life to this type of career, I have compiled/blended various real accounts and reflections into this book. As you'll see, many of these experiences are not mine alone, but involve the many men and women who have walked similar paths.

The stories will give you a better perspective of who we are, how we might think, and how our experiences shape our careers in executive protection – i.e., our "EP DNA." You'll also get a sense of the fact that we, the protectors, are not (yet) robots, machines or infallible – we are human.

Additionally, those serving as protectors often play many roles (e.g., confidants, facilitators, messengers, gatekeepers, gate openers, listeners, procurers, investigators, analysts, witnesses, medics, sometimes babysitters, sometimes friends and, in rare cases, even more). The jobs we have been asked to do can range from the simple to the incredibly complex, and from the very dangerous to the humorous.

Most of the time, principals and even other practitioners are never aware of these backstories, but they can be interesting, informative and sometimes just entertaining. My intent is not to sensationalize the content or the experience, but to bring relativity and conceptual clarity to the subject and topics by including these behind-the-scenes stories.

Over the years, I have watched many organizations and private entities struggle to find the right level of executive protection for their principals. They lose valuable time and, in some cases, increase the risk profile and anxiety of their protectees while experiencing high personnel turnover in their security details. This turnover sometimes leads to potential exposure of sensitive information about their clients. My goal in this book is to help principals avoid such stress and costly mistakes.

In the pages that follow, I will also address threats, risks and various uncertainties regarding the world in which we live today. Like others in my profession, I'm sure my perspectives and commentary might be a product of my security-focused training, experience and exposure. But let's be honest – if these global dangers didn't exist, there would be no need to write this type of book. We wouldn't need a military, police, private protection, security technology companies, or even the need to have locks on our doors.

Given this, you might get the sense I am a pessimist at best and a fatalist at worst, but I am neither. I am mostly a realist with tempered optimism which I utilize to create physical and emotional environments in which clients can feel safe. In spite of the subject matter at times, you'll realize I don't like to use fear as an emotion to control our lives or make EP decisions. Fear may be the *catalyst* to consider protection, but I prefer simply to be informed and make educated decisions about protection. We'll explore the subject of fear in more detail later on.

Ultimately, no EP book can ever address every individual situation or scenario that would compel someone to seek protection. The best approach should include an honest conversation and review of risks and consequences. I want readers to be inspired to review their current level of involvement and perspective regarding EP (whether receiving or providing it) with intent to inform, adjust, improve or just confirm your own protection methodology – i.e., how EP fits into your world and provides everyone involved with a better quality of life and peace of mind.

PROLOGUE

ALFRED HERRHAUSEN:
A WAKE-UP CALL

ON A BRISK LATE AUTUMN MORNING just outside Frankfurt, West Germany, bank executive Alfred Herrhausen started his day off just as he always did. After being picked up from home by his protective detail, his three-car security motorcade proceeded along its standard route through a beautifully manicured and wealthy suburban neighborhood, with Herrhausen himself in the rear right seat of a heavily armored Mercedes sedan.

It was November 30, 1989. Herrhausen was 59 years old and had risen to become both the head of Deutsche Bank and a close friend and advisor to Chancellor Helmut Kohl. In addition to his work in banking, he was a member of the Steering Committee of the Bilderberg Group, a small and secretive association of European and American leaders (which has remained of great interest to many conspiracy theorists for over 50 years).

As Herrhausen's motorcade approached the intersection less than 1,000 yards from his home – like it had done hundreds of times before – a blue and silver child's bicycle sat inconspicuously next to the sidewalk railing. This bicycle had been seen periodically at this same spot – so much that it had become part of the landscape and had not drawn attention or concern.

However, on this day, a small satchel had been attached to a rack behind the seat of the bike. Unbeknownst to Herrhausen or his protective detail, a small group of determined individuals had put a plan into action months before what would be his last departure from his home. As the lead vehicle in his motorcade passed the bicycle, someone watching from a safe distance nearby initiated a remote infrared beam across the road.

Seconds later, Herrhausen's armored vehicle broke the beam, detonating a bomb made of approximately 22 pounds of explosives. A copper cone-shaped plate about eight inches in diameter had been placed inside the satchel beside the bomb. As the explosives ignited, this plate was launched with the accuracy of a sniper's bullet, tearing through the right rear door of the armored Mercedes at a speed of two kilometers per second. The copper plate penetrated the armored vehicle and nearly severed Herrhausen's legs. Within minutes, he bled to death from his injuries.

(Kai-Uwe Wärner/picture-alliance/dpa/AP Images)

At the very moment of this attack, I was just 21 miles away (near Darmstadt, West Germany) along with Air Force OSI Special Agent Jack Smalley. As a young sergeant and security specialist in the U.S. Air Force, I was temporarily assigned to the Air Force Office of Special Investigations (AFOSI) Detachment 7024 at Ramstein Air Base. A trained security driver at the time, I was a member of a protective service operation (PSO) and the primary driver of a Level B7 armored Mercedes.

Our principal was a U.S. Air Force brigadier general and air division commander. This particular general also served as the Kaiserslautern Military Community commander, overseeing a group that included approximately 100,000 members of the U.S. Armed Forces and their families – the largest military community outside of the United States. Not all Germans were friendly toward the U.S. military at that time; perhaps some resentments still lingered due to our continued presence throughout the country after World War II.

Within minutes of Herrhausen's assassination, we received notification of the attack and were immediately placed on high alert. Additional resources from our AFOSI detachment were dispatched to our location to assist with an alternative route to our base, which was 75 miles away at the time. Our concern was that this could be part of a larger plot, and we feared others would be targeted – including our principal, the General.

Nothing quite like this level of sophistication had been seen before in the EP field; in fact, this event was considered a "wake-up call" for executive protection teams around the world. It has been nearly 30 years since the Herrhausen assassination, but the case is still considered one of the most effective teaching examples for anti-terrorism, close protection and defensive driving courses today. Similar bombs have been used countless times in war zones throughout the world, though with varying levels of sophistication and effectiveness.

This particular assassination had a deep impact on me and other team members. Earlier that year, we had received an intelligence report that the German Federal Police had raided a safe house belonging to suspected members of the Red Army Faction (RAF), a West German leftist terrorist group. In this safe house, a floppy disk had been recovered that listed seven people the RAF wanted dead.

Herrhausen was their number-one target. Their previous threats had led to Herrhausen's adoption of a heavy protective detail. Nevertheless, Herrhausen had been known to challenge this group of ideological Marxists by telling them they would never kill him.

But Herrhausen was now dead. And, as it turned out, our principal was also on that list. The killing of Herrhausen made the possibility of an attack on our principal much more real to us. Were a group like the RAF to succeed in killing the General, who commanded the largest concentrated group of U.S. military personnel in Germany, it would bring a great deal of attention to their radical efforts to push the Americans out.

After this, each time we approached bicycles, cars or any other unattended item along the road, or spotted suspicious activity at intersections, we could only hold our breaths – and would exhale huge sighs of relief each time we passed unscathed.

A few weeks after the assassination, I drove to the attack site to see it for myself. I wanted to examine the very spot we refer to as the "X" – the exact location where an attack is initiated. As a security driver, I wanted to know what this spot looked like and why the assassins had chosen this particular location.

I walked the area and along the road to get a sense of the terrorists' visual perspective and operational advantage. What surprised me the most (and what I believe shocked the investigators as well) was how so many warning signs had been missed. This sophisticated attack had required careful planning, surveillance and a considerable amount of preparation. The assassins had marked the road where the exact location of the attack would occur and had run wires under the street. This odd construction had been noticed in previous days by local residents, but it had neither been reported nor investigated.

Near the site of the explosion, it was reported a note was found bearing the famed symbol of the RAF (a red star with a Heckler & Koch MP5 across the middle). While two members of the terrorist group were listed as the only real suspects (and a few other theories have been speculated over the past couple decades), no one has ever been charged with the assassination. Many believe the sophisticated design of the bomb and trigger elements had all the markings of the former East German *Staatssicherheitsdienst* – more commonly referred to as the Stasi. It had long been known the Stasi had provided training and resources to the

RAF when it furthered their goals. It was also known that members of the RAF would often hide out on the east side of the Berlin Wall.*

The RAF was known to have close ties to several Middle Eastern terrorist groups, and some believed the bomb-making technology might have come from Lebanon. Only eight days prior to Herrhausen's assassination, René Moawad, incumbent President of Lebanon for only 17 days at the time, was assassinated by a similar attack using a remote trigger device. That bomb was concealed in a roadside shack and included nearly 400 pounds of explosives. It destroyed his motorcade, killed ten of his bodyguards and injured more than a dozen others.[1]

On November 9, 1989, just 21 days before Herrhausen's assassination, the Berlin Wall came down, allowing thousands of East Germans to cross the border that had separated them from the western side of their country for over 28 years. Along with the new tide of freedom, large financial rewards were offered for any information leading authorities to the arrest of anyone in the RAF. I had a poster in my office that the German government distributed listing the most wanted members of the group; I recall marking off their names (sometimes weekly) as the East Germans collected their money. Because of this effort, the terror group was fundamentally dismantled over the next several months, and no major RAF attacks or targeted killings took place again.

I have always wondered: If the Berlin Wall hadn't come down during this time, would the RAF have continued with their efforts to assassinate my principal (the General)?

The fall of the Berlin Wall marked a new era in our history and began the softening of the hard lines of the Cold War. With this change came significant developments and an increased sophistication in

---

* If this were the work of the RAF, it wouldn't be their first attempt to assassinate a U.S. general on German soil. On September 15, 1981, General Frederick Kroesen and his wife were being driven in their armored sedan near his work at the U.S. Army's European headquarters in Heidelberg. Suddenly, suspected RAF members fired a rocket grenade from a hillside near an intersection, striking the trunk of his armored vehicle. Fortunately, the assassination attempt failed, and the General and his wife sustained only minor injuries. Just weeks prior, the RAF detonated a bomb in the U.S. Air Forces in Europe (USAFE) Headquarters at Ramstein Air Base, injuring 20 people.

killing still employed today in all parts of the world. My close proximity to that one crucial event in time had a significant influence on the foundation of my mindset and established my approach to executive protection, which I have maintained since I dedicated my career to the individuals who are *the protected.*

"OUT OF INTENSE COMPLEXITIES,
INTENSE SIMPLICITIES EMERGE."

- WINSTON CHURCHILL

CHAPTER I

EXECUTIVE PROTECTION IN A COMPLEX WORLD

YOU WILL NOT FIND definitions in Webster's Dictionary for executive protection or close personal protection. However, these terms can be defined as *measures taken to ensure the safety and security of a person or persons who may be exposed to elevated personal threats, risks and/or vulnerabilities as a result of their title, position, employment, public profile, wealth, associations and geographical location.*

In other words, executive protection (EP) involves a person with specialized skills – as well as a particular mindset and sense of dedication – keeping another person safe, even at their own peril. Of course, people in the profession understand it frequently goes even further. Often, experienced and polished EP professionals will also provide their principals with a limited level of executive and personal assistance while on travel and serve as coordinators and facilitators to ensure itineraries, travel and events are kept on schedule.

If we take the definition another step further, it could also be described as providing principals with a certain peace of mind regarding their personal safety, security and privacy that allows them to focus on their executive roles and leadership responsibilities.

Principals requiring protection today are a more diverse and dynamic group than ever before. While wealth isn't the only motive for someone to request or require personal protection, it is often the reason for it. The number of ultra high net worth (UHNW) individuals and families has been on the rise for many years now. In March 2018, Forbes identified 2,208 billionaires from 72 countries and territories. In the U.S. alone, there are over 500 of these ultra-wealthy people.[2] CNBC reported that there is a new billionaire somewhere in the world every two days, with Asia leading this growth.[3]

But you don't have to be a billionaire to need or consider a level of executive protection. People using EP can often require various levels of assistance to facilitate their very active lifestyles, travel and exposure. They may represent governments, organizations, corporations and/or influential family dynasties, but can also be key decision-makers and social influencers. Some live to push the limits of exploration and invention, taking dangerous but calculated risks as a part of their norm.

The EP programs that protect such people usually evolve over time, beginning with the individual and then extending to the family; in most cases, coverage includes an office and one or more residences. Normally, the protection at some point involves travel support and begins to slowly cover other aspects of a principal's life. As it does, the need for additional security facilitation by trained professionals grows with it. Eventually, if a program is developed for a corporate executive, a separate program for the family outside of the corporate program may be necessary to meet the security requirements.

Policies and procedures help establish an operational foundation and maintain consistency, but it is still important to recognize that EP encompasses more elements of an art than a science. Every principal, every family, every threat and every individual's risk appetite is different. *If the only standard of achieving effective close protection was keeping someone alive, the evaluation process would be simple – but flawed.* Executive protection goes well beyond just protecting another life, and it's in this area that there can be major variances in the capabilities of those providing these services. Therefore, principals should have the right expectations of the EP provider(s) they have hired. When capabilities and expectations don't match, just like with most services, the result will be eventual disappointment on both sides.

No individual or program can predict with 100 percent accuracy when and where close protection may be required. Organizations, executives, officials, UHNW individuals, families and everyday citizens can and will occasionally find themselves at the wrong place at the wrong time, as we have tragically witnessed in many places around the world.

In some cases, it might be a matter of preemptive response or reaction by you or your EP team that makes the difference. In June 2017, we witnessed this type of successful response when three Capitol Police special agents assigned to House Majority Whip Steve Scalise were on site during a congressional baseball practice session in Alexandria, Virginia, for an upcoming charity game. On this very early summer morning, an unstable and politically disgruntled man arrived at the ballfield armed with a rifle and the determination to kill; he began to open fire on Republican representatives who had only ball gloves in their hands to defend themselves.

When the dust had settled, many were injured but fortunately only the attacker died from return fire by Agents Griner, Bailey and Cabrera, who were supported by responding Alexandria police officers on the scene. It was immediately determined that if the protective agents had not been there that fateful morning and prepared for duty with the proper training and mindset, Congressman Scalise may have been killed – and likely many more might have been injured as well.

Sometimes, EP may seem unnecessary, cumbersome or intrusive – and, in most cases, you'll never be provided advance notice of the need for it. But in the right circumstances, your EP may actually hold the line between life and death.

A Brief History of Executive Protection

Throughout history, literature and folklore, there are thousands of examples of people in one of the world's *other* "oldest professions" – i.e., one human protecting another for a cause or compensation. As long as people of means or status have secured protection against those wanting to cause them harm, there have been the protected.

Today, this job is often referred to as executive protection. Perhaps not much has changed over the course of history as far as the need for protection. But what has changed dramatically are the levels of sophistication involved, the means of protection, and in some cases the number and nature of global enemies or threats – thereby creating even greater risks and challenges in defending principals.

As we travel the world, we can find many examples of early influences on modern-day executive protection. Europe has a long and storied history, from those selected to protect Alexander the Great through to the Roman Empire and medieval states. In the early 1600s, the French had the Musketeers of the Guard (also known as the King's Musketeers), which formed the royal guard for the monarch anytime he would venture outside the royal residences.

Equally well-trained and loyal were the Japanese samurai – which are still a symbol many EP organizations and professionals identify with today. Throughout Asia, you will find other similar groups who were entrusted with protecting royalty, dynasties, leaders and nobles.

In Central and South America, you can find examples among the Inca and Aztec civilizations, with small groups designated as bodyguards to protect their rulers. The Middle East, Eurasia and regions of Africa have also seen dedicated groups of fearless fighters that, over time, evolved into protectors of the realm.

Today, we are able to witness firsthand centuries-old organizations like the vestiges of the Yeomen Warders at the Tower of London and the Swiss Guard at the Vatican. In recent times, the Swiss Guard, the Vatican Police and the London Metropolitan Police Protection Command are just a few examples of highly trained specialized close protection units having been created within longstanding organizations.

One example of these forces in action was during Pope Francis' official visit to the U.S. in 2015, where the United States Secret Service worked in coordination with the Swiss Guard to protect him during his stay. Fortunately, modern advancements and cooperative mindsets have allowed for greater collaboration between many countries' professional protective organizations. Nevertheless, few know this security event took two years to fully plan – though the Swiss Guard itself has had a few years' head start over the Secret Service (the Guard officially started providing protection for the Pontiff in 1506).

The Secret Service was given its mandate to provide protection after the assassination of President William McKinley in 1901. While there are many other international organizations responsible for protecting high-profile individuals and world leaders (many of whom do so with incredible proficiency), few have the level of experience, training and resources to protect them better than the U.S. Secret Service. The United States has several government and military organizations charged with protecting VIPs and visiting world leaders, but the Secret Service's number-one and number-two clients are the President and Vice President of the United States and their families. Considering we have witnessed the assassination of four U.S. presidents and attempts on at least a dozen others, it's safe to say no one would take the job without a Secret Service detail.

Along with the Secret Service, there are many federal and state agencies, non-governmental organizations, corporations and private security firms throughout the world who have developed and implemented various levels of executive protection programs. However, the benchmark used in their creation has often been the U.S. Secret Service.

My own career path included protective details with the U.S. Air Forces in Europe (USAFE) and later the CIA as a close protection specialist and special agent. I often worked alongside the Secret Service, Department of State, National Security Agency, Department of Defense and other fine international organizations. My advanced training and depth of experience came from my time with the CIA. Because of the Agency's unique mission, the skills, training and tradecraft we used might vary slightly from the typical government or private-sector organization, and so might our "toolbox."*

My training and experiences with the CIA have served me (and others like me) well because of our ability to quickly scale up or down depending upon the principal or mission – and with limited or reduced resources at times. Because of some environments and missions, we

---

* For example, in April 2018, CIA Director Mike Pompeo traveled to North Korea on a secret mission to meet with Supreme Leader Kim Jong-un on behalf of President Donald Trump. From an EP perspective, this was surely not an average assignment.

might not have been able to use our badges, credentials or principals' names to influence our requirements and facilitation for the better. At the CIA, we would often only use that type of leverage as a last resort and preferred to use other means first, which could require a lot of creativity and protective tradecraft.

Through the centuries and even recent decades, our adversaries, weapons, transportation, training, tradecraft and equipment have all evolved significantly. In my career, I have broken bread with my fellow protectors from around the world – and yet, in spite of historical time and distance, our conversations probably resembled those of the people who performed this job long before us. Many of us are drawn to this profession by the sense of mission, camaraderie, lure of adventure, travel, training, accomplishment and loyalty in seeking to be modern-day knights, samurais and royal guardsmen.

The Current EP Landscape

Now that we've established what executive protection is and briefly looked at the forms it has taken throughout history, let's look at the global risk environment and other broad influences regarding your personal security.

To some, the concerns and trends I write about could sound overstated or divergent from your own opinions or perspectives. To others, they may be the very reasons you have or are considering a level of EP. For the rest, these could be subjects you need to discuss internally while viewing the future with a new lens regarding risk.

Executive protection can normally be broken down into two major categories: *required* and *requested* services, with a few shades of grey in between. Once you've determined which category fits your needs, you can then begin to consider other questions to help identify your specific EP requirements.

The highest levels of close protection are generally reserved for the President of the United States or other country-level leaders due to the extreme risks associated with their roles. Other government officials have similar levels of protection that vary based on their position. Some high-level corporate executives also fall under a broad mandate for protection based on company policy. Certain organizations and entities may also be required to provide close protection for individuals working in extreme or high-risk areas under a *duty of care* responsibility.

Protection isn't always a formal requirement. In some cases, UHNW individuals may feel their wealth and profiles expose them to such high levels of risk that they need to hire protective services. Some corporate executives who are not automatically covered by company policy have even negotiated certain levels of protection in their contracts. In other cases, fear or anxiety might simply compel individuals to hire executive protection services to soothe their feelings of personal danger. (We'll explore fear and anxiety as justifications for EP later on.)

No matter who the principal is, from the perspective of those providing EP, the job will always be a matter of personal *service*. Even the President's Secret Service has it in their title.

You'll see throughout this book that every principal and EP situation is different, but the common thread running through each arrangement is that EP is a level of protection for one's self and/or family that:

1. is proactive and reactive;
2. involves a keen sense of situational awareness;
3. includes approaches that are both physical (e.g., people, barriers) and cerebral (e.g., intelligence analyses);
4. is determined by risk factors, personal desires and decisions designed to counter concerns; and
5. allows for more freedom of personal movement, not less.

A few years ago, I was in Beverly Hills for a meeting. While standing with a few associates in the Beverly Cañon Gardens outside of the Montage Beverly Hills hotel, we noticed a few kids had gathered and were playing soccer in the grassy area. Still having our conversation, I couldn't help but notice the small crowd nearby taking cell phone videos of the scene.

There was one kid wearing a baseball cap who appeared slightly larger than the rest. At one point, he kicked the ball too hard for the small space, causing it to fly toward my group and some people enjoying lunch on patio tables outside. I stepped outside my group and stopped the ball with my foot before it hit a table. As the young kid with the hat came running over, he was already apologizing. I chastised him for being too aggressive with the little kids and told him, "Please don't kick the ball into the tables because there are plates and glasses on them." When he got closer, I realized why everyone was taking pictures and videos – that young kid was Justin Bieber.

I looked at the other tables nearby and there sat Oprah Winfrey having lunch with friends. As anyone can imagine, both of these individuals have what we might refer to as *high* profiles, but they were still able to enjoy a day out in public. Yes, they had their EP teams with them, but they were providing adequate space to allow them to be as normal as possible in a public environment. Such principals probably wouldn't be able to get away with that level of exposure everywhere, but in places like Beverly Hills, Aspen and Monaco, they fit right in with all the other "high profiles" while getting a little fresh air and sun.

Introduction to Risk

Whether you are high- or low-profile, single or a family, a corporate executive or private person, the threats and risks relevant to you – i.e., your "risk landscape" – will depend on many factors that include *who you are* and *how you live your life*, in broad terms.

For example, if you only travel via commercial airlines, you may not be concerned with trending numbers of private aviation accidents and security incidents. If your company doesn't create or manage intellectual property, you might not care much about espionage. If you have an extremely low profile, you might not worry about attracting the attention of a person with certain mental health conditions and/or criminal intent to cause you or your family harm.*

If you don't travel internationally, evacuation plans or major medical assistance in foreign countries may not be of importance. But if you do travel abroad, you might be concerned with local criminal activities and the regional political climate. You might also care about unique customs, cultural norms and laws of which your ignorance or misunderstanding could result in negative consequences. Traveling senior executives are often distracted and don't normally pay attention to their surroundings – statistically increasing the risk of an unfortunate event.

Relatedly, everyone must give more attention to the possibility of email or devices being hacked and sensitive personal or company information being compromised. In all these cases, EP normally plays an expanded role beyond just close protection, becoming "chief facilitator" for principals. We'll explore all this and more throughout the book, but professional and judicious facilitation plays a major role in close protection when and where risks exist.

If we broaden our scope some, we start to see factors which are comparatively more out of our control than lifestyle or travel habits. Terrorism is a good example of this. As we have witnessed too often in recent years, terrorist attacks and other violence in public places is no longer limited to isolated areas of the world. This increase in unconventional violence and the diverse choice of weapons (e.g., vehicles, knives, explosives, poison) is leading to a change in the term that we once used to describe such acts – i.e., it's now "active violence" instead of "active shooter."

For many principals, the risk from terrorists or organized criminal elements (other than wrong-place, wrong-time events) are the least of their concerns. But unless you live under a rock, you'll always have

---

* Note that your profile can never actually eliminate this risk; it can just reduce it.

some level of risk associated with criminal activity. And while it may pose a much smaller risk, terrorism still is a factor to consider in our risk assessments.

All this means (with or without EP present) that it's important to have a keen sense of situational awareness and vigilance in *any* high-risk areas or situations where you're personally exposed – e.g., large crowds, unsecured areas of public transportation, major event venues or unfamiliar locations. We'll discuss terrorism in more depth later in this chapter, but most importantly, you should have a reasonable plan, even if only mentally.

In addition, incredibly rapid growth and changes in technology continue to thrust most of us ever faster into the 21st century – but have also left others far behind in many parts of the world. Balancing the needs of principals who may operate, live or travel between developed and developing countries can present many challenges in today's EP environment. (We'll dive deeper into technology later as well.)

These and other factors – large and small – will determine the level of experience and sophistication an EP professional will need to have at his or her disposal (or in their toolbox) regarding their principal's security. I'm not trying to minimize anyone's capabilities, but there are situations where the talent and experience required to provide more-than-adequate protection may vary.

You may only need a qualified driver who has security training. In other cases, principals might require or request a full physical security presence at their home, and only for their family. Others may have an EP agent escort them from door to door. Some principals may request (and their risk assessment may support) a full complement of the above, possibly due to a qualified threat. Bottom line: There is no such thing as "EP in a box."

We often look for an "easy button" to accomplish the difficult. But if you are designing a full-time and dynamic EP program, there are no shortcuts. Whether as a principal or security manager, you need to be involved with reviewing your threat environment and assessing the factors most relevant to your program. You need to know what you're doing, why you're doing it, and the potential risks you'll face along the way – as well as the important mitigating plans to address them.

Just like in business, a key part of developing any security strategy is considering recent events and the lessons that can be learned from them. Analyzing history and projecting future trends will allow you to adjust your existing security program sooner rather than later – and it'll keep you one step ahead of what you may face in the future.

It's easy to look at national and global events in isolation as stories catch our attention for a brief moment in time and then disappear. But, as it has been throughout history, considering past events as part of our whole assessment allows us to see important trends that might be in our future.

In order to provide an impartial perspective on this subject (as well as check my own perceptions), I contacted a former colleague now at TorchStone Global, a premier global risk mitigation and security firm. TorchStone's management team has been in the trenches for decades helping to protect others – from the President of the United States to corporate executives and their families.

I asked TorchStone if they could contemplate the global environment and create a summary of current conditions and a predictive analysis going forward regarding today's security and EP landscape. TorchStone agreed to my request, and VP of Protective Intelligence Samuel D. Ward, CPP, and Senior Protective Analyst Malique L. Carr, PhD, produced the analysis of the global technology, risk and security landscape that appears in the next few pages.

While only reasonable projections, perhaps they might shed some insight on how past events can shape and contribute to future trends that could affect personal security for principals and their families.

After TorchStone's analysis, I'll provide my own thoughts on these issues and trends. Our analyses aren't quite the same, but I think each complements the other well. In this business, it's important to be able to reach out to others with different areas of expertise and bring their viewpoints to the table. Your conversations – and level of security provided – will be better for it.

TorchStone Global Analysis

Technology, Risk and Security in Tomorrow's World

Security is a multibillion-dollar industry showing no signs of reversing course. The global physical security market is estimated to reach $110 billion in annual spending by 2021.[4] Cumulative cybersecurity spending from 2017 to 2021 is estimated to exceed $1 trillion.[5] Changes in technology and the global threat landscape will heavily influence the future directions of executive protection and security for ultra high net worth (UHNW) families. How will the global threat landscape change in the coming decades? How will the security services in the UHNW sphere evolve to continue to effectively protect people, physical assets and information? We evaluated the future of *technology, risk* and *security* in this essay to explore the answers to these questions.

Future of Technology

Changes in technology drive changes in our society. These changes directly impact both what we aim to protect and how we provide protection.

We are approaching the obsolescence of passwords, photos, signatures and Social Security numbers for identification because biometric data will allow for greater accuracy. There may come a day when every individual's DNA can be instantly scanned and matched in a global database for accurate identification. While these technologies may serve to improve safety and security in many ways, protecting biometric and biological data will become increasingly important. Biological data from UHNW clients may be particularly sought after by those with malicious intent.

Usage of credit cards and cash are down in favor of biometric technology and embedded devices. Workers in Sweden already use embedded microchips for timekeeping, food purchase, unlocking doors and accessing computers.[6] Companies will continue to move away from the bring-your-own-device model as implanted technology becomes more common. Like microchipping and invisible fences for pets, embedded devices will enable protection specialists to prevent and/or quickly ascertain if unauthorized individuals are nearby. Embedded device hacking would be a major concern.

We are merely scratching the surface of our technological connectivity and reliance on cybertechnology. We will find new, enhanced ways to promote our experiences on social media. We will record or livestream through contact lenses or embedded devices so others can remotely and intimately share in our experiences. This type of footage may be beneficial for executive protection details, as it would allow for remote surveillance through the eyes and ears of a UHNW client or individual of interest, but will also bring up issues related to privacy and hacking.

We are also entering a world of augmented, virtual and mixed reality (AR/VR/MR). Optical head-mounted displays will lead the way, but technology will improve, giving us light-field smart glasses, smart contact lenses and eventually implanted devices. Imagine a 4D social media network where you can be anywhere in the world: You could be dancing in the front row of a concert by your favorite musician without leaving your home.

Some may think operating from a virtual world or using augmented reality within a safe space may eliminate the need for physical and executive protection. As we have witnessed, the brain treats experiences in virtual space as real; consequently, there can be real emotional risks involved with verbal or perceived physical assaults in a virtual space.[7] In the future, we may have virtual agents protecting UHNW clients in such an environment.

As communications technology and transmission methods improve, AR/VR/MR technology will revolutionize standard operating procedures for everything we do – from college education to cooking and construction. Enhanced reality will become more attractive than our natural reality and may become our baseline environment. We will scroll through our to-do lists with blinks of our eyes while we travel in driverless cars, planes, hovercrafts and hyperloop trains. While this technology will make our days more efficient and enjoyable, the more our world becomes dependent on cybertechnology, the more exposed we will be to cyber risk.

As technology improves, so will our understanding of the human body. Implanted devices will provide alerts for health incidents. In the future, internal devices may also monitor brain activity and physiological measurements, registering changes from a baseline. The devices could send alerts about emotional experiences and pre-incident indicators. For example, certain patterns may signal anger or aggression. Executive protection agents could be alerted when UHNW clients experience fear. Law enforcement may also be able to stop crimes or identify at-risk individuals who exhibit atypical neuropsychological and physiological responses to situations (e.g., characteristics of psychopathy).

Future of Risk

The world is undergoing multiple transitions. Risks like wealth disparity, social instability, ineffective governance and difficulty adapting to environmental and technological changes will contribute to increased sociopolitical polarization and tension for the next few decades.[8] Top global risks include: extreme weather, large-scale involuntary migration, natural disasters, terrorism and interstate conflict.

Weather will become more extreme. Only the privileged will be able to afford climate-controlled homes in the most habitable areas. The underprivileged will be increasingly faced with life-or-death situations. They will be forced to migrate to more temperate climates, exacerbating conflicts around immigration and between the UHNW and underprivileged. Ultimately, people will fight to survive.

The risks of interstate conflicts and terrorism will continue to evolve with societal changes and technological advancements. Countries will continue developing more sophisticated weapons. How will world powers maintain peace if developing countries threaten to use these weapons to assert political and economic influence?

Modern terrorism is driven by energy surrounding sociopolitical events and is thought to occur in waves.[9] Which energy will drive the next wave is unknown, but terrorism expert Jeffrey Simon hypothesized[10] the next wave will be defined by the role technology will play in promoting terrorism. We do not yet fully understand the risks associated with the world's increased dependency on all things cyber. We live in a world of increased hacking and decreased privacy where electronic surveillance and virtual robbery are prevalent. The potential risk and global impact of cyber-enabled economic warfare grows as more people move to exclusively electronic currency.

It is likely that in the future, terrorists will engage in multiple types of warfare: conventional, use of weapons of mass destruction, cyberwarfare or all the above.[11] They will adapt attack methods from the expensive and complex (bombs and stealth planes) to the simple and readily available (knives and vehicles). Extremists and sympathizers will continue using the Internet, social media and other cybertechnology to recruit or inspire vulnerable individuals, fundraise, surveil targets, cyberstalk and harass. In the future, there may also be a resurgence of biological warfare and agroterrorism, which could devastate entire regions.

As the vulnerabilities for physical, emotional and financial security become known, those with resources will pay for protection. Protective intelligence will remain key for executive protection agents to remain aware of sociopolitical strife, biological threats and terrorism to best prepare for the risks their UHNW clients face.

Future of Security

It seems likely the most impactful and well-funded security programs of the future will aggressively adapt technology to identify and mitigate risk. Cybersecurity professionals will remain early adopters of technology as the field moves forward with quantum cryptography and key distribution.[12] Similarly, downward pressure on costs and slimming profit margins will drive physical security specialists toward advances in remote monitoring services, robotics and artificial intelligence. The rest of the security industry, including executive protection and protective intelligence, will need to similarly adapt to address new vulnerabilities and remain relevant.

Scanning tools capable of prescreening people who interact with a protected individual will accompany advances in biometrics and embedded technology. Background checks across global databases will be easier and more reliable. Risk assessments will be increasingly automated and include big data and analytics. Universal translators and audio enhancers (potentially embedded in an agent's ear versus an external device) could improve intelligence and security operations abroad. More covert and powerful drones with advanced audiovisual technology will be used to conduct route analyses. Remote monitoring centers will send data and instructions – via real-time augmented reality – to executive protection professionals in active threat environments. Non-lethal weapons could be used to overload an embedded chip in an attacker's body. Clothing will become increasingly resistant to explosions, gunshots, stabbings, acid burns or other chemical pollutants. AR/VR/MR will power immersive training simulations, allowing protection professionals to practice under a myriad of conditions.

The primary drawbacks to these technologies are the potential for cyberattacks (e.g., a denial of service attack on a moving vehicle) and hacking (e.g., manipulating biometrics). Additional vulnerabilities include protecting one's privacy and sensitive information from ubiquitous audio-enhancers or hacking into embedded livestream and recording systems. Determined attackers will find a way to use whatever tools are available to cause the greatest harm.

Conclusion

Tomorrow's risks – including increased polarization, climate change and terrorism – coupled with rapid technological expansion ensure the necessity of security providers in the future. Protective intelligence and related services will be needed to identify vulnerabilities and flag potential threats as early as possible. Protection specialists must adapt and maximize emerging technology if they expect to remain relevant, while also continuing to learn how to operate if all electronic systems fail. There will be a greater need for cyber-security and technology experts to set up safe systems and reduce harm when systems fail or are penetrated. While many will focus on securing technology and systems, there will always be a need to protect UHNW individuals through physical security and executive protection in real life and virtual worlds. In sum, we agree with a quote attributed to American five-star general and Medal of Honor recipient Douglas MacArthur: "There is no security on this earth; there is only opportunity."

A Complex World and Influences on EP

The TorchStone analysis provides a stimulating assessment of where we are today and the direction in which we are heading regarding technology, risk and security. Their analysis may also provide certain considerations that might influence your decisions regarding EP now and in the years to come.

Now, I'd like to add my perspective on the topics they covered and some others.

As anyone who has been in this profession more than 20 years will tell you, even with all the new technology and fancy gadgets at our disposal, it has never been more difficult to identify all the risks to our principals that exist in the world today.

It is my desire to carefully thread the needle between responsibly addressing many of the current and emerging risks we're facing and balancing my honest optimism that, as a society and profession, we're able to handle them. Most in my field have seen a lot of bad (and some of us very ugly) things, but I'm still not a pessimist. In spite of negative events and the existence of some very evil people in our world, I'm hopeful about things to come.

While there is a constant barrage of 24-hour news reporting on every horrible thing happening in the world, there is positive news too – you just need to look harder to find the fascinating, inspiring and exciting people and events. One television event I enjoy is a particular international network presentation called *Heroes*. This show honors individuals who make unique and extraordinary contributions to humanitarian causes around the world and in their communities. For a few hours, this show illustrates the good that goes on in the world today and leaves you inspired to do more yourself.

With that being said, let's look at some examples of influences and global factors that can increase your level of risk to some degree – including technology's rapid development, the evolving face of terror and the current-day scope of insider threats. Based on your lifestyle and risk appetite, these topics may be considerations when working out your *personal why* you want or need EP.

Technology: The Good, the Bad and the Ugly

Almost all new technologies have upsides and downsides. Marc Goodman, the founder of the Future Crimes Institute and a best-selling author, summed up this complexity well when he said during an interview, "Fire was the first technology, right? It could keep you warm at night, heat your food – but it could also be used to burn down the village next door."[13]

The speed at which new and emerging technology changes requires constant adaptation and additional consideration regarding our protection programs, as well as in our individual lives. Often, we don't fully understand the ramifications of new technologies until weeks, months or even years after they're released. For example, a 3D printer is a new groundbreaking technology that can do good (e.g., make medical devices, produce human implants or contribute to other new inventions) or bad (e.g., make a plastic gun or other weapons undetectable by security screenings that could be used by someone with malevolent intent).

A lot of old-school security and EP professionals resist embracing new technologies, but the traditional skill sets of weapons proficiencies, self-defense, driving, etc., are no longer enough. Many of the changes that have impacted EP (as well as all of us) over the past couple decades have been the result of rapid advancements in technology. Whether we like it or not, technology is permeating our lives in almost every way, affecting both our personal security and privacy. EP professionals need to keep up.

Technology: The Good

Possibly more than any other invention, the Internet has brought us a whole new world of exploration, information, learning, access to businesses worldwide, conveniences and connectivity. Each day, we use it for routine communication, higher education, medical information and advice. We rely on it for political facts, news, weather, important public alerts, professional work portals, movies, music, videos and travel information. It helps us find lost relatives or new life partners, gives us cooking instructions, and shows us how to repair car engines, roll cigars or build paper airplanes. It is sometimes impossible to imagine how we ever survived without it.

Today, the Internet is even more powerful because of an even more revolutionary invention: the smartphone. Smartphones have given us immediate access to an inconceivable amount of web-based knowledge, a growing pool of over 1.5 million apps to utilize every possible distillation of that knowledge, and enable real-time communications with almost anyone in the world. If I had described this technology 100 years ago, they might have tied me to a pole and burned me alive.

In today's fast-paced and connected environments, smartphones have allowed many a savvy EP operator to become a rolling command post through constant contact with administrative assistants, limo drivers, pilots, yacht crews, doctors, and principals and their family members. We are able to handle everything from the simple (e.g., last-minute schedule adjustments, reservations, weather monitoring) to the highly important (e.g., reviewing remote video camera alerts at residences and offices, checking real-time intelligence updates, tracking our principal's flights in real time), all on our devices.

Often, these requirements must be dealt with while on the move and in the streets, with usually incredibly accurate GPS directional guidance being sent to a wireless piece in our ears as we follow driving directions on a small map on our wristwatch – all with our hands on the steering wheel.

On one occasion in New York, my principals made a last-minute request to attend the sold-out U.S. Open tennis tournament. While on the train with them to the stadium, my ops team searched for and purchased tickets online. Within 45 minutes, they were able to have them hand-delivered to the EP team as they entered the stadium without any interruption in their stride.

Here's the best way I can describe the significance the smartphone has had on our profession: It used to be if you had to rush out the door to follow your principal, you would immediately reach for your weapon first. Today, the smartphone would probably be the first item most agents grab – weapon second.

The Internet and smartphones are the most visible technologies impacting our daily lives, but technology's revolutionary effect on us, our brains and our EP missions goes far beyond.

As we are already witnessing, our skies will continue to be filled with commercial drones making deliveries and providing other useful assistance in ways we haven't even yet imagined. We already use them to transport supplies and medication in emergency situations, assist first responders in disasters, and give law enforcement immediate "bird's eye" views during crises and crime situations. Drones are now also invaluable in assisting firefighters with structural and forest fires to locate trapped victims and determine hot spots that would otherwise be inaccessible.

Ground travel is already affected by technology on so many levels, seen and unseen, but in the not-too-distant future, the cars next to you on the road won't all be driven by humans. Once perfected, driverless vehicles relying on advanced detection electronics such as cameras, lasers and radar will vastly reduce traffic accidents, injuries and deaths due to the elimination of basic driver errors, distractions, impairment due to drugs/alcohol and poor driving practices. Though I personally love to drive, this is one area of technology where I see tremendous benefits for our society.

Without a doubt, there will be challenges and unique risks that will require refinements along the way. Developers are still trying to solve how cars will avoid potholes, manage detours, deal with construction sites, navigate impromptu parking lots, and adjust for heavy rain, snow and other types of unexpected road conditions. Sadly, we have recently seen how people unexpectedly crossing the street can still not be reliably detected fast enough by driverless cars to avert a terrible accident.

Some may argue these experimental driverless vehicles will be the cause of many deaths. But to keep it all in perspective, we must acknowledge that motor vehicle accidents *in the United States alone in 2017* were the cause of more than 40,000 fatalities for a second straight year – with human drivers.[14] Some countries will develop their capabilities faster than others, but the billions of dollars spent globally on research and technology development will continue to fund the race to make these vehicles mainstream in most countries this century.

It might sound crazy, but the driverless car concept could one day even apply to autonomous air taxis, though some aviation experts have expressed some doubts due to the difficulty of perfecting a viable commercial vertical take-off and landing aircraft. However, in March 2018, the Kitty Hawk aviation company unveiled the Cora, a flying car that operates on battery power and is designed to transport passengers without a licensed pilot. This is not just a concept: It is flying *now*.

As the TorchStone report highlighted, another major new development can be seen in medically implanted radio-frequency identification (RFID) microchips. These devices are implanted in the soft part of the hand between the thumb and index finger for things like unlocking doors to homes and offices, logging onto computers, and making purchases with a simple wave of the hand. They are catching on quickly, especially in Sweden, where thousands of early adopters are lining up to simplify their lives with this technology. There are still many questions that need to be addressed about protecting the privacy of the data on these chips, but they are likely to be as ubiquitous as the smartphone at some point in the future.

Some of the biggest benefits of technology we are witnessing are in the field of advanced medicine. Even the information EP professionals now have access to has been nothing short of life-saving. Automated external defibrillators (AEDs) and other medical emergency devices are becoming so small, effective and portable that EP teams are carrying them in their backpacks, allowing them to administer crucial medical support to principals within seconds.

We now also see the miraculous creation, repair and replacement of body parts, as well as instant access to global research through supercomputers that will ultimately provide revolutionary treatments previously unknown to most medical practitioners. Promising cures and treatments for illnesses and diseases which have plagued us for centuries are now available or will be soon. Watson, IBM's supercomputer, is now even being used to link real-time medical data and global research results so as to educate doctors in new treatment options – and, in some cases, even producing cures not previously available.

Finally, no one can deny the benefits which crowdsourcing and mass communication technologies have provided to law enforcement. Instant communications with thousands of citizens through apps or crime-stopper tip lines as well as mass alert texts for critical events (e.g., "active violence" or "AMBER Alerts" for missing children) have helped save lives, solve crimes and arrest criminals.

All these (and so many more) exciting advances mean that technology is evolving at speeds never before seen. Many will have a significant and positive impact on our world, our security and EP. In some cases, these advancements or new developments might only be days old before becoming obsolete due to competing technologies. Others may rapidly need improvements and version updates – all before most of us can even learn how to use the 1.0 version.

More exciting changes are coming our way at speeds as fast as a Hyperloop – stay tuned.

Technology: The Bad

While I can't imagine living without the convenience technology brings to our everyday lives, we must acknowledge the serious risks to our privacy and security that comes with it. For all the good the Internet and related technologies have given us, we're now exposed to a whole new world of risks and threats unimaginable just a few decades ago.

Cybersecurity and Privacy

You might think cybersecurity isn't the purview of EP professionals, but you'd be wrong. Any EP program lacking appropriate consideration and coverage of cyber threats is risking their principal or organization's privacy, safety and security. Depending on a principal's corporate or government position, cyber espionage could even mean the loss of intellectual property and corporate/state secrets.

We look to cybersecurity to defend against the risk or threat of hackers infiltrating systems from the personal computer to the corporate mainframe. If you think these aren't serious dangers, just talk to any IT manager. These professionals are challenged every day by threats ranging from individual cybercriminals to an *army* of hackers looking to cripple their principal or organization. Failure to protect an organization's cybersecurity can result in major loss of revenue, intellectual property (IP), resources or consumer confidence. It can also affect critical infrastructure and, in some cases, result in the loss of lives.

At the annual Overseas Security Advisory Council (OSAC)* conference held at the State Department in late 2018, cybersecurity ranked high on the list of topics, as it has for the past three years. Panel members and speakers included members of the U.S. Secret Service, FBI, State Department, Office of the Director of National Intelligence, and many private-sector and Fortune 500 CSOs and security leaders. They all expressed concerns about the sophistication of evolving tactics of foreign state-sponsored hackers, the increasing number of individual online profiles being targeted by spear phishing, and the hacking of large corporate accounts.

Cybersecurity vulnerabilities can easily be the result of unintentional actions on the part of those inside the EP umbrella – i.e., bad "cyber hygiene." No matter who you are, you put yourself and others within your company or family at risk every time you open an email or text from someone you don't know well, or which even seems like it's from a friend but feels strangely not like them. Clicking on an unverified link or downloading a document you aren't sure you can trust is just like opening your door to a stranger who is casing your home with bad intentions. Logging onto free or unknown wireless hotspots

---

* A federally chartered public-private partnership on matters of international security managed by the U.S. State Department's Bureau of Diplomatic Security

or what you believe is a legitimate Wi-Fi connection (but actually is an "evil twin") is no different than walking into a strange place and putting all of your sensitive data right out in the open.

Companies routinely spend millions of dollars to detect, track, report, investigate, resolve and defend against these concerns. Gartner, a global research and advisory firm, has estimated cybersecurity cost the world nearly $93 billion in 2017.[15] Many other cyber experts put this number much higher and predict a significant increase in cyber-crimes year over year. Interestingly, most of these funds are spent on just defending against attacks and protecting sensitive information, not preventing the attacks in the first place.

In 2015, Ginni Rometty, IBM's chair, president and CEO, was addressing the IBM security summit in New York City, where she theorized that if data is the world's new natural resource and is the new basis of competitive advantage, then "cybercrime, by definition, is the greatest threat to every company in the world."[16] If the threat is this significant to companies, it will also prove to be substantial to individuals and families.

Here's how cybercrime can play out in the real world. One common method hackers use against their cyber targets is "spear phishing" – i.e., disguising oneself as a trusted source via email or other communications in order to gain sensitive information or passwords. Spear phishing can involve malicious URLs disguised as normal links, or it can simply involve impersonating someone close to the target and getting them to unwittingly reveal private information.

Another tactic sometimes used in combination with phishing is the use of "ransomware," where attackers use malicious software ("malware") to block or "kidnap" data and then demand large sums of money for its return. Such attacks are sometimes seen against individuals, but they occur daily against many big companies. More often than not, they aren't reported, so it's hard to get accurate numbers on them.

These attacks result in millions of dollars paid out to criminals and hundreds of millions of lost or stolen personal documents each year. According to the FBI, these figures are increasing rapidly.[17] Most cyber experts and IT directors I talk with say we're in a constant state of catching up and are playing a very frustrating and dangerous game of *Whack-a-Mole*. Alarmingly, as these bad actors succeed in distributing this ransomware, experts caution such attacks will increase.

Many senior U.S. officials and other risk analysts believe one of the most serious threats to our country and our democracy occurred in the months leading up to the 2016 U.S. presidential elections. Our intelligence community states that hacking of the Democratic National Committee's emails and other accounts took place under the direction of a Russian-backed cyber effort, which even involved such simple tactics as spear phishing.

Further details of this attack will continue to be brought to light long after this book is published, but one thing is certain: Cyber warfare has escalated, and the Russians and others will increase their already-extensive efforts on this "battlefield." This is one area of concern which can easily go from bad to ugly very quickly and will only get worse in the years to come, no doubt leading to significant changes in the Internet and "Internet of Things"[18] alike.

What exactly does all this have to do with EP? Breaches in cybersecurity and/or misinformation about a principal or company (e.g., by a hostile actor or foreign nation) could easily put them at a higher risk. As such, EP programs today must include social media and cyber monitoring as part of their protective intelligence efforts. These efforts must be closely connected with company or personal IT teams.

From an EP perspective, the best defense is to have daily backups of all critical data, refusing to pay ransoms and totally resetting all infected computers. Many companies and EP teams even use social media monitoring software that constantly scans enormous amounts of data in search of a "needle in the haystack" that can provide advance warning of any potential risk to their principal.

On a general level, EP managers need to devise and stick to policies and procedures involving the online handling of corporate or personal information. As has been seen repeatedly in recent years, all of your careful cybersecurity efforts can be instantly undermined by simple carelessness.

We are all growing painfully aware that the more dependent we become on technology, the greater the risks to our security. For those subject to high levels of cyber risk from state-sponsored or corporate espionage efforts, the prevalence of web-connected technology *everywhere* in our lives (e.g., in our cars) requires a well-thought-out mitigating strategy. Countermeasures might include the use of secure communications devices normally only available to government agencies but now available to the private sector as well.

I should also note that privacy is not just an IT concern: Our principals and executives are also vulnerable while traveling and often let their guard down when they are technically the most exposed. On more than one occasion, I have passed a note (notice I did not send a text or an email) to my principal while in a vehicle in a foreign country reminding them the conversation they were having on the phone or with a fellow passenger might not be advisable based on the risk of listening devices or even lack of control over our assigned local driver. I know that in certain countries, local intelligence agencies have more often than not interviewed our drivers after our principals have headed home.

Automotive Cybersecurity Risks

Given the speed of technological advancement, automotive cybersecurity is another fast-approaching risk that governments and industries will need to address soon. Wi-Fi and Bluetooth technologies in our vehicles have advanced rapidly; driverless and electric vehicles in particular require an enormous level of connectivity.

But our ability to protect these systems is not as advanced as the technology powering them. EP professionals need to take this gap seriously. Because these technologies are becoming standard in many automobiles, we must be cognizant of the risks to connected vehicles and, by extension, our principals. Principals under physical or IP threat from adversaries may find their vehicles hacked while moving or experience certain automobile functionalities disabled remotely.

In 2016, the Institution of Engineering and Technology released a report providing a thought leadership review of risk perspectives with regard to connected vehicles.[19] This report explained how connected vehicles will make travel safer and more efficient, but also warned that these vehicles and the people in them could be at risk from online threats. In addition, attacks on smart infrastructure or interference with satellite navigation could "severely disrupt traffic in urban areas and bring large parts of a city to a standstill."

The same report outlined recent experiments where researchers from the University of California in San Diego and University of Washington tested their ability to monitor data processes within a smart vehicle and even to take it over entirely from afar. Beyond the threats this poses to individuals' safety, the report suggested hackers may target automobiles because they are host to a wealth of sensitive financial, social media, insurance, lifestyle and medical data.

It is also not unrealistic to assume certain bad actors have been working on the capability to exploit most, if not all, of the smart technology used in modern vehicles (e.g., keyless entry, Wi-Fi, Bluetooth, onboard computer systems relating to vehicle operations, etc.). These blind vulnerabilities can (and should be) of concern for many principals and EP teams. This is another area where the risks should be evaluated and managed by a capable cybersecurity expert.

Drone Dangers

The increased use of drones by the private sector and government can provide many benefits as I've already outlined. But the story is not all positive. Many citizens and governments have been forced to develop defensive measures against adversarial drones that present risks, threats and privacy challenges for our personal security, law enforcement and protective details. I've recently had to address this issue with clients regarding the growing use of drones by paparazzi. Even law enforcement doesn't know how to respond to these concerns because there are no major laws currently protecting citizens from such drone use.

Terrorist groups like ISIS and Al-Qaeda have been trying to perfect their use of crude but effective weaponized drones for a few years now. In 2018, an assassination attempt involving an exploding drone took place against President Nicolás Maduro of Venezuela. While the attack failed, it wasn't the first attempt using this method of assassination and it will not be the last of its kind – for many bad actors, this will be considered a trial run of a new weapons delivery capability.

In the future, capable and/or sadistic entities can and will use drones for deadly purposes. During a U.S. Senate hearing on homeland security in late 2018, sitting FBI Director Christopher Wray testified that the Bureau is convinced terrorist groups will use drones to carry out attacks on American soil.[20] All physical security programs should incorporate discussions of this potential threat vector (including any EP operations), and countermeasures must be considered as part of risk-mitigating strategies.

There are methods under development now to counter these dangers. I recently met with several proprietors of an emerging technology that allows you to be aware of a drone being operated in your immediate vicinity – even if it's invisible to the naked eye. The possibility of drones hovering overhead but out of sight often presents privacy and security concerns among high-profile clients.

Detection is only half of the problem. The rest of the dilemma is bringing bad drones down safely and legally without injuring someone on the ground. Innovative technology and products are constantly being created and tested to defeat a malicious drone, but the best way to defeat a bad drone just might be the use of a good drone with countermeasures. Just like with combat jet fighters, events with skilled drone pilots are popping up involving drone dogfights – or, as some refer to them, the *Game of Drones*.

Lastly, it pains me to acknowledge this, but it will probably take a tragic event and significant loss of life before any meaningful laws will be written and enforced regarding the use of drones.

Information Overload

As I mentioned previously, smartphones have brought such a positive, elevated convenience and electronic awareness to our lives that we'll never be able to be separated from them – until, as inconceivable as it may be now, the next level of technology replaces them. But in speaking with colleagues, clients and friends throughout the world, a consistent sentiment we share is that *we are all nearing a point of sensory overload.*

Because we are all so connected to the wide range of useful information smartphones allow us to find and receive, our obsession (or addiction) is creating new dangers for everyone. Thousands of deaths have already occurred on streets and highways as a result of distracted driving. Even distracted *walking* has caused injuries and deaths as people absorbed in their phones have walked in front of cars, buses or trains. People have even fallen off cliffs while taking selfies. The number of incidents has been serious enough that many governments are enacting laws to allow police officers to fine offenders and bring their attention to the dangers they are posing to themselves and others.

According to a U.S. Department of Transportation report released in 2018, 3,450 people were killed in 2016 and 391,000 were injured in 2015 in motor vehicle crashes involving distracted drivers[21]; some statistics lay blame on cell phone use for a quarter of such accidents.[22]

I'll go into this in more detail later, but we have to remember that being involved in a car accident is one of the greatest risks to our principals – more than any other real or perceived threat they may face (outside of travel to high-threat areas or because of a specific threat).

As we are all now becoming painfully aware, smartphones can also take our focus away from crucial work-related responsibilities. Many corporate policies do not allow smartphone use at the office (or severely restrict it), as businesses understand the level of distraction and addiction these tools create. According to a recent study, the need for access to smartphones can be as addictive as drugs and alcohol for some people.[23]

A recent phenomenon related to smartphone addiction is what's called "phantom vibration syndrome." This syndrome, which has been the subject of many behavioral studies, makes people think their smartphone is vibrating when it's not. This occurs to me often as well, even when I don't have my smartphone with me.

More and more, studies are showing the seriousness of the psychological and/or neurological response from the overuse of a smartphone, which can result in subsequent withdrawal symptoms. Our brains are changing and adapting to the constant connection with our fingers when using a smartphone. If you have any doubt about this, watch a one-year-old child play with your phone once they have observed you using it and see how quickly they master the finger movements necessary. It's amazing to realize those born today will never know what it was like before these powerful little devices.

According to Adam Gazzaley, a neuroscientist at the University of California in San Francisco, this nonstop interactivity is "one of the most significant shifts ever in the human environment."[24] Some people may be able to manage all of this potential distraction, but it is becoming very obvious that many can't. The next time you're in a restaurant or on a plane, take a look around and notice the numbers of diners or passengers who are not engaged with each other, but rather have their attention immersed in their smartphones. In recent years, I have been in many airports and couldn't help but be amazed at even the number of security and law enforcement officers who succumb to this dangerous distraction.

I have also seen a growing number of EP professionals falling victim. We may rightly expect EP practitioners will always be very aware of their surroundings in carrying out their important responsibilities. But they, too, can sometimes exercise poor judgment regarding smartphone usage. This inward focus instead of outward awareness is not a positive trend, as lack of attention has been the reason for many lapses in security in recent years. For example, I am aware of a principal who was robbed of his cell phone on a busy sidewalk because his EP team was distracted at the time by their smartphones. Even trained security drivers or hired chauffeurs are vulnerable to using smartphones behind the wheel.

When, where, how and why security professionals use their phones does require judgment, discipline, planning and even training. I've had many principals tell me one of their biggest complaints about their EP agents is that they're on their phones too much (reading, talking or texting) – even while walking in public. In some cases, multitasking while with a principal is part of the job, but, in *most* cases, this is totally unacceptable behavior by EP professionals. This sends an immediate message that what's on the phone is more important than being aware of your surroundings and protecting your principal.

As security and protection specialists, we *must* be proactive, knowledgeable and sufficiently distant enough from technology to objectively evaluate new innovations and changes in order to be properly prepared and make necessary accommodations to better protect our principals. New technologies can be very exciting and advantageous to the EP profession, but they can also bring significant risks and vulnerabilities. It's imperative we consider all the associated ramifications and not blindly fall into the trap of *bigger, better, faster, more.*

Technology: The Ugly

As we already know, all things that have been and will be invented for good can also be used for malicious purposes. In the wrong hands, almost anything can have deleterious effects on societies and even result in deadly consequences.

With all the bad news we are exposed to every day, it can be difficult to make a distinction between what is just bad and what is really ugly – though I believe there is a difference. I'd consider the ugly to be any events, whether natural or man-made, intentional or unintentional, that cause widespread or severe disruption, destruction, anguish and death. This may include technology's misuse or even unintended negative consequences of its proper use. It could mean the deployment of devastating weapons of mass destruction like biological, chemical or nuclear armaments.

Moreover, as we explored in the previous section, technology seems to be taking over our lives more than we can keep up with it. This ubiquity in some cases leaves us exposed to incredible personal and societal risks which would have been unimaginable just a decade or two ago.

As we delve further into the types of ugly threats/risks that we may encounter, I would like to make a respectful suggestion. Individuals who provide protection and often those who are being protected can have a high level of confidence and pride in their expertise and capabilities. Ironically, it is this very level of confidence that can create a barrier to understanding and knowledge where another expert opinion is required to make sense of these complex issues. Therefore, it is important to keep in mind there is no shame in "tapping out" when a concern extends past your capability or previous exposure.

Artificial Intelligence

It's not my intent to put all future artificial intelligence (AI) technology in one basket of "ugly," since I'm sure AI developers and engineers will continue to advance ever more fascinating and sophisticated innovations with many beneficial uses. It's safe to say there will be unintended consequences resulting from such an invasive technology that also involves human-like interactions and "thought processes" – just as there are when real humans are in charge. As it progresses, AI will probably be "responsible" for bad decision-making and linked to harmful events or those associated with negative ramifications.

Not long ago, Elon Musk and Mark Zuckerberg got into an interesting tiff on Twitter over the potential risks of artificial intelligence. Musk warned that AI could eventually become a threat to humans; Zuckerberg clearly didn't agree. In fact, Musk has frequently warned about the dangers of AI, saying it could even threaten humanity if not developed correctly.[25] During the 2017 Web Summit technology conference in Lisbon, Portugal, physicist Stephen Hawking stated that the emergence of AI could be the "worst event in the history of our civilization" unless society finds a way to control its development.[26] Even he admitted: The future is uncertain.

Artificial intelligence can be broken down into two major categories: (a) artificial narrow intelligence (ANI) or "weak AI" and (b) artificial general intelligence (AGI) or "strong AI." ANI focuses on a particular area or task and does not come anywhere close to human cognitive capacity. AGI, on the other hand, is the type of artificial intelligence that causes security experts more concern, since these advancements will allow technology to think on its own and make independent intelligent decisions like a human. The positive and negative implications AI could have on EP or security in general will continue to be revealed and deliberated as the technology emerges, but there is no doubt AI will have an important impact on personal security.

One major concern regarding AI relates to the increasingly aggressive and sophisticated hacking of computers, devices and systems across the world. Hacking a residential Wi-Fi network or personal email account may be inconvenient, annoying and/or an invasion of one's privacy, but hacking critical AI with malevolent intent could lead to significant and destructive consequences that could include the loss of life and major civil disruption.

This emerging technology will also intensely challenge our laws and courts regarding privacy. In a Rand Corporation perspective on the topic of AI, Osonde A. Osoba and William Welser IV state: "The legal standards of reasonable or acceptable privacy need renegotiation to accommodate new technologies that are being adopted at pace and scale."[27]

Regarding national security, Osoba and Welser write, "The application of AI to surveillance or cybersecurity for national security opens a new attack vector based on this data diet vulnerability. Adversaries may learn how to systematically feed disinformation to AI surveillance systems, essentially creating an unwitting automated double agent." This also opens up a risk for personal security, and EP professionals of the future must be aware of the dangers to personal and company AI systems.

Just like some medications that were initially developed for good but later caused unforeseen negative side effects or social impacts, AI is definitely going to be another game-changer. For now, we're going to have to wait and see where it takes us – and eventually deal with the consequences.

The Internet as a Propaganda Amplifier

The use of the Internet and social media to recruit individuals for nefarious purposes, legitimize evil behavior and spread propaganda is a troubling and growing concern. This phenomenon places our global societies in a constant struggle to maintain our freedoms while trying to work against this spread of evil. It also provides a unique challenge to those running EP programs.

Before the Internet and social media, if an individual or small group felt or acted in ways considered antisocial, unacceptable and even illegal, they would normally do so alone or in a small geographical area. With these modern tools, they now have the ability to connect with and belong to larger associations (global in most cases), all inside the safety of their homes. In many ways, this newfound acceptance of depraved thoughts or urges serves to legitimize their feelings and can make them feel like they're part of a larger and even *acceptable* culture. This can often be dangerous or deadly to companies, employees and principals, as well as our society and our world.

Though terrorists in the traditional sense are not the only ones taking advantage of this new phenomenon, the terrorist group ISIS is probably the most prominent recent example. In the last few years, little has been more troubling than ISIS's ability to assemble an army through mass dissemination of online propaganda and a call to arms to join their sadistic cause. In essence, ISIS has created perhaps the first international "franchise" for terrorists. Their propaganda and messaging tactics have fueled far too many lone wolf actors who feel they have been called to violence against innocents and even civilization itself. ISIS's instruction to their followers to kill with bombs, vehicles, knives, hammers or any means available takes humanity back several centuries to a time of truly barbaric behavior.

To capture or neutralize one terrorist or many is one thing. But to control or eradicate the spread of a deadly ideology to millions of people through the Internet via a few strokes on a keyboard is something altogether very different and requires specialized "soldiers." Back in 2014, the U.S. State Department initiated a multimillion-dollar effort to challenge ISIS with a countermessaging campaign called "Think Again, Turn Away." Not everyone viewed it as being effective, and some even commented that this campaign may have given more attention to ISIS and their propaganda machine. Either way, it highlights the level of effort and cost to counter dangerous messages that can have a devastating effect on safety and security.

Again, this sort of campaign goes well beyond ISIS. The power of the Internet to amplify dangerous messaging can also be seen in the continued rise of "fake news." In fact, there has never been a time when false and/or damaging information could be shared as quickly as it can now via the Internet and social media. A fake story can spread virally and cause uproar in a matter of hours (or even just minutes). In some cases, it can be the source of disrupting violence and even death. During these volatile events, EP teams must pay particular attention to their principals and their routines to ensure they don't unexpectedly become a victim of sudden turmoil. This can be of major concern if a principal is high-profile and/or traveling; such a threat can emerge without warning and can produce any number of flash points in many parts of a city – not just a single location.

The Dark Cyberworld

As we've explored, the Internet can be a powerful force for good. But it can also be a horrific and terrifying place. Child abuse and/or pornography communities, underground human trafficking rings, hate groups with twisted ideologies, and other dangerous associations operate within the Internet, on social media outlets and on the dark web. These people legitimize dangerous criminal behavior and can have significant negative consequences on anyone. In recent years, many reprehensible activities or services that would have previously only been found on the dark web are slowly making their way to mainstream public domains and chat rooms.

For anyone not yet familiar with the term "dark web," it's the sewer of the Internet where layers of networks live and breathe, where anything can be acquired, and where some of the world's worst troll for illegal and despicable goods, services and clients. It can be akin to going underground in major cities to places where you can meet anyone willing to do anything, and where procuring information or an abysmal act is only a matter of price. (In some limited cases, the dark web can also be used by whistleblowers and for other legitimate activity where anonymity is critical.)

Knowing what lurks in the dark world of the cyber underground regarding a protectee can sometimes be essential to a program, depending upon the principal and their profile. As an EP director, you should be aware if your principal's name or association ever appears on the dark web. More importantly, you should know the context in which their name was mentioned and the reason (for example, your principal may be the target of extremist, hateful or threatening speech online).

This level of professional Internet trolling for protective intelligence should only be conducted by experts who really understand how to navigate the dark side of the web, what specifically they are looking for and why. What you might find in this dark space of the Internet are individuals willing and able to retrieve very sensitive data on your principal or offering to sell what they might have on a person. This may include compromising pictures, stolen emails, sensitive personal records or anything else that could be used in a negative or dangerous manner.

A good friend of mine who once worked for the Pentagon had the unique task of carefully diving into the dark web to obtain vital protective intelligence on his newly assigned principals and their families. The years he spent in this space communicating with some very disturbed individuals changed his personality to someone who became increasingly paranoid and concerned about the world around him.

While the most nefarious sites and services exist solely on the dark web, we witnessed not long ago the hacking of a more mainstream website whose business model included assisting married people seeking to have affairs. This popular website legitimized this unfortunate behavior and connected people interested in these services. Their mass marketing had a devastating effect on many people's lives – and arguably contributed to many suicides. While I'm not suggesting we should implement an Internet "morality police" (it's needed but not enforceable), certain activities just push the envelope. Others are outright dangerous and threaten to break down the fabric of civilization.

Cyberbullying and Suicide

I have never drawn hard lines between what is providing close protection with my full-time principals and what is potentially "putting your nose where it doesn't belong." As an EP professional, sometimes you have to address sensitive and even taboo subjects that might seem to cross the line of privacy – some of which we can't ignore in the performance of our jobs. Admittedly, it's a difficult balance.

One area where this flexibility is important is in the realm of cyberbullying and suicide. For decades, the teenage suicide rate was going down. But since 2007, teenage suicides have been on the rise.[28] In recent years, more and more families have been forced to deal with what has sadly become an epidemic among our teenagers.

Suzanne Barber, Director of the Center for Identity at the University of Texas in Austin, once told me, "The Internet and social media environments have become our modern-day examples of the 'Wild Wild West.'" Until certain authorities, controls and even laws are put into place, the greatest risk to individuals and the general public is the anonymity of the web and social media for those who have nefarious intentions and can act with minimal perceived risk to themselves. Bullying, physical and emotional threats, and stalking through virtual contact have been growing concerns over the past decade and have even triggered congressional hearings on the topic.

I, too, have experienced the devastating phone call that too many have received, when the beautiful 15-year-old daughter of longtime family friends of ours took her life due to high school bullying. There are no words to describe the pain and anger felt by all those whose life she touched.

According to the Jason Foundation, we lose approximately 100 teens per week to suicide (over 5,000 per year) in the U.S. alone. To break this disturbing number down even further, that's *one suicide every two hours in America*. The Foundation states that four out of five kids who committed suicide gave clear warning signs of trouble.[29]

Regardless of wealth or status, the devastating effects of bullying (and cyberbullying) are often the reason behind teen suicides, now the third leading cause of death among teenagers. A poll of 4,500 U.S. teens aged 12 to 17 conducted by the Cyberbullying Research Center[30] indicated that nearly three-quarters of them had been bullied at some point in their lives – and 44 percent of them reported it had been within the previous 30 days.

For all the good it does, technology helps facilitate this behavior far too often. The Pew Research Center recently found that 95 percent of teens have access to a smartphone. YouTube is used by 85 percent of teens, followed by Instagram, Snapchat and Facebook. Alarmingly,

24 percent say that social media has a mostly negative effect on their lives – and the Cyberbullying Research Center highlighted that more than half of cyberbullied students said "it really affected their ability to learn and feel safe at school."[31]

These facts are key from an EP perspective. Naturally, all of these teens having access to social media creates many opportunities for good – and very bad – behavior. In the end, we EP practitioners are responsible for the welfare of the children of our protectees; in many cases, they are our youngest principals. As EP professionals, we have a responsibility to report sensitive concerns relating to bullying and self-harm, and our principals have an obligation to listen as we work together to help children through some very difficult times. (Of course, every situation must be addressed on a case-by-case basis, and we should acknowledge every family is different.)

It may go without saying, but balancing our professional roles and understanding necessary personal boundaries with principals can be very challenging at times. In the EP environment, especially when families and children are involved, we are often put in the delicate position of deciding whether to advise parents of concerns associated with their children and when to maintain a certain level of mutual trust with our younger principals. It may be one of the biggest dilemmas we face with family EP details, and principals with children must encourage an open and nonjudgmental dialogue.

We'll talk more about this in a later chapter regarding family EP, but under *no circumstance* does any child, regardless of status or privilege (or lack thereof) deserve to be bullied to the point where they even consider taking their own life.

While I'm on the subject of suicide, I'm going to take some author's discretion and draw attention to the unfortunate number of veterans today who are taking their own lives. According to the Department of Veterans Affairs, total suicides among veterans did decrease slightly from 7,663 to 7,298 between 2015 and 2016, but that's still about 20 a day. Rates of veteran suicide have been higher among the age group of 18–34 and are reportedly increasing.[32] Veterans as a whole made up 18 percent of all suicides in the U.S., even though they are only 8.5 percent of the U.S. population.[33]

Whether because of depression, PTSD or substance abuse, we *must* publicly address this issue and devote greater national resources to help veterans who are coping with this adversity and eliminate the stigma associated with seeking help. I personally know several veterans who have committed suicide or lost their lives from the residual effects of PTSD. For many veterans, substance abuse disorders and addictions just compound their challenges. According to the Department of Veterans Affairs, approximately two out of 10 veterans with PTSD also have a substance abuse disorder, which greatly increases their risk of suicide.[34]

My simple message to any veteran who might be reading this book and having similar thoughts or doubts about the future: Reach out and keep talking to those you know who may understand what you're going through, especially other veterans. You made it through some of the toughest training and experiences known to man, not to mention perhaps difficult times even before joining the U.S. military – and you can make it through this.

If you or someone you know needs to talk to someone now, call the **National Suicide Prevention Lifeline at 1-800-273-TALK (8255)** and if you're a veteran, proudly tell them you are.

One person in emotional distress is one too many. We must increase our awareness and outreach to help lift others from hopelessness, bullying, PTSD and other mental health conditions which may lead to suicide. Even being successful and wealthy does not protect everyone from mental health struggles, as was evident when the iconic fashion designer Kate Spade as well as famed chef, world traveler and writer Anthony Bourdain both chose suicide over living another day and finding help.

In addition, drug overdoses over the years have taken the lives of many principals who had some degree of personal protection. These tragedies obviously illustrate that this is a serious issue that crosses into all demographics. While the exact number of drug overdoses every day is hard to quantify accurately, a recent *L.A. Times* article illustrated drug overdose numbers with a sobering analogy: The annual number of fatalities is so high, it would be similar to having a Boeing 737 aircraft crash and kill all on board – every single day.[35]

As protectors, there may be those rare times where we'll need to be prepared to save our principals from themselves and perhaps rally a group intervention. We strive to ensure that suicide or even accidental drug overdoses are not viable options.

Now that we've discussed the good, the bad, and the ugly sides of technology, I'd like to leave you with a final thought on the topic. In the world of EP, we often focus on the physical methods of protection (e.g., agents, weapons, vehicles and barriers) that help defend our principals from physical threats (e.g., assaults and accidents).

But we frequently underappreciate how technology fits into the overall security equation. In today's world, technology can help us strengthen the protective "bubble" we design for our principals. On the flipside, technological threats can penetrate that bubble and can cause as much harm as any physical danger – if not more.

In short, if you take anything from what we just discussed, it should be the extremely important impact technology will have on your security planning – good, bad and ugly.

With our discussion of technology now behind us, I'd like to explore other challenges you may have to navigate throughout the lifecycle of a protective program, starting with "insider threats" originating in both the cyber and physical worlds.

We'll also look at emotionally-charged topics such as terrorism, kidnapping and assassination; it is important to note that, for those who encounter these threats, the degree of impact will be extreme. However, fortunately for most principals, the risk of encountering these types of events will be low.

Insider Threats: Cyber and Physical

Insider threats can come in all forms and approaches and represent another level of risk that can turn from bad to ugly overnight. What is most concerning is the very nature of the term *insider*. These threats don't just have to represent physical risks for them to be dangerous or to wreak havoc. Cybertechnology has added a whole new dimension to insider threats, with far-reaching negative personal, economic, business and reputational results. In many cases today, a physical threat could even materialize from the results of a cyber threat, or vice versa.

Often, the physical security providers don't comprehend the extent of their protectees' vulnerabilities regarding cyber infrastructure; likewise, cyber experts don't always totally understand the risks associated with poor physical security controls. The two must complement one another to create a cohesive web of protection.

Most commonly, the word *insider* is used in a business context where a security threat originates from a current or former employee, contractor, business partner or associate. However, because we are referring to executive protection (including families under the umbrella), this list includes friends, other family members or anyone who might have trusted access to principals and their families, business networks, databases and other sensitive information.

Cyber Insider Threats

Prior to computers, servers and databases, the term insider threat had a very different meaning. But more recently, cyber threats may be the first thing people consider when they hear of insider threats.

Cyber insider threats are obviously very real, and they must be taken seriously. A common risk may come in the form of a disgruntled employee, an individual hired with a predisposition for criminal or malevolent intentions, someone who is deliberately targeting an organization, or a foreign bad actor.

These bad actors often use unprotected or poorly protected web networks as vectors by which to harm our protectees. For many executives and principals, the possibility of unauthorized access to personal emails or sensitive information can lurk in the background like those mostly unseen icebergs on the surface whose most damaging mass exists out of sight.

Risks may also come from a general blurring of the lines surrounding how we understand privacy today, as we must endure unrelenting requests for more and more of our private information in order to stay connected and relevant amidst a barrage of companies and services. They assure us our data will be safe with them – that is, until they are hacked or that data is sold. Even as we debate and legislate privacy and data rights, we often give up our protections by freely announcing our every move, thought and decision online. When it comes to EP, sensitive information floating around publicly on the web can be a serious danger in plain sight.

On an even more basic level, leaving your phone or computer unattended, unsecured and without a screen lock is *never* advisable. And if you want to see an IT manager lose their mind, plug a USB flash drive into your work or personal computer that someone gave you at a trade show (or found on the ground), or click on one of those phishing emails because you thought it was from a friend.

Additionally, many executives and their family members assume their private or home network is somehow protected under the corporate cybersecurity umbrella. This is rarely the case. When in doubt, it is highly recommended to bring in a trusted and vetted cyber expert to evaluate your home network and review your family's online presence and cyber hygiene. This effort is no longer just something you do once and don't have to think about again; in some environments, depending on your risk level, this analysis may be repeated several times a year.

Ultimately, no matter how diligent the adults may be regarding cybersecurity, your entire family's security and privacy can still be impacted by your children's unwitting behavior regarding social media, online presence and participation in risky online activities.

As an example, I know of an executive who spent a significant amount annually to protect his and his family's privacy. Information security and confidentiality were of the utmost importance to him. He and his family were always careful to limit knowledge of travel plans and itineraries only to those who had a true "need to know." They had proper tripwires in place and ensured members of the security detail were constantly scouring the Internet for information that could have a negative effect or generate a security risk.

On one occasion, all of these precautions were undone instantly by one of the children, who posted pictures of their travel on a highly popular social media platform during a family vacation. This post went undetected just long enough that it could have posed a significant risk to the family.

With nothing more than a simple click, a family member, friend or staff member can easily erase weeks, months or years of work and diligence in protecting sensitive information. In some cases, irresponsible posts can endanger the physical safety of principals, their families and their security details; at a minimum, their reputation can be damaged. Usually, this recklessness is not a result of malicious intent, but is due to young family members or naïve employees who wish to boast about their exciting experiences.

This story is often repeated with many high-profile or UHNW families and the children who can't resist sharing their exact travel location and activity with the world – thereby unintentionally inviting paparazzi and other unwanted attention. We have seen this situation played out far too often with certain reality stars or celebrities who use social media to remain relevant with their audience. Just like with an oversharing family member, their objective is not to bring harm or risk to themselves or their families. But the result is that, once the information becomes public, it is almost impossible to control those who repost, save and disseminate this information, regardless of the harm those actions may cause.

In the end, it takes a dedicated cyber specialist to navigate these dangerous waters and keep your privacy and cybersecurity "boat" from being sunk. No security program today is complete without a comprehensive cybersecurity initiative. While some individuals claim to be proficient in managing their own cybersecurity, it has been my experience that this is not an arena in which to be guided by amateurs. It takes a real subject-matter expert to actively ensure all your cyber vulnerabilities are evaluated, under control and being monitored continuously for risks.

It may start with a qualified third-party cyber risk assessment (CRA) to identify the potential vulnerabilities and gaps within your cybersecurity network. This would include your web networks, computers and devices, as well as your personal and organizational policies and procedures for managing your cyber presence. The CRA should include mitigating strategies and recommendations to consider regarding all your cyber concerns, especially while you are traveling, at home and in the office. In many cases, a good cyber expert can tailor a class or give personal instructions to improve your cybersecurity, password strength and storage, use of dual authentication logins and (most of all) improve your cybersecurity hygiene. And if your travels take you to high-risk countries, these experts can help set you up with a proper plan and secondary equipment to reduce your cyber risks and obviate a data breach or theft by overt or covert means.

Physical Insider Threats

As with cyber insider threats, those physically closest to us can have negative intentions or make very bad decisions that can cause harm or increase personal safety risks. Thankfully, this doesn't occur as often as in the cyber world due to the sheer volume of threat paths in today's cyber environment, but insider physical threats and risks do occur, so it is imperative to maintain awareness for signs of potential trouble.

With high-profile celebrities, these risks can come in the form of a staff member, vendor or contractor selling information to tabloids or paparazzi. If you are running a business that has sensitive information and intellectual property, you must be careful who has access to this information – whether at the office, while traveling or at home.

Too often, the calendars of corporate CEOs and executives are exposed to more people than they should be. In some cases, it can just be a matter of staff or employees – including EP personnel – disclosing too much private (or even confidential) information about their principals and their lives.

In 1999, Edmond Safra, a 67-year-old Lebanese Brazilian banker (whose net worth was around $2.5 billion) heard a commotion at the door of his Monaco penthouse apartment. He immediately went to his safe room and felt confident his protective detail would let him know when all was secured. Unfortunately, he probably didn't recall he had dismissed his detail earlier that day.

Safra's American nurse – a former U.S. Army Special Forces medic and part-time bodyguard – was with him in the apartment. Unbeknownst to Safra, he had started a small fire as part of a plan to convince his principal and other security personnel that he had foiled an attack. He intended to put out the fire and "save" Safra in order to gain his acceptance and that of the security detail.

It was later learned that the bathroom designated as a safe room in Safra's penthouse home was improperly designed; the space was not built to withstand heat or smoke and lacked proper external communications. Safra and a second nurse died from smoke inhalation after locking themselves in this room.

An associate of mine had been on Safra's protective detail two years prior to this event. He said Safra had been briefed many times on his security team's concerns regarding this medic/security officer. The medic had displayed strange behavior and an unhealthy and alarming level of "affection" toward Safra. According to my friend, the signs leading up to this tragedy were there but ignored.

While conspiracies and claims have surfaced over the years that others were involved with Safra's death or that the medic was pressured by Monaco police to admit to starting the fire, the medic was found guilty in 2002 and sentenced to 10 years in a Monaco prison. He was released in 2007.[36]

Consider this as well: In 1995, an employee and personal assistant to the American Tejano singer and songwriter Selena had been displaying serious personality issues. These issues were not directly addressed and, because of the lack of action to stop her, the assistant shot and killed Selena – another tragic loss that should never have occurred.

Admittedly, these are *extreme* examples of insider threats. Fortunately, they don't happen very often, and I feel most people have the best of intentions. Also, these illustrations are not intended to make you begin doubting everyone's loyalty or sanity, but to demonstrate the dangers of ignoring obvious signs of concern. In many cases, rather than physical harm, these situations more often result in embarrassment, financial loss, privacy breaches, damaged business relationships, risks to intellectual property and investments, and other non-physical threats.

Overall, the best advice is still "see something, say something." If you have a concern, assemble a small group of trusted advisors and discuss the situation. Consider outside counsel if needed to take the appropriate next steps.

It is imperative that EP details and their principals work together to avert, acknowledge and investigate legitimate concerns regarding insider threats. While efforts can be made to mitigate the risks associated with insider threats, I prefer a proactive approach. Many times, principals are hesitant to plan for such events – understandably, it can be difficult to believe those closest to you could betray you, but your family's physical and psychological well-being and, in some cases, their very lives, can be at risk.

Terrorism

Terrorism is real and so are the effects – and, as long as there are humans, there will be terrorism in one form or another.

No one will ever forget the attacks of September 11, 2001 – the images from that day are seared in our memories. Americans and the world are still feeling the effects of the attacks (physically and emotionally), even after nearly two decades.

Today, our news is saturated by attacks conducted by groups like Al-Qaeda, ISIS, Al-Shabaab and Boko Haram. But terrorism isn't new; these despicable groups are parts of a long line of terrorist organizations dating back decades. At various points since the 1960s, groups like the Palestine Liberation Organization (PLO), Germany's Red Army Faction (RAF), the Abu Nidal Organization (ANO), the Irish Republican Army (IRA), Hezbollah and others have all engaged in terrorist attacks. Some of these groups have survived and tried to remain relevant to their causes; many have dissolved or been eliminated over time.

The U.S. has not been immune to terror or extremist groups popping up within its own borders. Groups like the Weather Underground, United Freedom Front, Jewish Defense League, Symbionese Liberation Army (whose kidnapping and controversial coercion of wealthy heiress Patty Hearst in 1974 brought them widespread attention[37]), Black Liberation Army and Army of God all had their roots in the U.S. and operated actively for years. Some might even classify the Ku Klux Klan as America's oldest terrorist organization, with some of today's fringe groups taking up their charge.

Not long ago, the term "terrorism" had a simpler definition. Webster defined it as "the unlawful use or threat of violence especially against the state or the public as a politically motivated means of attack or coercion."[38] But the swarm of terrorist attacks around the world since 9/11 has left this simple definition lacking – at least toward our ability to understand all the motives behind terrorism today.

Even Dr. Bruce Hoffman, Professor at Georgetown University and the Walsh School of Foreign Service – a man who has been studying terrorism for decades – explains that it is not always easy to use one definition of terrorism. The U.S. government itself often struggles to stick to one definition.[39] *

---

* It's reasonable to believe the U.S. and other governments are resistant to put one specific label or definition on terrorism, as they want to have the necessary latitude in their response options, capabilities and funding.

The recently deceased global historian, political commentator and distinguished scholar Walter Laqueur concluded many years ago, "No all-embracing definition [of terrorism] will ever be found, for the simple reason that there is not one terrorism, but there have been many terrorisms, greatly differing in time and space, in motion, and in manifestation and aims."[40] * Laqueur stated that there are over one hundred definitions of terrorism in existence. He also wrote:

> *Terrorism is largely a generational phenomenon and, even if defeated, it may recur at a later date. There is no good reason to expect the disappearance of terrorism in our time. In an age in which large-scale wars have become too dangerous and expensive, terrorism is the prevailing form of violent conflict. As long as there are conflicts on earth, there will be terrorism.*

You only need to look to recent homegrown terrorism in the U.S. to observe this recurrence. For example, towards the end of the 2018 election season, a man apparently fueled by the current political rhetoric and his own mental health issues sent pipe bombs to various high-profile individuals and a large news organization. These bombs were fortunately intercepted before they detonated.

As I mentioned in the beginning of the book, I want to give readers some background as to where those in my profession gain their experiences and form their perspectives. My proximity to many terrorist attacks and even a few terrorists over the years has definitely created a certain sensitivity about the subject for me, and I'm sure for others as well.

I got my first real introduction to the many terrorist groups and ideologies during the mid-to-late 1980s while stationed at Ramstein Air Base in Germany. I often worked alongside agents of the Air Force

---

* I'd even add that the British believed the American revolutionaries (1775–1783) to be terrorists.

Office of Special Investigations, Air Force intelligence officers, German police and others; this served to expand my knowledge of investigations and intelligence regarding groups deemed a threat to Americans or our interests.

At the time, the ANO, PLO and RAF caught much of my attention. I took a keen interest in these organizations and their modus operandi, affiliations and reasons for existence. I kept a calendar hanging on my office wall that recorded all past terrorist attacks over the recent decades at that time. This calendar was monitored regarding potential anniversary attacks which might affect our base or my protectee.

Just a few days before Christmas 1988, Americans and the world were shocked by the bombing of Pan Am Flight 103 over Lockerbie, Scotland, which took the lives of 243 airline passengers, 16 crew members and 11 individuals on the ground. Of the 189 Americans on this flight, many were members of the military, CIA officers (including the Beirut deputy station chief), State Department diplomatic security agents, and other U.S. embassy security officers.

Ramstein had one of our own on the flight that sad day: Edgar Howard Eggleston III, a 24-year-old Air Force sergeant from Glens Falls, New York. Sgt. Eggleston was a fellow airman whom I met when teaching a course regarding remote security measures for those assigned to sensitive communications sites and high-risk facilities. Like most of those passengers, Edgar was going home for Christmas – in his case, to see his ailing stepmother.

While several terrorist organizations jumped to claim responsibility, many believe Libya's Muammar Gaddafi gave the orders to take down Flight 103. Others believe Iran had a hand in the attack.

Regardless of who planned or gave the orders to blow up Pan Am Flight 103, I can still picture Edgar's car in the parking lot near the communications building where it sat, untouched, for several months following the bombing. As I drove past his car every day, I was constantly reminded of our loss and that horrific attack on humanity.

Neither this book nor EP are about waging war against terrorism; our profession *cannot and does not* take an offensive posture in trying to defeat it. Rather, we take a *defensive* stance or strategy of avoidance – which is what we'll discuss in the next few pages.*

Terror Today: Being in the Wrong Place at the Wrong Time

Your mathematical odds of being at a location when an unexpected attack occurs are so small as to be almost incalculable (unless you are living in a part of the world where they obviously occur with regularity). For those who are not operating in these environments, we should realize the odds of ever being a victim of terrorism are on the same scale as that of being killed by a tornado.[41] Instead of victimizing ourselves via the mere thought of being targeted or caught up in a terrorist attack, remember that millions of public events occur every single day around the world without incident.

But that doesn't mean we should ignore the threat. Many corporate executives and UHNW families are frequent international travelers and can often find themselves at popular locations and events – thus increasing the odds of being a victim, even if ever so slightly. As EP providers on travel with our principals, we are now, more than ever,

---

* Even so, the vast majority of EP teams do not specifically try to defend against terrorist activity. Those EP teams that are at a heightened state of anti-terror awareness involve those whose principals have some degree of relevant personal prominence or the need/desire to travel to high-threat locations.

forced to consider and mentally prepare for our options regarding such events. Many attacks may not even be terror-related – in many cases, they are unprovoked, random acts by mentally unstable individuals or those with other twisted ideologies.

A determined, relentless and sadistic adversary – whether an organized group or just a lone wolf – can be difficult, if not impossible, to predict, detect or defend against once that person or group has initiated their heinous plan. Our challenge is to know when, where and how to reasonably adapt to these changing times and attack methodologies, while not allowing them to control our lives or the lives of our principals. It's a delicate balance. EP professionals must resist the urge to overcompensate just because these events seem to occur more frequently – and yet be ready to articulate concerns rationally when we want to increase the level of security around our protectees.

On the most basic level, EP professionals and principals alike must develop their own internal plans of action for reacting to a terror-like attack. As EP leaders, we should prepare by running through potential attack scenarios to which our principals and teams may be exposed. We need to consider and know our primary and secondary escape routes, hospitals, hotels, airports, embassies and consulates. We might be looking for at least semi-safe rooms or secure locations where we can sit tight as we determine our next moves.

In some cases, it's not just enough to survive an attack – additional risk factors may present themselves in the chaos that follows. Secondary attacks, mass confusion, stress and tactical mistakes can sometimes be as dangerous as the initial attack itself.

Unfortunately, we can't always identify the *wrong place at the wrong time* before something terrible happens. If your principal is ever specifically targeted or you are operating in high-risk terror environments, *you must ensure your EP program has an effective strategy regarding your principal's safety.* For everyone else, terrorism is another part of our planning, mindset and resources – i.e., the *what if* scenarios we run through before any movement, trip or event.

The right mindset and preparedness came in handy in 2015, when three Americans were forced to subdue a suspected lone gunman on a high-speed train in France who was armed with an AKM assault rifle, a pistol and a box cutter. This individual, who planned a killing spree on board the moving train, was stopped by the three American passengers who were determined not to let it happen. Their brave actions no doubt saved dozens of lives.

Another famous incident that took place in India demonstrated the value of the proper mindset and preparedness. On the evening of November 26, 2008, ten terrorists launched well-planned attacks on locations throughout the city of Mumbai, killing at least 164 people over almost four days before being stopped. These attacks came without notice and caught everyone off guard, including the Indian government, intelligence communities and thousands of tourists exploring this enchanting city.

I personally know several security and EP specialists who were in the city at that time and who had to quickly jump into action with the very response for which we always prepare but hope is never required. Some of these individuals have been recognized for their efforts and can be credited with saving the lives of their principals and others who gratefully fell under their protective umbrella on that terrible day.

Sadly, several individuals did not heed the specialists' advice and attempted their own escape without assistance; in some cases, they were killed during the the chaos while trying to get to safety. Others found themselves barricaded in a room until a better plan and rescue could be organized and executed.

A few years after this attack, I was given a guided tour of the Taj Mahal Palace by one of the hotel's longest-serving employees. On the day of the attack, this gentleman was just leaving the hotel when gunfire erupted. He quickly ran back inside for cover and spent the next several days hiding out and trying to help other employees and guests do the same. He led me and a colleague on a detailed tour as he recounted the events and what was still the very vivid trauma of what he and so many others experienced.

It was both overwhelming to consider the mass chaos and confusion that occurred as well as confounding that 10 individuals could cause such devastation over a four-day period throughout this city before being stopped by police and the Indian Special Forces.

It is events like these that make you realize: It might be just a matter of your EP team's training, preparedness, situational awareness and all the advance work they do that will give you enough time to react, adjust and recover as they try to keep you out of harm's way.

Ultimately, the best response to wrong place, wrong time events is to be one step ahead regarding your safety and security planning and mindset. I can tell you firsthand that how you respond immediately after these events in certain locations and countries might affect whether or not you are able to share your stories later.

Years ago, an extremely high-profile principal of mine had to travel to a particular country on business which was not considered to be especially tolerant of his specific religious beliefs, background and political position. On this trip, he had meetings and even a small public media event that would be aired locally on the same day. The local country management wanted him to attend additional business meetings and a dinner following the media event, as well as spend the night at this location.

My first instinct was to question why it was important for him to remain in this country overnight – especially given the news reports that he was here, which would raise his profile and attract those who might want to target him before his departure.

I shared my concern with him in a way that I figured he would appreciate as a businessman. I said I didn't see the "return on investment" (ROI) regarding his extended and overnight stay at this time due to the associated risk factors. His response was, "I trust you and it's your call."

Needless to say, we finished the media event and headed directly to the airport, where we implemented our backup plan for our overnight stay at another location while continuing his regional business travel. While I wasn't popular with the local management team (as they wanted their time with the boss), it was my professional opinion the ROI was not worth his personal risk.

Throughout my career, I have found if I have articulated my thoughts on a threat, risk or concern to my principals professionally and intelligently with alternatives and solutions, in almost all cases they have heeded my warning and/or advice and accepted my recommendations. Word of caution to EP providers: Your credibility is crucial when suggesting major changes to executives' schedules and programs, so make sure you have all your facts first and do a strong gut check.

Separating ISIS from Islam

Our faith, like yours, commands mercy, peace and tolerance.
It upholds, as yours does, the equal human dignity of every
person – men and women, neighbors and strangers. Those outlaws
of Islam who deny these truths are vastly outnumbered
by the ocean of believers – 1.6 billion Muslims worldwide.

– His Majesty King Abdullah II bin Al-Hussein
of the Hashemite Kingdom of Jordan

Over the last decade, ISIS has ramped up our society's fear factor, and many have grown worried a terrorist attack could happen at any location where crowds are gathered. Some Westerners harbor an unreasonable level of fear of all Muslims since ISIS claims to represent the Islamic faith.

This concerns me, not just because of this specific ISIS-related sentiment, but, just as importantly, how we handle the next "ISIS" with a similar ideology. We must remember that world history is full of examples of people committing major atrocities in the name of their religion or deity. Just as in the case of ISIS, these small factions of misguided religious zealots haven't represented all those of their faith, whether Christian, Jewish, Muslim or something else.

While I met some friendly opposition to the inclusion of this topic in the book, I believe it is relevant to the EP profession. I've unfortunately witnessed unwarranted fear or concern among some in our own field when providing protection in countries where Islam is the primary religion. Some EP agents have difficulties separating what ISIS (and other similar groups) represent from the rest of the world's over one billion Muslims.

With that said, the anxiety is understandable on a practical and basic human emotional level if you can't automatically distinguish between a good person or bad person wearing the same clothes. Many EP practitioners are former military or security contractors who have served in various Muslim countries where they have been in combat – and may have experienced terrible events that reasonably can alter one's perception.

It is important to remember these difficulties are not unique to Islam or Muslim regions, as many in the U.S. have formed and maintained similar emotions and opinions as a result of wartime experiences in other countries (e.g., Japan, Germany, Korea, China, Vietnam, Russia and even Britain at one point). By the same token, many across the globe have not always agreed with American policies or our involvement in their countries; therefore, they often have their own suspicions and even loathing of Americans. For EP professionals of all nationalities, we sometimes feel this awkwardness when working in various places throughout the world.

The threats and risks we face from ISIS or likeminded extremists today – or the next ISIS under another extremist or religious banner tomorrow – are very real. ISIS is obviously not the first terror group, nor will they be the last. At the same time, it is important to recognize there are many outstanding Muslims fighting and often dying on the front lines in coalition forces and others who work diligently behind the scenes to put a stop to terror. According to the Pentagon, this number includes over 5,000 wearing U.S. military uniforms.[42] Hundreds, if not thousands, of U.S. soldiers and special operators have relied on their Muslim interpreters and counterparts throughout the world – and, in many cases, each have helped save the life of the other. Overwhelmingly, those of Muslim faith are just as concerned for our mutual safety as we non-Muslims are.

It doesn't excuse the attacks or take away the pain of a loved one's death due to terrorism, but one could argue that no group has lost more in life and irreplaceable cultural heritage as a result of the barbaric atrocities committed by ISIS than Muslims themselves.

Even today, with all the concern over ISIS in the U.S., our memories are fading with regard to the April 1995 bombing in the heart of Oklahoma that killed over 168 of our own citizens and injured hundreds more. This attack was perpetrated by former U.S. soldiers belonging to the same faith as a majority of Americans (although one was a self-described atheist who later converted to Christianity). Regardless of their professed religious beliefs, they too were motivated by a misguided and extremist view of the U.S. government that led them to kill and wound hundreds of innocent American citizens and children of all faiths.

The Oklahoma bombing was an outlier event regarding domestic terrorism and cannot be compared with the concentrated threats from other formidable enemies with a religious edict to destroy or convert. The point is that hate and even evil can come from *all* types of religious and secular ideologies. We need to remember that a shared religious belief was not the common thread behind these attacks – the *intent to kill* was the motivation.

As far as Islam is concerned, I have traveled and lived in various Middle Eastern and Islamic countries for many years. I have worked day-to-day beside those of Muslim faith, have been invited into their homes, solved complicated issues together and celebrated together. In some cases, I have depended upon them to protect me and my principals.

As EP professionals, we must assume a logical role of calmly guiding our protective programs and principals through these confusing periods of increased terrorist attacks. We must have a plan that is effective but reasonable, use prudent courage, avoid becoming a victim of fear, and refuse to submit to intimidation.

Kidnapping and Assassination

Kidnapping and assassination are among the worst-case scenarios that EP services protect principals against. These risks are extremely rare, but they're part of the landscape – and if you're still determining your need for EP, the thought may have occurred to you at least once.

Here are some insights on how to assess and approach these unique risks – again, most of which are extremely unlikely for the vast majority of principals.

Kidnapping

We often see reports of child kidnapping on the news and posters in public places showing yet another missing teenager. Movies like *Taken* can raise your concern and, yes, fear. Over the past few years, there has been no shortage of real-life kidnappings occurring in places like the Middle East and Latin America. Many play out openly in the media, and too many have ended in devastating murders. It is no surprise that the fear of kidnapping can grip anyone's mind – especially a person with a high profile.

Kidnapping is one of society's worst crimes and a horrific event for everyone involved. It should also only be handled by a professionally trained negotiator. As a former colleague, friend and retired FBI agent with experience in over 100 hostage negotiations once told me, his last negotiation was no less disturbing than his very first. Most of his negotiations took place in Mexico over more than a decade. It is important to note that all of his victims survived their ordeals.

In the summer of 2015, the White House announced there were approximately 30 Americans being held hostage abroad. This topic was brought to the forefront after many families whose loved ones were being held publicly voiced their struggle and frustration with our own government's longstanding policy against any "negotiation" with terrorists for the release of Americans being held hostage. Ransom is still a sensitive subject, as many believe if our government starts paying for kidnapped Americans (as is the practice in many other countries), the dangers to Americans traveling abroad (especially in high-risk areas) would increase exponentially and place a price tag on U.S. citizens everywhere. While this is a reasonable viewpoint from a macro level, for the family members of those wanting their loved ones returned, any cost or effort expended is worth it.[43]

In some countries, kidnapping is a daily concern, with criminals using it as a tool for extortion and profit. The risk will vary from country to country; Mexico, India, Pakistan and Iraq often top the list. We should note that most individuals kidnapped are from the same nationality of the country in which they are taken.

While kidnapping *for ransom* is rare in the United States, we are not completely immune from the risk of other types of kidnapping. According to the FBI National Crime Information Center (NCIC), there were 464,324 entries for missing children in 2017. The National Center for Missing & Exploited Children (NCMEC) reported it assisted in more than 27,000 cases during that year, which it categorized as follows: [44]

- 91 percent endangered runaways
- 5 percent family abductions
- 3 percent critically missing young adults, ages 18 to 20
- 1 percent nonfamily abductions
- Less than 1 percent lost, injured or otherwise missing children

Many other attempted or actual kidnappings routinely go unreported or are unknown to the public. As a result, the authorities believe the statistics regarding actual kidnappings are slightly higher than are reflected in official reports. While I will not mention names, I am aware of several other more recent global kidnappings of high-profile family members. But they are still extremely rare.

We've also seen a significant increase in "virtual kidnapping." This is where a criminal demands ransom over a phone call or text for someone they falsely claim to be holding as a hostage (generally a younger family member). Normally these kidnappers ask for an amount small enough that the unwitting family member can send or transfer it easily and quickly for the release of the "captive."

The FBI has warned citizens to be more aware of these extortion scams, but they still continue today. They advised that many of these cases are on the Pacific Coast and involve criminal groups from Mexico claiming to be members of a cartel – thereby instilling more fear on the part of the family being extorted. The FBI reports an increase in instances of this scam in many other states such as New York, Nevada and Texas. Many scammers target seniors now, as they are perceived to be easier to dupe.

The FBI believes the best way to avoid the scam is to be alert if you receive one of these types of calls and to slow the conversation down by asking for more time. After this, attempt to call or text the victim or their friends to locate them and confirm they have not been kidnapped, then contact the police.

So how does the kidnapping landscape impact a principal? The first thing to know is that an individual's financial status or worth is *not an automatic factor for targeted kidnapping*. In fact, many criminals in kidnapping-prone countries target foreign travelers of any level of wealth or position. These kidnappers can be especially dangerous because of their lack of sophistication. They are often unconcerned with being caught or whether or not anyone is harmed in the act, and they might not be aware of the wealth status of the person they are targeting.

In fact, I agree with many of my colleagues and other experts: Those individuals with extreme wealth and political connections (the presidency, FBI, CIA, law enforcement, international diplomats, etc.) might actually be the *last* group a kidnapper would want to target if they had any reasonable expectation of enjoying their ransom. Kidnappers know that, in most cases, a UHNW individual would use their influence and empty their accounts to ensure justice was meted out to those who harmed their family members.

However, this is not universally true. Some criminal organizations and gangs are so large that those at the top have less concern of being caught or prosecuted, since they direct others to perform their heinous work. In addition, some individuals or groups might target UHNW individuals for political, criminal or publicity gains regarding their cause or claims (the Lindbergh baby and John Paul Getty III come to mind). There are also those who might prey upon high-profile individuals for self-gratification, including some sort of personal revenge.

While the kidnapping risk can never be completely dismissed, it is important to analyze the actual likelihood of this occurring to you or a family member. Given the total number of UHNW and high-profile individuals and families around the world who are *not* affected by this crime, the actual risk of being kidnapped for simply having wealth is still miniscule. Statistically, you or your children have greater odds of choking on food, getting hit in a crosswalk, being robbed on the street, being bitten by a dog, getting struck by lightning or falling off a ladder, than being targeted for kidnapping.

Factors that might increase this otherwise small risk include your profile, accessibility (low security) and fixation by a disturbed person to do harm or exact revenge on you or your family. Certain behaviors on the part of a UHNW family member will also always elevate the danger. These include high-risk travel exposure, interactions with nefarious individuals, questionable business affiliations, or associations with others who might take advantage of the relationship, trust and proximity (i.e., the insider threat).

While still extremely rare, the associated concerns and consequences are the very reasons many individuals and families will at least occasionally consider the kidnapping scenario. The risks and dangers must be realistically examined as part of a holistic EP program to ensure appropriate consideration, protection and response measures are in place. While we can't address everyone's risks in this book, I encourage a healthy but reasonable discussion with a protection professional as part of your overall dialogue on this topic.

In the case of corporations, they must at least acknowledge the risk in order to meet their *duty of care* for their employees and staff traveling to dangerous areas. This requirement is a growing concern for many companies and is becoming legally complicated as to how much responsibility a private business should assume. I suggest that corporate security managers spend some time with each principal's general counsel to ensure their program meets the corporate responsibility and good faith effort to protect executives and employees where safety and security are issues – regardless of whether or not high-risk areas factor into the equation.

There is also something to be said about your own presence of mind as a principal in relation to this topic. In recent years, I've had the opportunity to meet and provide occasional support to an internationally recognized supermodel and businesswoman, her husband, and their beautiful family. I was surprised to learn that, while traveling to Europe for work during her early years of modeling, she narrowly escaped being kidnapped herself. This young model used her basic human survival instincts and skills that students are taught in the Survival, Evasion, Resistance and Escape (SERE) training that I received in my own previous military life. Her attention to detail, situational awareness and quick action very possibly saved her from a terrible outcome.

In most cases, your greatest chance of escape and survival is taking *immediate* action upon being kidnapped to resist and get free. In most cases, the initial hands-on kidnappers have a specific role of grabbing and getting you to those who are better prepared to keep you for as long as they need – i.e., people who use specific resources and methods that will make escaping much more difficult.

At the end of the day, you can't allow kidnapping to consume your thoughts or generate unreasonable fear. Nevertheless, kidnapping is one area of risk where the right measure of prevention will *always* be better than any level of response.

Assassination

For most readers of this book, like the subject of kidnapping, the subject of assassination is the furthest thing from your mind. I am only going to touch on the topic because it really requires specific and direct discussion if you *ever* believe you could be a target of assassination. While it is *extremely* rare, it does occur and cannot be ignored when protecting high-profile individuals.

While assassination is always considered murder, murder is rarely considered an assassination. Cause for a targeted assassination normally falls under political/governmental, religious, criminal or ideological reasons. Assassins are often motivated by money, power or insanity. Targets include presidents, royalty, religious leaders, business decision-makers and often spies. Celebrities have been targets as well, but normally by those who are mentally unstable. We've also seen several recent examples of individuals who posed a threat to certain world leaders becoming victims of assassination, including Kim Jong-un's own brother.

For most protectees, assassination is not a concern; however, high-profile figures can never rule out a personal attack from someone suffering from a psychotic condition or episode. And while terrorist-related assassinations would still fall under the above-mentioned motivations, most principals will not find themselves on these target lists.

That being said, a few years ago, Al-Qaeda released an online magazine that called for the killing of a number of American businesspeople in lone-wolf attacks. I will not refer to any names but, trust me, their security and our government were (and still are) aware of these threats. Similarly, ISIS has listed the names and addresses of targets, including some members of the military, and has ordered the same style of attacks and assassinations.

In December 2016 in Ankara, Turkey, the world watched video of the moment an off-duty police officer assassinated Andrei Karlov, the Russian ambassador to Turkey. This assassination was politically motivated, as the killer was heard shouting "Do not forget Aleppo! Do not forget Syria!" Whether or not this was the only objective or if he had deeper motivation is still undetermined, but the result was the same for the ambassador.

Any trained close protection specialist must always consider assassination as a possibility, regardless of a potential assassin's motivation.

While principals have never been attacked under my or my team's protection, I do believe there have been times in my career, both as a solo practitioner and as part of a team, that I/we may have avoided a possible assassination or planned attack. I have also had more than one principal who became a potential target of assassination. The risk requires a serious and immediate recalculation regarding a principal's activity and exposure while a proper protective counterapproach is applied until the danger can be mitigated.

If you've done this type of work long enough for certain principals, you may never know how close you've come to a potential assassin. Consider this: Before John Hinckley Jr.'s assassination attempt on President Ronald Reagan, he stalked President Jimmy Carter. In 1980, Hinckley attended a public event where President Carter was speaking; it was reported he later told the Secret Service he had a pistol and was going to shoot Carter. While standing in line only a few feet from the President, he felt a Secret Service agent make eye contact with him. In his paranoid state of mind, he decided not to attempt the assassination.

During periods of surveillance or while scanning a crowded hotel lobby or audience, I myself have sometimes made eye contact with persons of interest (POIs) and dispatched a team member or host nation's security to investigate further. In some instances, we felt enough reason for concern and changed our plans regarding our principal's movements.

One more thing to be aware of on this topic is the aversion close protection specialists have to many arrival and departure locations (hotels, restaurants, airports, offices, etc.). In addition, lobbies, escalators and elevators can present challenges to control and secure.* Hotels (especially large ones) can be one of the most difficult types of venues at which to conduct EP operations – so these sites are near the top of the critical list to get right.

---

* To our higher-profile and higher-risk principals: This is one of the reasons we prefer to check you into the hotel ahead of time and have your hotel keys with us so we can take you directly to your room. Sometimes we may suggest you use a side or back door for entry. Depending upon the location and event, we EP types get a little nervous if you decide to stop to chat with a friend, colleague or admirer on your way in or out of a hotel for too long.

Why do hotels concern us? Consider Robert Kennedy in 1968, Ronald Reagan in 1981, Margaret Thatcher in 1984, hotel attacks in Jordan, Mumbai, Islamabad, Kabul, Indonesia, Mogadishu and Tripoli, and even the 2010 assassination of Hamas military wing leader Mahmoud Al-Mabhouh in a Dubai hotel. Regardless of the reasons, methods or the people behind planned assassinations, these attacks show the level of vulnerability, access and predictability associated with hotels and certain similar venues whose visiting security and EP don't normally have enough resources or time to provide comprehensive security coverage – therefore requiring us to tighten the protective circle around our principals.

The Profile of Assassins

In trying to counter the threat of assassination, you may wonder whether there is a certain profile to look out for – i.e., can assassins be identified ahead of time based on certain characteristics? The answer isn't simple.

Dr. Robert A. Fein, a forensic psychologist specializing in threats and violence, has worked with the Department of Defense and the U.S. Secret Service for two decades. During this time, he has personally worked on hundreds of protective intelligence cases involving possible threats to the President or people of similar stature. His 1997 Exceptional Case Study Project regarding attempted assassinations since 1949 did not reveal any particular demographic profile common to assassins. Rather, it showed various *reasons* and *behaviors* that lead a person to attempt this act – something that is much harder to track.

In 1975, 28-year-old Lynette Alice ("Squeaky") Fromme could have assassinated President Gerald Ford before being restrained by a U.S. Secret Service agent if her Colt .45 pistol actually had a round in the chamber. According to Fromme, she intentionally ejected the cartridge earlier and had not really intended on killing the President. Either way, Squeaky Fromme, who was dressed in a red robe that day, did not look like someone who you'd imagine as an assassin.

In 1981, John Hinckley Jr. attempted to assassinate President

Reagan with a .22-caliber pistol. Afterward, the world got a view of Hinckley and his background, physical demeanor and lack of training. You wouldn't have thought someone like him would be able to fire six shots in less than three seconds and hit four individuals within 20 feet, including the President, all before the U.S. Secret Service could reach him.

In 1995, Prime Minister Yitzhak Rabin of Israel was being protected by the very capable and highly trained Shin Bet (Israeli Security Agency) while leaving a rally in Tel Aviv in support of the Oslo Accords. As he was preparing to get into his waiting security vehicle and while surrounded by his protective detail, a young Orthodox Jew named Yigal Amir, who opposed the signing of the Accords, stepped into close range and fired three bullets, hitting the Prime Minister twice. Later that evening, Rabin died from his wounds.

When a killer is able to breach the inner circle of a high-profile principal's detail, it's the ultimate catastrophe for these professional protective organizations. The American, Israeli, Egyptian, Pakistani, Indian, Saudi, Lebanese and other national security services have all had their share of failures, lessons learned and, in most cases, significant program improvements in response to these types of assassinations – but at a high cost.

Even after evaluating hundreds of assassinations like those above, Dr. Fein has concluded that trying to create a definitive profile of an assassin is almost impossible. As he wrote in a 1998 book entitled *The Psychology of Stalking: Clinical and Forensic Perspectives*, "The reality of American assassination is much more mundane, more banal, than assassination depicted [in movies]."[45] Not long ago, I spoke to Dr. Fein. He believes the facts are the same today when it comes to profiling an assassin.

Unfortunately, once a determined person or persons have, for whatever reason, decided to commit an assassination, they have two major advantages: their choice of location or venue and the element of surprise. These advantages are also the most difficult to defend against. So, rather than trying to identify *who* is a threat, your focus should be more on *what you can do to reduce your vulnerabilities*.

In most cases, the first thing you should do if you have reasonable suspicion of any potential targeted attack is to immediately alert state and federal authorities. These initial meetings will help you as you consider your best options moving forward. You should then assemble the best team you can (e.g., experienced professionals regarding intelligence, criminal psychologists and profilers, probably current or former FBI agents, and highly trained close protection specialists) as you work with the authorities to mitigate your threat.

Again, if a principal has *any* risk of being the target of a personal attack or specifically a threat of assassination, this possibility should be taken extremely seriously. Principals need to articulate their reasons for being targeted (if known), as this information could help the EP professionals and authorities to better profile a potential assassin and their methods, along with planning mitigating strategies.

Doomsday or Catastrophic Events

According to the *Bulletin of the Atomic Scientists* report, after over 70 years of countdown, it is now "two minutes to midnight."[46] This idea of "doomsday" and the mindset it often generates adds a new dimension to the field of executive protection, and I know several EP teams who operate in various spheres of preparation. While I'm not necessarily personally adopting the notion of an impending doomsday event, I also can't ignore various events around the world which make you pause and consider: *What if?*

The Doomsday Clock was created in 1947 by scientists who helped develop the first atomic weapons in the Manhattan Project. The intent was to monitor and calculate the only threat at that time which could bring about a global apocalypse: a nuclear exchange. The editor of the *Bulletin of the Atomic Scientists* describes the purpose of the Clock as follows:

> *The decision to move (or to leave in place) the minute hand of the Doomsday Clock is made every year by the Bulletin's Science and Security Board in consultation*

with its Board of Sponsors, which includes 15 Nobel laureates. The Clock has become a universally recognized indicator of the world's vulnerability to catastrophe from nuclear weapons, climate change, and new technologies emerging in other domains.[47]

According to Dr. Rachel Bronson, President and CEO of the *Bulletin*, the biggest current-day concern is the lack of progress world leaders have made in the face of continuing geopolitical turbulence, especially regarding nuclear weapons. Climate change and technological risks are also major factors causing the Clock to be the closest to midnight it has been since 1953.[48] The escalation of tensions with or pending denuclearization of North Korea could conceivably add or subtract more seconds to the Doomsday Clock in the next annual report.

Whether you believe the world is a safer place today or you're one of the doomsday preppers will depend upon your perspectives, philosophies and perhaps theological beliefs – and in some situations, you can probably easily make a case for either scenario. Because we all have differing perceptions of the risks we face and the world around us, these beliefs will often color the way we make decisions regarding our preparation for personal security.

For those who may not subscribe to a global doomsday event or concern, we can all agree there is always a risk of a geographical "doomsday-ish" event worthy of consideration in EP security plans. If you were in San Francisco during the 1906 earthquake, LA riots of 1992, New York during 9/11, the 2004 tsunami in Indonesia or the 2008 Mumbai attacks, you lived through what could be considered a doomsday type of event.

While these might be considered nightmare events and not the "end of the world," the unfortunate truth is that EP may not be able to save you or your family in the case of a global catastrophe. However, there are smaller, significant events for which EP teams should have a game plan in place to counter. Consider, for instance, our reliance on technology to power every part of our world – a dependence which could present a "single point of failure."* In Ted Koppel's recent book, *Lights Out*, he brings much-needed attention to our and other nations' power grids, critical infrastructure vulnerabilities and general lack of contingency planning, which could easily be devastating on many levels in the event of a major successful cyberattack.[49]

Koppel's book is a hard message to digest, but we do need to consider the implications of these scenarios.** Most experts on this subject feel it's not a matter of if, but when, how long such a disaster lasts and the fallout that will ensue. As Koppel also wrote in a recent public letter, "Simply put, the Internet is, at one and the same time, the most wonderful and the most dangerous invention of our age."[50]

Every CSO, EP director or security manager should consider these types of scenarios (even if just conceptually) as part of their security program's preparations so, if the lights ever do go out, there is a plan for communications and even basic survival – not to mention that principals have been briefed and/or trained as needed.

The concern over a potential doomsday event has been elevated recently – and not just from a group of former military and survivalist types that come to mind from movies, books and even the recent reality TV show *Doomsday Preppers*. These individuals and families live a life off the grid and stockpile food, water and ammunition. Recent reports illustrate this movement is wide-ranging, attracting many regardless of wealth, education or social status.

A 2017 article in *The New Yorker* magazine by Evan Osnos reported on what he titled "Doomsday Prep for the Super-Rich."[51] In this article, Osnos addressed the UHNW individuals living in New York and

---

* For more evidence of the power of technology to cause terror (even accidentally), consider the emergency alert sent to residents of Hawaii in early 2018 warning of an incoming ballistic missile. This emergency management message caused immediate panic and mass confusion, sending people to their basements and seeking shelter. Technology could be positively credited for being able to notify thousands of citizens to take important action during a crisis, but it also demonstrates what could happen if the same technology were used by bad actors.

** If you have doubts on this topic, pick up a copy. After reading and at least considering the likelihood and reviewing the facts and testimonies of international experts on the subject, your level of rejection might be slightly altered.

Silicon Valley who are preparing for the worst. As one CEO stated for the article, he focused less on a specific threat such as an earthquake, pandemic or a dirty bomb than with the aftermath from "the temporary collapse of our government and structures." This level of prepping involves dual passports, extensive fuel storage, decommissioned and converted Cold War missile silos, large air filtration systems, weapons, and stockpiles of food and supplies which could make Costco feel like a convenience store.

The U.S. and other world governments also have plans for such events. The Department of Homeland Security and FEMA refer to this as Continuity of Operations (COOP). This plan is described as an effort within individual executive departments and agencies to ensure Primary Mission Essential Functions (PMEFs) continue to be performed during a wide range of disasters, including localized acts of nature, accidents, and technological or attack-related emergencies. Some corporations have a similar plan and I know of a few UHNW families and family offices with a condensed version of a COOP strategy. More people and organizations should consider this important exercise and prepare an initiative as it might relate to natural or man-made disasters.

As an example, a typical "doomsday prepper" might lift an area rug on the living room floor and enter their bunker. Or they might take a short drive to a cave or underground shelter they've been working on for years. For some UHNW preppers, their doomsday plan will include a more robust response and will, in most cases, involve helicopters, planes, boats, hundreds if not thousands of acres of land, contract security forces, doctors, chefs and other specialists who can help make the end of the world more tolerable.

Maybe the best statement about all this was summed up by John Jay, American statesman and one of the Founding Fathers of the United States, whose words have been requoted and adapted throughout the centuries: "Let us hope for the best and prepare for the worst." If I could add a word to this quote, it would be to "reasonably" prepare for the worst.

Fear, Anxiety and the Unknown

The oldest and strongest emotion in mankind is fear,
and the oldest and strongest kind of fear is fear of the unknown.

– H.P. Lovecraft

As the NFL was approaching the playoffs in late 2015, I had a conversation with my friend and colleague Jeff Miller, then the NFL's senior vice president and chief security officer. We talked about some of the major security precautions and changes the NFL has made over the years to address some of their known concerns (e.g., fans carrying weapons into stadiums, airborne threats, crowd control, negative alcohol-related behavior). But despite all the problems that have since been addressed, he said what still kept him up at night were the threats and risks he couldn't anticipate. Many of my colleagues in the intelligence community and law enforcement would agree with that sentiment.

While the unknown concerns some, it might be surprising how many people consider today's world far safer than in the past. Many argue we are safer today than ever before due to a higher level of public awareness and our government's increased defense and response capabilities since 9/11. We have cameras on almost every street corner and in most buildings. Generally speaking, we have more police training and presence in public spaces and, while our officers are being stretched thin in many places, their capacity for emergency response has improved immensely over the past couple of decades.

Christopher Preble, Vice President for Defense and Foreign Policy Studies at the Cato Institute, highlighted the "are we safer" debate in an article entitled "The Most Dangerous World Ever?"[52] As he pointed out, we are bombarded 24 hours a day by bad news that leaves us feeling less safe. Preble mentioned there is little focus on the "threats that no longer threaten." While the argument will not be settled in this book, the topic does partially overlap with the influences on a principal's level of risk which can determine the level of protection they seek.

All of the changes and unknowns of the 21st century tend to generate two things that can greatly influence any EP program: fear and anxiety. While it's not my intention to delve too deeply into the subject, I do believe a better understanding of these emotions is instrumental in the final decisions that will be made about any level of protection.

Fear is an unpleasant emotion caused by the belief that someone or something is dangerous, is likely to cause pain, or is a threat. *Anxiety* is similar: a feeling of worry, nervousness or unease, typically about an imminent event or something with an uncertain outcome. Though anxiety can be subtle and fear is hard to miss, both are powerful emotions that influence the way we think and what we do.

I'll be the first to admit, you can't talk about personal protection without addressing fear. But despite the very real conversations around it that need to take place, my intent is *never* to use fear as a prime motivator for making most EP decisions. When speaking to my principals or clients, I would rather concentrate on helping them make comforting and rational decisions regarding their safety, security and privacy.

There are many times the element of fear can keep us safe or prevent us from making dangerous decisions. The world is full of examples where a person listened to a little voice inside them which helped to avoid a tragic ending. But it's not the fear we want to concentrate on here – it's the *reason* for it. Our justification for our fears is what helps determine the requirements for protection.

For example, traveling can often be the source of security anxieties which manifest themselves in conflicting feelings of both excitement and dread. Many principals and EP agents are most concerned when we're in unfamiliar territory and have a reduced amount of control and comfort. Though I would (almost) never discourage a principal from travel and exploration, I might make recommendations to ensure they have addressed certain risks and concerns before and during their journey – all designed to make their experience more rewarding while addressing the specific reasons for their fears.*

EP management should review all itineraries, travel plans and relevant crime reports (including OSAC and other travel warnings and intelligence). In many cases, they should contact local EP practitioners, who are often keenly aware of nearby risks and threats. The local EP team should have all the necessary vetted resources and contact with authorities as well as assets to provide direct support as needed.

As Preble states, the world will never be free from dangers, but we should aspire to understand them clearly. It is much better when the protectee and protector are on the same page and can find a common ground on which to agree. Without it, the yo-yo effect regarding the levels and degrees of protection will exhaust everyone involved – until the string breaks (i.e., patience runs out) and the principal has to start all over again with a new team and new program.

So, what's my point? Fear is a very real and important emotion and can be the impetus for making many decisions, including those relating to security. It is important to recognize that, in the space between actual and perceived risks, our perspective is what causes the pendulum to swing in the decision-making process regarding the size and scope of our protection.

My goal with any principal or client who has any level of fear has always been to listen to their worries, try to bring a degree of rationality into our discussions (if necessary), and design an acceptable and balanced approach to address their concerns. The very root of the fear may actually be different than what might surface in conversations, so if the response is not in line with the real reason for concern, I will not dance around the issues. In some cases, the unaddressed fears can metastasize very quickly, affecting the quality of life of everyone involved.

---

* When I worked for Director George Tenet at the CIA, he would never ask whether or not he could travel to any particular country. Rather, his chief of staff (or Dottie, his executive assistant) would come into our offices and tell us he needed to travel to a particular place. It was his security detail's responsibility to determine how to do it safely and securely. Trust me, there were many times that, if we'd had a choice, we would have preferred to send his proxy, but that was never an option.

No one can ever offer complete protection – not the EP specialist, police, military or government. What we can do is provide knowledge and convert fear to information in order to help make balanced and rational decisions, as well as take appropriate action toward our security and the goal of attaining greater peace of mind.

As President Dwight D. Eisenhower once said, "If you want total security, go to prison. There you are fed, clothed, given medical care, and so on. The only thing lacking is freedom."

Addressing the Hype of Fear

While sometimes we believe we have a handle on our emotions, the news media can promote information or a depiction of a scenario that may cause us great stress. As a real-world example, I've recently been assisting others with managing anxieties related to the fear of becoming a potential victim during a period of increased crime and violence in a foreign location.

In March 2018, a few reports surfaced as they do each year listing the "most dangerous cities in the world."[53] This list gets published and distributed by various global news agencies as well as other travel and security-related articles and outlets. As you can imagine, the titles and narratives are modified to fit the slant of the individual editorial piece. This particular year, the list ranked Cabo San Lucas, Mexico, as the most dangerous city in the world. In 2016, Cabo wasn't even listed. What happened?

This annual report is primarily based on available figures for murders per capita. Like all news reports, including the headline alerts hitting your smartphone with every "breaking news" event, if you don't take the time to read past the dramatic and *usually misleading* first line, you don't get the full story – the all-important background and details are clearly missing. If you looked past the headlines relating to this report, approximately 13 lines down you would read what factors were behind the increase, the root causes, who was targeted, and who was not.

Cabo is located on the southern tip of the Baja Peninsula in what has otherwise been a peaceful region and popular tourist destination of Mexico. Yes, this area saw a dramatic increase in cartel activities – murder rates went up nearly 500 percent, according to reports from 2016 to early 2018. In any area, this major increase would be a reason for concern – thus, Cabo's status atop the list.

However, when evaluating any type of risk, you must consider all the factors, not just the headlines. In this case, nearly all of the murders were between rival cartel members or Mexican assassins (*sicarios*) over territorial disputes – and, no doubt, included many local Mexicans who were caught up in this brutal but isolated conflict for various reasons. These murders were designed to be intimidating and retaliatory and were committed to create fear in anyone trying to interfere with cartel activities, including the local and federal Mexican government.

As I have explained to clients, we actively work with multiple sources of intelligence and security professionals to better understand the risks and monitor for shifting trends that may increase our immediate concerns for individual safety. We watch for indicators that cartels or other criminal elements might be changing their tactics in a manner that would elevate risks for tourists and expats living in this region (e.g., burglaries, kidnapping, extortion, etc.).

At the time of the completion of this book, the case for listing Cabo as the world's most "dangerous" city was an inappropriate and inaccurate portrayal of this small Baja community. While accurate and reliable crime statistics have been difficult to obtain and trend in Mexico, the murder rate in Cabo has now significantly decreased from the numbers listed in this report.

Of course, statistics are just one element of reporting. In small towns where hundreds of people have been murdered in a short period of time, it simply doesn't go unnoticed by the public or the authorities. When the murders stop or significantly decrease, the same is noticed, and the city will also respond more positively to the reduction of violence with a gradual return to normalcy. For Cabo, an increased military presence, a permanent Marine base, more professionally trained federal police, improved intelligence sharing and possible truce agreements between warring cartels might all account for the reduction in the murder and violent crime rates witnessed toward the end of 2017.

It is important to take into consideration what factors constitute "danger" and might be an influence on EP-based decisions. There are places both in the U.S. and abroad that have a high rate of automobile accidents due to poor road conditions or design which pose a much greater threat of injury or death than the likelihood of being caught in the crossfire between rival cartels. Other dangers can present themselves in street crimes, extortion, burglaries, disease or lack of immediate access to reliable medical care in the event of an emergency. The article on the "most dangerous city in the world" would have to take these and other factors into consideration if it is to reflect accurate information.

Make no mistake, Mexico has some dangerous cities and regions throughout the country – mostly due to cartel-related violence. However, the citizens and tourists in other international cities might strongly disagree with the idea that Cabo San Lucas is the "most dangerous city in the *world*" ahead of, for example, Kabul, Baghdad, Caracas, Lagos, Aleppo, San Salvador, Sana'a or Karachi – or even St. Louis, Chicago, Detroit and Baltimore. If you attempt to make a legitimate comparison of Cabo San Lucas with just the small sampling of the cities above, you have not personally been to Cabo or any of the other places mentioned.

The southern end of Baja, Mexico, is home to thousands of expats and welcoming to more than a million tourists each year. I lived there myself for nearly a year and often continue to visit. I still consider this unique region as one of the jewels of Mexico and have felt as safe there as I do in most U.S. cities – sometimes safer. This doesn't mean it wasn't disturbing or sad to witness this increased level of violence in such a beautiful area, but it is important to keep all factors in proper perspective when calculating your associated risk and making decisions to travel to any city in the world.

With a lack of accurate reporting, at times we can find ourselves spinning our own narratives. I have also experienced my own difficulties with overemphasizing risk at times and have had to be cautious about making certain predictions that could be considered overzealous.

In July 2018, Mexico voted in a new president. Only time will tell whether or not his policies and approach to cartel-related crime will be effective. My hope is that Cabo San Lucas preserves its charm and will continue to be an attractive place for those who live and visit there.

Avoiding Fear as a Motivator (But Listening to Its Wisdom)

I've lived through some terrible things in my life,
some of which actually happened.

– Attributed to Mark Twain

Generally speaking, fear can be a major influence regarding why security is requested or needed. This is especially true when our personal and family's security is in question. However, I have learned that when EP is not approached correctly, the protection intended to reduce anxiety can actually be the cause for increased fear and frustration – and *raise* anxiety.

Security and/or EP managers, contractors and vendors should *not* resort to scare or fear tactics to justify their EP existence. Instead, they should take a realistic, holistic and pragmatic approach when communicating with their client or principal. EP managers may express all the benefits of having a true protection professional by their principal's side, but they should be honest about the potential risks their clients face. Unless they are providing EP to a high-profile individual with *credible* risks or threats, they should not try to convince their principal they will not live another day without their protection.

One of my personal pet peeves is when security managers or EP practitioners and/or contractors use fear as a motivator to manage their programs, budgets, resources, travel and very existence.

Like many elements of life and even arguments in these pages, there is always a counterpoint to consider. In the widely acclaimed book *The Gift of Fear* by Gavin de Becker,[54] the author takes his readers through various relevant examples and statistics regarding the subject of fear. His illustrations help explore the fact that we all have this internal instinct inside us to anticipate the presence of danger or potential violent behavior, and we have to listen to those instincts and take action.

I agree with de Becker – we all have a sometimes trained or just intuitive "sixth sense" that calls out to us when something is wrong. This might be partially related to what we have seen, experienced or been exposed to in our lives. On the other hand, I've been with people who seem oblivious and naïve to risk and dangers around them, and I can only assume they've lived a fairly sheltered life or just have not tapped into this basic instinct. Others can seem hypersensitive to even the hint of risk, and something tells me they've been exposed to a few bad situations in their lives or have overactive imaginations. Combine both and you have a case for high anxiety.

In any situation where fear is present, the very fact that we feel this sensation may help encourage necessary precaution or immediate reaction which might save a life – maybe your own. I also agree with de Becker when he said, "Our judgment may classify a person as either harmless or sinister, but survival is better served by our perception."

De Becker's follow-up to *The Gift of Fear* was *Fear Less*,[55] where he articulated the exhausting number of press organizations and outlets that often sensationalize bad news and the epidemic-level rush to be first to report "breaking news" – which could be argued might be more psychologically damaging and potentially dangerous than the event itself.

As a principal, be cautious if your EP seems to be resorting to such fear tactics to manage your protection. If in doubt, have an honest discussion to be better informed and understand the concerns.

As a practitioner, serve your clients without bringing unnecessary fear into the protective equation, but be authentic and balanced about legitimate fear.

The Future of EP?

Even though close protection is one of the oldest professions in the world, and while our weapons, gadgets, equipment, training and technology have evolved throughout history, the hands-on skills and mindset of protecting another person have changed very little since the days of samurais, knights and warriors.

At the current speed of technological development and social acceptance, the EP professionals of the future might not have blood running through their veins, but chips, wires and cables – and they may be operated by advanced and sophisticated human-level AI software.

When I entered the Air Force in 1984, if you had told any pilot at that time they would one day be sitting in a building on the ground with a monitor and a joystick controlling an unmanned aerial vehicle (UAV or drone) with the capability of delivering supplies, conducting surveillance or dropping a guided missile on a target, most would have just nervously laughed. But these functions have been reality for some time now. In the future, we will probably even see unmanned drones of various sizes carrying troops or passengers.

Could the future of executive protection push humans out of the profession? Unless there is a major backlash to advanced technology in our future, I believe within my potential lifetime, a scenario similar to the following could take place:

> An executive or principal will step outside his or her home to an awaiting luxury sedan being "driven" by an AI android or human-like robot. This entity will be specifically designed to act in the capacity of a trained human security driver, using sophisticated software applications as it does its job.
>
> Standing near the rear door will be another EP android constantly analyzing every situation and movement around it for potential threats. It will greet the principal, open and close the vehicle door, and step inside – possibly with specialized equipment to defend against a human or electronic adversary. This EP android will not need to eat, drink or sleep, nor be distracted by its smartphone or similar advanced device yet to be developed or available on the market.
>
> As they depart the residence, the gate will open. Another residential EP android will step out to provide a friendly wave to the principal. It will remain at the residence's entry control post to greet and allow

authorized vendors, contractors and guests onto the property while updating family members and staff at all times.

Upon arrival at the principal's work, the principal will be met by an office EP android who will identify them through biometrics and advanced facial recognition software. The android will provide a personal greeting and maybe soft tease because it has been programmed to follow the principal's favorite sports team – who might have lost their game the night before.

This office android will have already been tracking the principal's vehicle since it left the residence and would be prepared to make any emergency notification if required. It will remain posted outside the private office to control entry based on protocols. It will be equipped with the same advanced intelligence software as the other androids and will constantly be scanning and providing uninterrupted physical and technical security by using a database of persons of interest the EP administrator has already uploaded to each android.

And even with all that technology, somewhere nearby or miles away, a human EP program manager will sit in a room with a screen and control device, providing input and monitoring the principal's environment by utilizing other advanced software still to be developed. If they are lucky enough, they might be preparing for international travel or a special occasion where the EP robots will not be going – just yet.

I believe a human element will always be necessary in the business of executive protection – because only humans (in theory) can truly understand other humans in their care. However, if you've seen Sophia, the first AI robot to "become a citizen" during an event held in Saudi Arabia in 2017, you might begin to doubt that as well.

Like airplane pilots thirty years ago who thought they could never be replaced, it's for similar reasons that I, too, want to believe it could never happen in the EP profession. As we consider the speed, progress and acceptance of AI technology, I also must realize one day soon portions of the physical EP human skillset will slowly be encroached on by this advanced technology. The pure imagination of the 1973 futurist film *Westworld* will converge with modern technology in developing lifelike AI robots in our not-too-distant future.

It does make you think.

> "HE WHO HAS A WHY TO LIVE
> CAN BEAR ALMOST ANY HOW."
>
> – FRIEDRICH NIETZSCHE

CHAPTER II

Determining Your Personal *Why*

I HOPE NIETZSCHE WON'T MIND if I modify his quote to drive home a very important point about personal security, but if I may: "He who knows his 'why' can appreciate the 'how' when it comes to building a close protection program."

Principals, you might wonder why I spent the last chapter talking about the world around us, causes and effects regarding security, risks, threats and vulnerabilities, and the things that shape the personal perspectives of practitioners when it comes to your personal security needs. The reason is that if you're exploring executive or personal protection, you'll first need to answer this question: *Why am I considering executive protection in the first place?* Answering this *why* question means considering a wide variety of circumstances.

With this context in mind, we're now going to explore the many more *personal* variables that factor into the initial decision to establish an EP program, as well as the startup decisions that need to be made along the way. The reader should come out of this chapter with a better sense of his or her own mindset regarding executive protection – which is important, as it informs the entire character and structure of any program eventually established.

Where to Begin

Whether you are in the beginning stages of an EP program or you are looking to transform your current program because of concerns or inefficiencies, it all comes down to an honest and accurate assessment of the requirements, plan of action, execution and effective management.

Executive protection programs are designed to increase awareness, remove the unknowns, create measured responses and provide proactive solutions to threats against a person or persons. These programs are responsible for mitigating threats/risks and reducing vulnerabilities regarding the safety, security and reputation of an individual, organization, key executive leadership and key employees where applicable.

As it should be, EP is very confidential and private in nature. Because of the privacy factor, it can be difficult for those needing protection to find trusted information. This leads to an important question: To whom do you turn when you need protection and who do you ask the tough questions for honest answers? You might ask a friend who currently has a level of EP protection, and this can often be a good place to start your Q&A process. You might also reach out via a recommendation to someone who has years of vetted EP experience who can help guide you.

There are any number of companies who advertise their EP services, but I would seek a strong referral before picking a company from the Internet who might be paying for advertisement in order to be placed at the top of your search. At the same time, there are many good companies, advisors and consultants who can help guide you through the process – just do a little homework first.

Either way, it starts with a human interaction and should include a lot of questions and answers until you're comfortable understanding your needs and articulating a formal request. Depending on the complexity of the protection you're seeking, it could take awhile until you become confident with the process.

Before an EP program can be developed, certain internal evaluations must be completed and constructively discussed among management. This includes the all-important Threat, Vulnerability and Risk Assessment (TVRA) that focuses on the actual principal(s) or protectee(s) – and which we'll review in the next section.

The following is just a sampling of other components of EP programs:

- Authority to act and rules of engagement (ROE)
- EP manager, agents and officers
- Operational budgets
- Continuous proficiency training and equipment
- Supporting policies and procedures
- Open communications with key stakeholders
- Knowledgeable EP regional security managers (for global organizations)
- Vetted and contractual relationships with third-party global EP providers
- Real-time inbound flow of relevant and actionable intelligence
- Global security operations center providing 24/7 support

If the proximate risk is against an organization as a whole, a different approach may need to be considered that would include increased security presence (e.g., armed officers, patrols, EP support, etc.).

A well-structured and managed program should reduce inconsistency, provide clarity and avoid confusion while promoting confidence in those whom it supports. If at any time clients or principals feel like their EP coverage is inconsistent, confusing or generates a lack of confidence, a reevaluation may be needed to identify any troubled areas of the program or service provided.

The Importance of a TVRA

One of the initial things you can do to identify your individual *why* is to conduct a Threat, Vulnerability and Risk Assessment (TVRA). If a company or EP practitioner begins making recommendations and adding any level of service or headcount before they've had the chance to make a valid needs assessment (a TVRA), be forewarned.

There is a good reason you'll see TVRA referenced over 25 times in this book – *it's that important.* When done properly and accurately, it can help you address the subject of fear more reasonably by identifying appropriate risks and emotionally and rationally putting them in the right category of likelihood. This effort should help you in managing your life more suitably without using fear as the motivator.

When I spend time with corporate or private EP details and managers, I can quickly determine if they have had a TVRA or even any level of assessment done within their program's history. Many programs adjust "on the fly." With the travel and special event tempo of many protectees today, unless someone is specifically tasked with managing their protectee's evolving TVRA through a protective intelligence program, the need for (or prior existence of) a TVRA can often go undetected, unrealized or in some cases just unacknowledged – until some event or information causes an immediate issue that must be addressed. A *proactive* approach will most often be better than a *reactive* approach.

There are many TVRA-style models and methodologies for considering your risks by identifying your threats and related vulnerabilities. Many individuals will try to make this process very complicated, but I prefer to keep it simple where possible.

1. **List Assets:** This list shouldn't only include tangible items like residences, vehicles, collections and aircraft. It should cover *everything* important to you, like your family members, anonymity, company brand, personal and family reputation, privacy, etc.
2. **Identify Threats:** Examples may include an angry customer or an outsider with malicious intent, or perhaps a disgruntled employee/staff member or other insider threats, earthquakes or other natural hazards.
3. **Determine Vulnerabilities:** This could mean access to your listed assets, individual people, gaps in physical barriers, distribution of personal calendars, social media presence, lifestyle choices, cyber infrastructure, etc.
4. **Consider Consequences:** Possible consequences include physical danger, loss of life, psychological damage, reputational damage, loss of wealth or profits, loss of privacy, etc.
5. **Assess Likelihood:** Finally, you must examine the likelihood of any consequence as a result of the identified threat in order to understand how to manage your risk.

When you list and create a matrix of all these factors, you will identify your *greatest risks* and *where mitigating strategies should be concentrated*. Some models might try to give each risk or threat a numerical ranking, but most often a *high*, *medium* or *low* ranking will be sufficient.

The more comprehensive and accurate the assessment, the better your results and data will be. To assist in determining your specific threats and vulnerabilities, principals should have open conversations with their EP/TVRA advisor or consultant. They should clearly articulate the options that will effectively meet the goals of protecting the principal(s).

A TVRA is like going to the doctor. You might believe you have a serious problem. But you would also assume your doctor would want you to undergo an examination, various tests and evaluations in order to provide you with an accurate diagnosis – and to create a plan of action to address the issue or concern and help make you healthy again. Such an evaluation could save your life. It's the same where your security is concerned.

As a principal, if you don't take this approach, you will be gambling on the appropriate and effective levels of protection for you, your family and your company. I have seen principals simply request the same type of protection used by someone else they know. But EP is not "one size fits all" – the outcome and results of your individual TVRA will help determine the priorities and resources necessary to meet your objectives. Most importantly, it should address all of the reasons you're looking for executive protection in the first place – i.e., your *whys*.

Bottom line: It is critical to conduct a baseline TVRA with an appropriate subject-matter expert to assist in determining the level of protection required and generating key information for your program's first steps. You should also have follow-on discussions with important stakeholders to ensure you have full support regarding your program, approach, budget and authority.

Know Your Enemy

While I don't intend on quoting lines from Sun Tzu's *The Art of War*, it *is* important to know who you are defending yourself against before you get started. Understanding the realistic risks and threats you face is the first step of the decision-making process for any level of security or EP program. In most cases, this should be well established during your initial TVRA.

Due to 24-hour news coverage, most people are numb to the daily reports of crime, attacks and deaths occurring around the world. Some people become so numb they believe it simply cannot happen to them. But in other cases, fear of these things happening leads people to acquire unnecessary levels of personal protection. This is where your *individual why* must be carefully defined regarding your level of security.

I can recall my first meeting with a principal who was very interested in what I thought was his family's biggest threat. While I had some speculations, I asked him to give me a couple of weeks and then we could set up another time for an in-depth conversation. I then conducted a very thorough TVRA and lifestyle assessment. I also arranged for a "Red Team" to conduct an independent assessment for a week to reveal additional concerns and vulnerabilities I may not have noticed.*

I gave this Red Team only his name and they took it from there. They conducted research on their target, gathering as much information as possible via social media and other online open sources. Someone with nefarious intentions can easily obtain an unfathomable volume of information on a target with the aid of search engines, web-based interactive maps, social media and blog sites. Depending on someone's ability to navigate the web (including the dark web and by assuming certain fictitious personas), a bad actor can gather more than enough information to plot the first phase of an attack – all without leaving the comfort of their home or country.

The Red Team in this case identified routines and routes of travel by the principals and vulnerabilities in gaining access to the residence. These items were included in my overall risk assessment and follow-on

---

* A Red Team in this case is normally a small number of individuals (two to six) with various skillsets, depending on the tasks. They assume the role of "bad actors" who want to do harm to a person, family, event, location, etc., but are hired by good people to exploit the vulnerabilities and gaps in security in order to address the deficiencies. If done correctly, this is one of the most important and essential elements to the overall TVRA.

recommendations, which we used to map out an agreed-upon approach to the family's security and privacy.

Determining Your Risk Appetite

How much EP do you really need? According to the Institute of Risk Management, risk appetite is defined as "the amount and type of risk an organization is willing to take in order to meet their strategic objectives."[56] When we refer to an individual's risk appetite, it's very similar – but instead of an organization, we're referring to individuals and/or families existing as they prefer to in their personal security environment.

As previously mentioned, many principals today operate in a dynamic environment that includes foreign travel, extreme sports and very active lifestyles. The amount of risk an individual or family is willing to take with or without any level of third-party personal security (including advanced medical support) to reach their personal objectives (e.g., experiences, personal goals, fun) would be defined as their personal "risk appetite."

There are many factors we face today regarding risk, but one trend I've noticed is the difference between what some individuals consider risks worth addressing and what others do not. This difference is often based on an individual's experiences and perspectives, which play a vital role in your risk appetite.

Here's where this comes into play in practice: Your EP program will invariably come with a range of tradeoffs. For example, in order to comprehensively address the risks you face, you may need to accept a reduction in your public

DEFINING YOUR RISK

Insiders | Natural | Outsiders

THREATS

Technology | People

VULNERABILITIES

Assets |

MANAGE RISK

Health | Psychological | Economic

CONSEQUENCES

ASSETS

Properties | Reputation | Staff

exposure. If you can't do this, you may need to accept a greater level of risk.

The strategy you and your EP advisors devise may also result in the addition of a large amount of staff and operations involved in your life – e.g., dedicated security drivers, close protection agents, armed or unarmed agents for your children, countersurveillance efforts, travel security support, varying degrees of residential security upgrades, IT and cybersecurity initiatives, and protective intelligence. How much security at the cost of perceived inconvenience and/or loss of privacy you are willing to accept is up to you.*

Properly determining the appropriate level of protection for a principal requires a degree of finesse and sometimes healthy creativity, and so the efforts must be flexible and tailored to their needs. In many cases, risk interpretations or perceptions will vary from principal to principal; therefore, the level of protection provided should be individually based.

Each principal will take away their own opinions and perspectives on these subjects. You and your family will have a unique perception of how these risks and concerns fit into your individual lives – and how the methodologies and recommendations can fit (or don't fit) regarding your personal security.

These perceptions might even vary within families. Many times, I have seen a major gap in the risk appetite or the perception of risk between spouses in protected families. In such a case, you must try to find a level of agreeable protection based on combined perceptions so your EP program will not constantly be vacillating between levels of coverage. It *is* possible to have two distinct programs within one family, but there will be challenges and compromises in most cases; communication, coordination and planning will need to be elevated to ensure the appropriate coverage is being applied when necessary.

As a principal, your risk appetite can and will change over time. In most cases, it will be constantly evolving across periods of elevated

---

* I'm not suggesting that preserving a degree of privacy is more important than your personal security. Rather, you need to be aware of this tradeoff in your decision-making – privacy will become a factor and, in most cases, your personal "tribe" will grow more than you expect it to.

concerns and include various levels of security. Sometimes there might even be a significant reduction in or elimination of certain levels of protection. Again, if your security is more than just personal *facilitation* and is truly a risk/threat-based program, the needs and level of coverage will fluctuate over time.

Few people in the world are required by law or decree to be protected. For everyone else, it comes down to balancing your "risk appetite" against many other factors – and making a decision.

Learning to Live with EP ("The Reluctant Executive")

While many executives appreciate the ease of transportation and overall lifestyle facilitation that EP can provide, most resist the invasion of privacy or inconvenience. Perhaps it's a new executive or CEO with an increase in their profile or extreme personal significance in their corporation's success. In some cases, these executives are themselves the repository (or human vault) of the business's intellectual property and vision – and are therefore key to its prosperity and require personal security for the company's sake.

This scenario may best describe a late icon of the tech industry I had the privilege of working for during his last days – or as I like to call him, "The Reluctant Executive."

I will never forget the day he was photographed in front of his home while standing with the assistance of a medical aide just a few weeks before he passed away. I remember this day because in many ways I felt responsible for the unflattering image. At the time, I was Director of Protective Strategies for a large security company. Our security firm had become a vital partner to this executive's company over the years; we were responsible for much of their corporate security and other special activities, which included this special security assignment.

As this icon's health began to decline and the inevitable end was looming, we were asked to assemble a security team to provide ongoing coverage of his home and assist the family as needed. The news of his worsening condition gained more publicity as local and international press (along with the paparazzi and some fans) began to descend on his property like vultures, including some with delusions of grandeur.

This executive was known over the years to resist any level of personal security or protection. At this time, though, it was rightfully determined that a dedicated level of 24-hour security be managed around his residence. We set up a command post in a nearby hotel and assembled a team of dedicated officers to be stationed near his home. Our primary goal was to support his family in any way we could, including protecting their privacy.

In this particular case, we used mostly off-duty or retired law enforcement officers because we knew we would have direct contact with crowds of civilians, and the level of protection and public interference required was best suited to a police officer's demeanor and skills. In addition, the residence faced two public streets with almost no setback and was surrounded by some of the most expensive homes in the country. Occupants of the surrounding properties included CEOs and founders of many well-known companies and other UHNW families. It was important the protective detail integrated seamlessly with the neighborhood, and they did a fantastic job of becoming security "ambassadors" for the company and for this family.

As time passed, I began to see in this executive someone who combined a personal philosophy and maybe even a little theology mixed in with someone who had a strong opinion about his personal security. He demonstrated a mindset that reflected a position something along the lines of: *If a determined person wants to get to me or cause me harm, so be it. If I have to live in a bunker and can't go where I want, when I want, without being told how, I choose not to have any level of protection or personal security.*

He would occasionally take a stroll in his final weeks with assistance on the sidewalk around his home. Because sidewalks and roads are public property, it was virtually impossible to protect his privacy in these circumstances. Despite these conditions, we did everything within the limits of the law to prevent pictures from being taken. On most occasions, we would confront the photographers and ask for their support in giving this person his space and allowing him to enjoy some privacy. Most would cooperate with our requests out of respect for him and his family.

Despite our efforts, one day the sensitive and unflattering photo I spoke of earlier was posted on the Internet and, within minutes, it was globally broadcast. This was a devastating blow to our whole team. We felt we had let our principal, his family and, frankly, our company down in our efforts.

Because I didn't reside in the state where this executive lived, I would travel there to manage the corporate and private client, work with our team, and coordinate with local law enforcement. I was in town this particular day and felt fully responsible for this violation of his privacy.

It wasn't long after the incident that the executive discovered that there was conversation within his family to replace our team, but he immediately put an end to the discussion by stating that it was *his* decision to go outside. He thought he saw a person in a passing van take his picture the moment he walked out to the street but, on that day, he boldly stated he would not be a prisoner in his own home and it was his decision alone to go outside.

On the day he passed away, a few others and I coordinated with his family and the company's management to ensure this innovator, husband, father and friend was taken from his home without incident, with dignity and with privacy. Thanks to the patience and professional assistance of the local police department and chief of police, as well as their neighbors and family members, our detail continued a dedicated 24-hour security vigil for several months. Often, we had to create a physical barrier to the home while thousands of onlookers a day (including some fans who came from around the world) visited a little corner of his residence along the public street in order to lay a symbolic gift, light a candle or take a picture within 50 feet of his front door.

While some may have considered the image of this executive during his final days to be unflattering, to me and the team, the picture represented an individual who was well in charge of his life, including his security decisions and privacy. For that reason, it is also an image of strength and defiance. I know the men and women who supported this detail and his family would agree he was his own man, fully in charge until the very end. I became a bigger fan that day.

Principals, this story in no way represents an opinion or recommendation to throw caution to the wind when it seems prudent to protect yourself and your family. But it should underscore how, in most cases, the decision is ultimately *yours to make* and you should be at peace with your protective decisions.

"THE FIRST STEP TOWARDS
GETTING SOMEWHERE IS TO
DECIDE YOU'RE NOT GOING
TO STAY WHERE YOU ARE."

- JOHN PIERPONT "J.P." MORGAN

CHAPTER III

STARTING OR TRANSFORMING
A PROGRAM

THE FOLLOWING PAGES CONTAIN information and guidance on creating or revamping an EP structure, enhancing your current state of protection and improving employee travel safety programs. I'll explain in more detail the fundamentals that make up an EP program and provide personal insights regarding the areas I believe are essential – including pitfalls, lessons learned and some collective perspectives from other global EP professionals. The concepts, principles and methods provided in this section represent examples of best-practice standards, benchmarking and my personal experiences.

Because there are so many elements of each program that need to be adapted to suit everyone's unique risks, it can become overwhelming to comprehend it all. By breaking the process down to the three basic steps illustrated in the following diagram, it can be easier to understand. In short, these steps are (1) determining your program requirements, (2) planning and implementing your program, and (3) managing your program.

Going forward, I may refer to executive protection as a "program" but, in general, many companies and their executives prefer a less obvious name – e.g., Executive Support, Protective Intelligence, Protective Strategies or some other appropriate title. Regardless of the name, the dynamics, capabilities and results of any program should be the same.

**Determine
Program
Requirements**

▼

**Planning and
Implementation**

▼

PROGRAM MANAGEMENT

Some of the following sections and information may be aimed more at the professionals but absolutely should not be ignored by principals or clients. Bear in mind: I will illustrate more features than a typical EP program may contain, since the specific needs of a principal will dictate which of these elements will be important or relevant.

The "SAFE" Approach to EP Planning

From the moment you start to build your EP program or plan a mission, you'll need to use a methodology that works. At every stage of your program, the options you choose to address your risks should do so in a *sustainable, acceptable, flexible and effective* manner – what I call the "SAFE" approach.

- **Sustainable:** If a version of your plan cannot last longer than the concern, you'll need a new plan.
- **Acceptable:** If all parties involved don't agree, especially the principals, it won't work for long.
- **Flexible:** If your plan is not reasonable and scalable, you'll need other options.
- **Effective:** If it doesn't work or do the job, don't use it.

Make sure the plan you develop addresses and meets these goals immediately. If any of these elements are left out, you'll find yourself revisiting the plan – and often increasing everyone's anxiety as you do so. Properly following the SAFE approach should allow you to merge your experience, intelligence and available resources to devise an effective strategy.

If you're a principal considering a full-time, robust protective detail for any reason, you should take some time to be intimately involved with the entire process of selecting and implementing the program. At a minimum, you should be routinely briefed regarding the process and have an active voice in key decisions. This important setup process ultimately leads to the selection of the person or persons responsible for protecting you, your family and your company – and who will become an important representation and extension of the same. This is crucial, as it relates to the *acceptance* portion of the SAFE approach. If you don't agree with the assessment, approach and staff selections, you will constantly be pushing back on the recommendations (and people) and may find they are not aligned with your *why*.

The Executive Protection Umbrella

You will often hear security professionals use the term "security umbrella." This refers to all the principals or protectees who may fall under the responsibility of the security program or detail. It is very important to note: This concept is often a point of confusion, frustration or concern for both the primary principals as well as the security detail.

Programs are usually designed to effectively cover one or perhaps a particular number of principals and will be based on the level of risk/ threat to or desired support for them. Confusion and risk will occur when the number of individuals unexpectedly exceeds the structure and capability of a security detail.

Ultimately, an EP agent's main responsibility is to his/her primary principals. If a situation involving serious danger requires a principal to be "covered and evacuated," a trained EP agent's primary objective is protecting the *principal* – not the entire group who might happen to be with them. This truth can be very difficult to accept at times because it is our human nature to want to protect everyone. But it is our job (or "charge") to protect the person or persons we are obligated to defend.

On a trip to the Middle East with CIA Director George Tenet,* we took him and other key intelligence officials across a border to a high-risk location during the middle of the night. As we departed the U.S. embassy in our small motorcade of SUVs, I was in the second vehicle (the "follow car") in the front right seat (the detail "shift leader"). Our vehicle was directly behind the Director's vehicle. My four occupants were high-level officials themselves and, as we pulled out of the embassy, they were engaged in serious conversation.

I turned, politely interrupted them, and asked for their full attention. I informed them that, while they were riding in our motorcade, our vehicle was tasked with one primary mission: Our role in the event of an attack would be to push the Director's vehicle with ours if needed. If his vehicle were disabled for any reason, our vehicle might become the Director's new primary vehicle and I explained how we would do this. I also

---

* George Tenet was Director of Central Intelligence (DCI) from 1996 to 2004. I'll mostly refer to him as "the Director" or "the CIA director" from here on out.

explained our SUV could be targeted first because of our obvious role. I further advised them that if we needed to put the Director in this vehicle for any reason, including any emergency (and I gave them examples), they either needed to be in the vehicle already or find another ride.

The bottom line was: Our security team's primary mission (including vehicles) was to protect the Director at all costs. I explained that we would do everything possible to ensure their safety, but they just needed to know where they ranked in our priorities. Eveyone in the vehicle was silent for the next several minutes as they digested my briefing and contemplated their positions in the organizational chart.

It is not always a threatening situation that can strain the EP umbrella. Members of an extended group may assume the EP agent is at their personal disposal. In many cases, the EP agents are treated like family themselves, making the dynamic even more difficult. They may task an agent to run an errand or ask for a special favor which can take the agent away from his or her coverage or compromise security for the principal(s).

Most of the time, these issues can be managed if not eliminated by the principal(s) advising extended family members, friends and associates of the boundaries regarding their EP team or providers. At the same time, it is the responsibility of the EP agent or detail manager/director to educate those individuals who may be unwittingly (or even wittingly) abusing an agent's presence for their own needs.

Layers of Security

Some terms you may hear in the EP and security fields are *concentric circles, convergence, defense in depth* and *layers of security.* These simply mean the multiplication of layers of mitigating strategies to defend against various types of security breaches and/or attacks (as illustrated below).

LAYERS OF SECURITY

Any level of protection may include physical barriers and natural layers of security (e.g., residences, offices, vehicles, etc.). Some are natural and obvious; some are added over time and are not as visible to the untrained eye. Some are designed as a deterrent (e.g., cameras, officers, K9, etc.) and others as a way to slow, identify and defeat a threat before it reaches a protectee (e.g., long driveway, path, gates, guard stations and other barriers to navigate). All layers should in some form provide an alert or trigger, allowing EP or security staff time to react, prepare, respond and take appropriate actions to mitigate the risk.

Each of these layers can be broken into various categories and specialties (e.g., materials, technology, people, intelligence) and complemented by training and procedures.

Before the world of computers and IT, "layers of security" or "defense in depth" primarily referred to defending against physical attacks. Today, IT/network security utilizes the same concepts; in this context, these principles refer to multiple IT strategies being in place to defend against various types of cyberattacks. While the measures and responses may be slightly different, they are all designed to identify, isolate and defend against threats – whether physical or against our IT network systems.

It is essential to any security program that these security layers are systemically and purposely designed and implemented. As a principal, one of the many questions you might have for your security manager or EP director is for them to explain the security architecture around you and how the components integrate with one another. It doesn't have to be complicated – in fact, once established and understood, this will reduce confusion and anxiety regarding the security in place around you.

The Four Pillars of Program Success

In the next few pages, we'll look more closely into the fundamentals of an EP program. Regardless of whether a program is for a corporation, organization or private family, the same core pillars of success will apply. While size, scope and intensity will vary based on the many factors I've already covered, once these things have been determined or decided, most corporate or well-established family executive protection programs operate on the same fundamentals:

1. **Policies, Procedures and Funding**
   - **Policies:** Corporate governance should provide support for various levels of security services designed to (a) protect and safeguard executives, employees and certain family members when higher-than-normal risks and consequences are present, and (b) to ensure business and corporate/family security continuity.

- **Procedures:** Guidelines and recommendations should allow and facilitate consistent and best-practice measures regarding the personal security of principals and employees.
- **Funding:** Policies and procedures, along with the three other pillars, should help drive most of the program requirements but without proper funding, the four pillars will have nothing to stand on.

2. **People, Training and Mindset**
   - **People:** Recruiting and assembling the right talent with relevant experience and proper management is paramount to any EP program.
   - **Training:** Many skills required by professional EP specialists are perishable. To remain current, prepared and motivated, continual training is a vital part of your EP program; the curricula should always represent the agreed-upon policies and procedures.
   - **Mindset:** Training is an often-overlooked requirement but helps to maintain the proper mindset within the EP team. This mindset works best when principals are in tune with it as well.

3. **Technology and Equipment**
   - **Technology:** Every EP program uses various levels and types of technology, systems and software to assist them in protecting their principals. Appropriately using the right technology can be as important as having the right people.
   - **Equipment:** You can't expect your security team to operate without the proper tools and equipment. These can range from the most basic requirements to some of the most advanced weapons, communications, vehicles and versions of protective necessities.

4. **Proprietary Information/Protective Intelligence**
   - **Information/Intelligence:** Current and relevant information and threat intelligence –combined with knowledge of

associated risks and vulnerabilities relating to a principal's position, event or travel – are crucial and will influence the health, safety and security of protectees.

It has been my experience that if one of these pillars is missing or insufficient, your program will be trying to balance itself on a three-legged stool. Eventually, you will have to identify which leg is missing or lacking and make necessary adjustments before a serious incident occurs.

1. Policies, Procedures and Funding

If an EP program is going to be effective and valued, it must be clearly outlined in some form of a policy or strategy. Policies help define the expectations of a program or members of an EP team. While these policies are frequently assumed and communicated verbally, greater understanding and compliance is achievable when companies are willing to articulate *in writing* the various levels of protection afforded to executives and employees. An understanding of these policy and procedural requirements is the very baseline regarding initial and annual funding and budgets.

There are many examples of what policies look like in an EP setting. For instance, policies could ensure any employee who requests travel to a country under a U.S. State Department warning or travel advisory must have approval from the director of security and be required to attend a country-specific safety and security briefing.

As far as procedures are concerned, consistency is important when deciding what level of protection is to be provided to an executive or employee during a situation deemed high-risk. Lack of confidence in an EP program can arise when executives or employees receive mixed support after similar requests for additional security. Confidence can also be jeopardized when security managers make recommendations for additional coverage that are not consistent or supported by current intelligence.

Standard operating procedures, if followed, can help improve confidence levels in any program. The intent is not to create corporate law or an absolute ruling on a particular situation but to provide best-practice guidelines for various scenarios that might require additional security or protection. Examples might include personal tracking systems, "meet and assist" procedures when traveling to a particular country, or even maintaining a separate controlled room for screening of all mail for principals.

Procedures should be based on findings from holistic assessments and intelligence and should be designed to optimize any follow-on recommendations or responses. Any recommendations should be based on analytical risk management methodologies. *If the approach and recommendations are not in line with certain policies and internal procedures, are unacceptable to principals, and cannot be woven seamlessly into the fabric of corporate culture and executive lifestyles, they may not be effective and will not support a sustainable program.*

You should review procedures often for relevance and effectiveness. Outdated procedures or guidelines are useless and can have a negative effect on the entire program, decrease the confidence of the principals, and fail to address the current threats, vulnerabilities and risks.

Finally, EP programs in general are designed, managed and controlled by many factors – e.g., corporate and CEO profiles, board mandates, corporate history and culture, or frequency of foreign travel. If you have a risk- and threat-based program, you should have a systematic structure in place to better respond to requests and provide the EP support required by specific situations.

Funding and Determining Cost

While cost should not be a factor in your safety and security, it does weigh heavily on many principals, families and organizations – and proper funding can be the difference between success or failure in any EP program. Unless the government or a corporation is paying for it, there will be an obvious personal financial cost that comes with executive protection. The actual cost will greatly depend on the level of coverage, resources and technology used, the number of security personnel utilized, and your activities (e.g., travel, size and location of residences, size of family under the umbrella of coverage, etc.). It can range from tens of thousands of dollars for short-term protection to millions each year for full-time programs.

As with any service, principals will associate cost with the actual or even perceived return on the security investment provided. But rarely have I seen cost be a reason appropriate security is not provided for principals or their families – unless it is a result of personal decisions by the principals or perhaps corporate executives and/or board members.

With the help of your CSO, security manager and/or outside security advisor, one of the first steps might be creating a list of all the reasons you are considering extra security and beginning to prioritize your concerns. If you haven't done this already, one of your next steps should be to seek a consultation with a recommended security professional with a strong reputation in executive protection. This person can help you navigate your concerns, decision and path forward with determining the necessary budget and funding for your program based on the level of protection required or facilitation desired.

Things get a bit more complicated where the corporate and personal security spheres intersect.

You cannot discount the corporate risk, public or shareholder reaction to and/or consequences of a security incident related to the CEO, the president or a senior executive. Any incident could negatively affect the company's stock price and the shareholders' confidence. Corporate management teams and security departments often have concerns regarding executives' personal security that typically include corporate espionage, public embarrassment, physical attacks or harassment, intimidation, extortion or attempts to capitalize on the unassuming or unprotected executive. In some cases, there may be other individuals who are critical to a company's success and considered essential to their business continuity; these people may require a degree of additional security.

Most security departments within an organization will not have a profit and loss component. But a major security deficiency adversely affecting executives, key personnel, IP, branding and future developments can indeed have a negative effect on corporate profits and losses.

More companies today are beginning to track key metrics that show how security in general affects a company's bottom line. For many companies, it is important to support and foster a creative environment so their employees will be able to think ahead and develop new and improved products and services. For security and EP professionals, our methodologies must include foreseeing undreamt-of threats that could affect our companies' and principals' well-being.

Approved services could include but are not limited to: a security driver, protection at the home and/or office, travel security and support via advances, certain security technology (including residential alarms and camera systems), an additional TVRA or expert examination of personal threats from a person of interest.

Certain additional decisions will need to be made by the board, CEO or executive receiving any level of corporate paid services after the assessment and legal consideration from the general counsel or outside legal advisor.

Whether the Sarbanes-Oxley Act, current IRS structure or any other regulatory rule survives under the current administration is still to be determined. Until then, you still need to consider federal and state rules and regulations when deciding how much to spend on executive protection. While this should *never* be a hindrance in ensuring any executive's safety, the reality is it may depend on how much of the cost is an authorized corporate expense and how much may need to be personally transferred to the executive receiving the service.

If you're an American corporate CEO or executive evaluating the need for extra security and you believe the company should absorb some of the cost of your personal (and in some cases family) security due to your corporate position, you'll need to have a third-party threat assessment conducted. You'll then need to submit the results as set forth under Title 26, IRS Code of Federal Regulations, Section 26, 1.132-5 regarding an IRS-authorized amount under the fringe benefits rules.

To avoid any potential tax liabilities, a bona fide risk must be demonstrated or identified through the assessment process. Your corporate attorneys, general counsel, CFO and coordination with your CSO or security management should able to help evaluate the third-party assessment results and keep you in compliance with IRS rules. Similar rules apply to government executives – there have been many examples where officials have been singled out for having the government pay for services that should have been paid for by the individual. Consequences have included personal reimbursements to the government, public shaming and, in some cases, resignations.

In certain instances, the risk assessment may include (or only recommend) a security driver, more accurately referred to as "secure transportation." If this is the case, the providers used must also meet the IRS code for providing secure transportation services. If they don't, this might just be considered a perk for the executive and therefore expose the principal(s) to financial responsibility for taxes on this service. I highly recommend you or your principal consult a trusted tax advisor on these topics as part of your decision process.

Companies and government offices will often spend millions of dollars on internal and external assessments to ensure their models and brands are relevant and in line with best practices regarding their message, products and overall success. They also need to give as much weight and attention to their protective program(s). As Mike Howard, former CSO for Microsoft, reminded the audience he was addressing at an American Society for Industrial Security (ASIS) event: "Security is a business and we should be applying many of the same business principles to make sure we are successful in our approach."

2. People, Training and Mindset

Just like in any profession, good people will always be the key to success. You should never skip the very important step of carefully vetting and qualifying candidates when recruiting and hiring your EP specialist(s). In my opinion, this is the most important element of your protection and program, which is why I will go into greater detail on this topic in Chapter IV.

Often, principals and even corporate security managers believe by hiring well-qualified and trained individuals, there is a reduced need for additional or continued training. While all types of training are necessary, proficiency training in the essentials is most important. Agents/officers may bring their hard and soft skills or qualifications with them when hired, but it is critical they continue to receive proficiency training to keep their skills sharp and relevant.

The lifestyle of the principal and a family must also be considered: Are you skiers, divers, boaters, extreme sports enthusiasts or hikers? Your EP specialist or team may need at least some basic training in these areas for the safety of the operation and to ensure all the right components are present and in good condition – as well as to have medical equipment and response measures in place, including medical evacuation.

I am a big advocate of agent physical fitness, including self-defense skills. As we all know, confrontation avoidance is our best skillset in the EP field. When avoidance is not an option and we are forced to quickly evaluate our contingency plan, that plan must include the use of force. Every agent needs to be ready and have a clear mindset and understanding of what their options are, including the legality of the action they might have to take. The one area in which I have seen many teams or individuals spend too little time training (at least compared with the other required skills) is self-defense, which helps to promote a well-rounded mindset. Self-defense skills, including a personal dedication to a particular martial art, are helpful and important – but highly perishable.

Perhaps equally as important as the physical skills themselves are the *mindset and mental preparedness* this skillset brings to an individual or a team. When needed most, your close protection specialist will not have the opportunity to take a "time out" and prepare for fast and accurate responses. They will need to react with the reflexes that can only come from training and repetition and, in most cases, require months if not years to develop.

In some cases, it's not all about using major physical force, but knowledge of a style and finesse – much like a matador in a bullfight who skillfully prevents a charging 1,500-pound bull with sharp horns from causing injury and even death by deflecting the bull's energy.

Often this skillset/training isn't as present among former or current law enforcement officers, military members and special operations personnel. I'll discuss this more later, but these types of professionals can be a bit out of their element in this regard when transitioning to personal protection programs. They are trained for force and/or combat – and if they're not ready for this changeover, they can potentially become more of a liability than a benefit to the principal. Ultimately, without proper training and "de-policing," former law enforcement officers operating in an EP role often have difficulty breaking off and escorting or evacuating their principals because they are trained to stay and address a confrontation.

When a potentially hostile situation presents itself to our principals, our job is to get them out of harm's way as soon as possible – not to stay and confront or apprehend. If you have the luxury of a large team, perhaps one team member's role would be to remain and deflect or prevent the adversary from following the other EP staff and the evacuated principal. But if you have a one- or two-person detail, your EP specialist's primary job is to remove the principal from the threat quickly and safely.

EP agents should be just as well-versed in *verbal* judo as they are with physical martial arts. This training should be mandatory and might be one of the best skills your EP agent can have. When a principal can't break away from a potentially uncomfortable or even dangerous conversation (or confrontation), an agent may need to step in. They may do this by gently grabbing the principal's elbow to lead him/her away from the individual or crowd in question as they explain they are "very late for another meeting" or "have an urgent telephone call" – all the while apologizing on the principal's behalf and assuming the role of "bad guy" for taking them away.

On more than one occasion, I have had to quietly and quickly step in between my principal and an overly enthusiastic fan, angry individual or irritating reporter who might not let go of a handshake or is holding onto my principal's clothes. In some cases, individuals were just too close to my principal and I understood they were looking for me to intervene or they felt physically threatened. Close protection specialists need to know how to appropriately act in these situations and break the contact with diplomacy and good sense. There are many ways to do this without making a scene or creating an embarrassing situation for your principal or yourself.

In most cases, if your EP specialist or team has done the job right, a physical altercation or response is not necessary. Just so there is no confusion as to what I'm communicating, I must emphasize: Most EP providers (with the exception of federal agents or sworn law enforcement officers) *do not have the authority or right to lay hands on anyone unless they or their principal is at risk.* The action by the EP provider should be performed with the minimum level of physical aggression that allows them to defuse the situation.

Every scenario is different, but *if* the justifiable and legal need for any use of force or defense arises, agents and officers *must be committed* to the accuracy and effectiveness of the technique to stop the threat and remove their principal from the affected area as soon as possible.

Part of my personal mental training is a variation of the military doctrine of *cover, fire and maneuver.* When arriving at a venue with my principals, I am constantly evaluating potential threats along the way: where or what we should use for cover, objects of distraction or weapons (especially if I'm unarmed), and barriers between the threat and my principal. I am considering what our next move would be if we were in danger – e.g., escape to a safe room, stairwell, office, vehicle, etc.

The number-one goal is to create distance from the threat. Agents should do everything they can to cover and evacuate principals when possible. With that said, there may come a time when these actions will not be enough, and agents may be required to use their hard skills to protect their principals.

Quick reaction time is essential in our profession. Repetition and confidence in our hard skills are paramount. While it is not necessary to be an MMA fighter or martial arts master, EP professionals must know how to execute effective defensive/offensive skills to create distance, deflect attacks, land strikes and counterstrikes, and in some cases defeat the attacker on the spot. We can maintain our edge, mindset and hopefully the upper hand by always learning new defensive skills and tactics, via consistent training through repetition and teamwork, and by putting ourselves in practice situations where we mentally respond to a threatening scenario.

While the aim is not to create an atmosphere of paranoia, a reasonable and managed level of situational awareness and an operational mindset are critical skills to have as an EP agent (and frankly for anyone else).

Principal Brief

Principals, a degree of the above is good for you to know and be aware of as well. Early in your program, your EP manager will conduct with you what we refer to as a *principal brief.* He or she will explain what your agent(s) would do in these situations so you are not shocked by the events that may follow – especially if the agent must grab you and move you to safety while pushing or pulling you in a direction and using verbal commands like "get down," "stay here" or even "run!"

As principals, if you have many questions, concerns and confusion about your EP coverage, you probably haven't had your initial principal brief. Not long after you start receiving any level of EP protection, your EP advisor, manager or lead agent should be very upfront regarding their methodology when describing your protective coverage and re-move all mysteries where possible. They should schedule a specific time on your calendar to brief you on the results of your TVRA and the mitigating strategies being recommended or implemented.

This briefing is your opportunity to discuss the specifics of your protection and a chance to ask the hard questions or voice concerns and get a clear perspective of how your day-to-day coverage, travel and other routines will look and feel. It's also a good time to talk about privacy issues and establish any potential restrictions. You'll want to create agreed-upon communication and reporting channels and determine how you want to handle communications (e.g., text or email, verbally, through an executive assistant, etc.).

As your program matures over time, your EP manager should always be providing you updates. At times, you may want to request an updated principal brief due to changes in lifestyle, health, children, marriage/divorce and so forth.

The relationship between principals and EP providers is like any other professional relationship where open communications are established and expectations are clearly defined, resulting in a comfortable and successful collaboration.

"Keeping it Real" with Training to Maintain Mindset and Reaction

During one of the CIA's Attack on Principal (AOP) drills, General John Gordon (the CIA's deputy director) and Executive Director Alvin ("Buzzy") Krongard actually joined us for our training at a location we affectionately referred to as "The Farm."

In one scenario, our motorcade experienced an explosion that could have taken out our principal's limo. During the drill, we evacuated both General Gordon and Buzzy to a backup vehicle – all under *live fire* and the response of a heavily-armed counterassault team (CAT) *also laying down live cover fire.*

The sudden assault and quick action immediately got everyone's attention and adrenaline pumping. I'll never forget when I jumped over the front seat to cover the General as we prepared to exit our disabled vehicle upon the command of my team members. I did all I could to keep General Gordon's 6'5" 250-pound frame from running off like a wild mustang and heading to the nearest barn for safety. When the exercise was over, the General and Executive Director brushed off the mud and adjusted their clothes, which had been almost yanked off by our team while trying to keep ahold of them and ensuring we had them covered and under our control.

It was an eye-opening and "energetic" experience for them both. They earned our respect for physically putting themselves through the drill – and I'll guarantee if a real "next time" event occurred, they would be better prepared for what would follow in order to save their lives.

3. Technology and Equipment

Just as we discussed in the beginning of the book, technology plays a major role in every day of our lives. And when it comes to security and personal protection, it plays a vital role in a holistic approach. Perhaps one of the biggest complaints I hear about our interest in, investment towards and use of security technology is our lack of true understanding of how to maximize its full capabilities.

An example might be expensive and robust social media monitoring software used by IT or marketing departments that isn't shared with security or EP intelligence team members. As I mentioned, social media and open-source monitoring for high-profile principals are no longer options – they are requirements. Many times, security or EP teams are not even aware the company they work for has this level of sophisticated software they could utilize.

Many of us are continually looking for ways to reduce the "noise" of it all so we can focus on whatever is most important to us. In the world of personal security and executive protection, this "noise" can contain critical information, but it can potentially be the reason for lethal distractions.

Associated with technology is the individual and team equipment required to provide adequate protection based on the current threats. As a former team leader/director, I've always supported having a reasonable amount of advanced equipment on hand; when a new or predicable threat emerges, you want to be sure you have the proper resources and associated equipment training. This could include various weapons and proper ammunition, vehicle light kits, drones, cameras with long lenses, radio communications, portable CCTV systems for hotels or remote locations, and other individual kit and travel bags.

When it comes to physical security technology and equipment (e.g., cameras, access control, lighting, medical automated external defibrillators, etc.), most command centers or operations are only using a small percentage of these systems' full capacities. In many cases, they aren't even aware a camera is more than just a camera – most digital cameras today have various analytical capabilities. In assessment after assessment, I find users not only don't use the built-in analytics, often they don't even know they exist within a system they operate every single day. The same can be said for radios, vehicles and other equipment on which operators have either not been properly trained or received only remedial training.

It can be shocking to witness the gap between actual use and maximal system capabilities, peak performance and optimization. It is not at all uncommon to find technology that has reached the end of its useful life still being used – i.e., technology well past its prime. Unfortunately, this situation may be very common due to the rapid rate of updates/upgrades in technologies.

Security technology is often tied to officer/agent procedures and, when the technology is outdated or inadequate, so will be the procedures and responses. Technology is only as good as those operating it; what once was used as an asset in your protective strategy can now become a vulnerability. In a previous position, my job was to exploit these vulnerabilities – and I can tell you with authority that bad actors love outdated (or even nonexistent) technology.

4. Proprietary Information/Protective Intelligence

Information and intelligence will both greatly influence any EP program and become the driving force behind most of your decisions, since both require active measures.

Proprietary Information

Proprietary information could be based on any of the following: corporate culture, past experiences, developments that raise a principal's risk profile, key executives' expectations regarding EP, budgetary considerations, and/or travel or event schedules which might require additional security. While intelligence might be the responsibility of a single seat within your EP team or your greater security department, information is something that should always be collected and shared appropriately to ensure your EP team is ready for last-minute changes and unplanned events.

Trust and mutual respect within the principal's inner circle are both key for the dissemination of important information. In this inner circle, it is important to never underestimate the power of the executive assistant (EA) in the chain of success of any EP program. A sharp and considerate EA can either make the life of the EP specialist and security detail work well or be a living nightmare. I cannot imagine doing this job without such a person communicating to us the ever-changing schedule of our principals. Whether the EA has just learned a principal is planning an international trip leaving tonight, the principal has received tickets for an NBA game starting in an hour, or they are planning to go holiday shopping with their children during the coming weekend, EAs can quickly communicate with the EP team to ensure uninterrupted protection. Even just a few minutes' heads up can make an enormous difference.

However, it is also important to recognize all information regarding principals' schedules and travel should be limited and controlled. At times, too many individuals have access to this information; a "need to know" policy should generally be utilized.

Protective Intelligence

Protective intelligence can be defined as information critical for determining the level and type of protection required for a person, event or resource and any necessary countermeasures. It is based on the collection and analysis of real-time data from a variety of sources that can impact the safety and security of the principals in their daily schedule or while traveling.

The process of gathering protective intelligence may begin with an event that triggers the need to collect and analyze information. It should include elements such as countersurveillance, investigations and analyses. It is also obtained from open sources, monitoring of social media sites and blogs for relevant insights. We are also utilizing software that further assists analysts in collecting and distilling relevant real-time information.

A good EP program should subscribe to and utilize various types of intelligence reports provided by reputable companies/sources. The decision to subscribe to certain paid intelligence reports will be determined by your corporate and executive profiles, budgets, functions, global footprint, and overall associated threats and risks. Regardless of your internal budget, it is highly important to establish a *timely* internal chain of review and dissemination of this information and how it affects your program, company, executives and/or employees. *Information received too late is just as bad as having never received the information at all.*

Examples of protective intelligence include:

1. An updated threat report highlights an increased security risk at a location the principal is visiting.
2. Suspicious persons or activities have been observed through countersurveillance.
3. A person of interest is posting threats against the company or an executive.
4. An anarchist group is planning on protesting or targeting a corporate event or executive.
5. Plausible threat information has been received through your personal or corporate mail screening process.

A Deeper Dive into Protective Intelligence

I outlined protective intelligence above, but this subject is so important in today's world that I want to take a deeper dive into it.

The EP profession and security in general has many buzzwords. Protective intelligence is one buzz phrase you might hear a lot, but unfortunately in some programs it is just that – a cool phrase. It should, however, represent the important compilation and analysis of information that can be utilized. Protective intelligence involves the methods used to identify, analyze and assess risks and threats, but it also *must* include the other important component of the process: *timely informing EP teams and/or principals in order to facilitate action when necessary.*

While you don't need to build a CIA Watch Desk or the Secret Service Protective Intelligence Division to help assess and manage the flow of information, an internal dedicated manager and/or reliable outsourced company may be what you need to keep up with the growing challenges we face regarding various threat vectors. Today, many corporate and EP details have established this capability within their programs. It is most often recommended to have a single seat assigned to a dedicated protective intelligence specialist who can focus on all the necessary data points and report any concerns to the EP manager in a timely manner for awareness or follow-on action if necessary.

Many factors will define the scope of protective intelligence for a principal's program. Some protectees may receive very few or no actual threats. On the other hand, while rare, I am aware of some protectees who receive thousands of threats a year. Some receive these same numbers in just months. If your principal receives a large volume of threats because of their corporate position, profile or controversial product or service, it is imperative to have a *dedicated* protective intelligence analyst and program in place to collect, investigate, analyze, assess, report, manage and act on these threats.

It may sound simple, but I have always treated protective intelligence as *the capability to know all things brewing*, then determining what actions should be taken to protect a principal's interests, privacy, reputation and safety.

Whether event-driven (e.g., receipt of a threatening phone call, email, letter or walk-in information) or an ongoing program, the process of working with protective intelligence should proceed similarly to the suggested intelligence flow outlined below.

- **Collect, Receive and Record Information**
  - o Identify potential threats or concerns through surveillance

- o   Review open-source information to reveal potential risks
- o   Receive reports from law enforcement identifying potential threats and risks
- o   Record information for historical and investigative purposes

- **Investigate**
  - o   Conduct background investigations, reviews of any persons of interest and additional surveillance
  - o   Coordinate with law enforcement
  - o   Document all combined information

- **Analyze and Assess**
  - o   Review data for correlations, accuracy and relevance; corroborate with multiple sources where possible
  - o   Determine potential threats or risks
  - o   Coordinate findings with legal counsel

- **Report, Manage and Act**
  - o   Report all information obtained and processed to the protection team
  - o   Aim to mitigate the risks or threats but, in all cases, actively manage situations until satisfactory resolution is achieved
  - o   Have information-receivers (in close protection or management) decide what actions are to be taken

The entire intelligence flow is important and critical value can be gained through a well-organized protective intelligence program. I have experienced it regarding my own and my principal's safety, and there are many practitioners in our profession who depend on daily reporting as a basis for effectively managing their principal's protection.

We EP types all face the challenge of not displaying too much alarm to our principals. When not used appropriately, protective intelligence can lead to a negative dynamic where credibility is lost and anxiety takes its place.

Situational awareness is a key component of protective intelligence.

Any program or effort must include the monitoring of real-time big data as well as growing trends that can ultimately impact your security. This requirement continues to grow at an incredible rate every day; even our government cannot realistically keep up with it all, let alone a small group of security professionals working for a company or family. Some components of a protective intelligence program will also be focused on persons of interest or real-time risks and threats associated with people, venues, events, activities and travel.

As EP managers, we also should be concerned with possible events or situations within our control that could have a negative effect on a principal's health or reputation. An example of this might be a bad actor gaining access to a stage where a principal is speaking for the purpose of causing harm or embarrassment.

Additionally, a true risk-based EP program must have some mechanism to collect intelligence, analyze it and make required modifications to the strategies already in place. The program must adapt to offset *potential* threats – which are the thoughts that keep us up at night.

But beware: Each escalation and additional measure should be designed for an approximate timeframe. If you operate in a particular heightened threat condition for an extended period, within weeks (or months) these elevated threat conditions become the new norm. In most cases, this is unsustainable. Over time, human complacency creeps back in as the reason for the escalation fades into the past. Most security experts understand complacency is often the worst enemy for individuals involved in the first line of security.

Post 9/11, I was entering my fourth year at the CIA and serving as an assistant team leader on the protective detail for Director George Tenet. From the moments immediately after the attack and in the months that followed, we had to consider there was a broader plan for attacking our infrastructure and key government leadership. Osama bin Laden already knew the CIA had been hunting him and was on his heels – after the attack, the Agency was on the tip of the response sword. Therefore, we knew they could target the Director and key leadership to potentially disrupt or delay our response. This was an intense time, with the Director's increased presence at the White House and more global travel. It wasn't long before several more principals were added to our protective responsibility and expanding our coverage.

This all meant we had become more vulnerable outside our headquarters in Langley. Each vehicle or foot movement, public appearance or clandestine meeting took on a different level of careful consideration and planning. We faced the dichotomy of managing increased levels of risk while still ensuring the principals could go about their business as normal. In addition, we had to ensure every protective detail and all assigned personnel maintained their heightened level of vigilance and readiness.

The CIA also issued threat briefings reporting that attacks on our principals were possible and, in some cases, imminent. These continued for over a year after 9/11. I often questioned the effectiveness of these reports and our untenable state of physical and psychological readiness. But, after these attacks, the last thing we wanted was to be caught off guard, and our attention to any intelligence report was in hyper-proactive mode.

As an operator, manager or principal, it is imperative that we not allow ourselves or our security details to live and remain in an amplified level of awareness or concern for extended periods of time. After a while (normally months), we can become exhausted and ineffective – both mentally and physically. Intensified levels of security are designed for short periods of time until the risks can be evaluated and mitigated. The goal is to return to a normal state as soon as possible.

While I continue to mention I do not appreciate individuals who use fear as a motivator for driving a protection program, there is the other side of this discussion: Some security managers put their heads in the sand and refuse to pay attention to growing threats. But threats *can* grow rapidly. They *can* ignite overnight and quickly turn into a crisis.* You have to strike a proper balance between the appropriate level of security and a state of self-imprisonment.

---

* This scenario is more common in foreign countries and for international companies but can also be of concern to a single family or principal.

"The Call is on the Ground"

In the summer of 1998, I was sent to Lagos, Nigeria, to prepare for the arrival of General John Gordon (the CIA's deputy director, or DDCI) and other senior intelligence officers traveling with him on an official overnight visit. While Lagos was not exactly a place I ever had on my bucket list, I didn't get to choose my assignments, as I was still a junior agent. My fellow agent Chris (whom I nicknamed "NASCAR") and I were tasked with arriving several days in advance and assuring this brief but very important trip went well.

Despite the less-than-ideal circumstances, this was the advance that made me understand the importance of planning for contingencies and having reliable protective intelligence. In this situation, I had to make an "on-the-ground call" using protective intelligence and resources in an unexpected but critical way to protect our principals and maintain important travel schedules.

This advance was a challenge from the time we landed in Lagos. As NASCAR and I stepped off the plane, a small group of local airport officials welcomed us. Our goal as CIA agents entering a country in advance of the Director or Deputy Director was to arrive without any attention or fanfare – so when we saw a "welcome party" on the tarmac, it left us feeling as if we had failed even before we had descended the jet ramp. Needless to say, this was not standard operating procedure. I looked at NASCAR as we were greeted and whisked through immigration and to baggage claim. Our escorts tried to make small talk about our flight, but it made both of us feel uncomfortable nevertheless. The group continued telling us about Lagos as we continued trying to figure out what was going on.

We had expected someone from the U.S. embassy to meet us at the airport, but by now we were sure this group was not them. As we made our way to baggage claim with our new Nigerian friends, I noticed someone dressed in typical U.S. embassy attire looking our way as if to say: *Are you my guys?* I stepped away and identified myself. At that point, he confirmed he was indeed there to pick us up.

I walked back over to the Nigerian who seemed to be in control. "I'm sorry," I said, "now that we know one another, can I ask you what you think we're here for?" With a confused look on his face, he said, "You're here from the United States FAA to inspect our airport for safety and security, aren't you?"

Ah-ha.

"Well, actually that's *not* why we're here. We don't work for the FAA," I said, "but I'm sure there are a couple FAA inspectors looking for a special greeting and a little assistance getting through the long immigration line you quickly took us through. Thank you."

With that, they all turned without saying a word and ran off looking for their *real* special guests. It turned out the Lagos airport no longer had FAA approval for American airline companies to land due to poor security conditions, so the U.S. officials were returning to inspect improvements – and it appeared things were off to a bad start.

Our American counterparts took me and NASCAR through an unsecured back door, after which we crossed a small parking lot to a vehicle waiting for us on the other side of a hole in the airport fence. As we made our way through, we had to actually step over a man who looked to have been deceased for several days. This was going to be an interesting advance, and no doubt the FAA inspectors were going to have their hands full.

After a long day of travel, I was exhausted. Upon entering my hotel room, I noticed a strong odor – it appeared the whole interior had literally just been painted. I thought this was odd, but I was done for the day and just needed to get a few hours of sleep. During the night, I kept hearing popping and cracking noises around the room, and even though I got up several times to identify where the sounds were coming from, I just couldn't figure it out.

As the dawn light streamed through my window, it became clear what the cracking and popping was: The paint was, for some strange reason, actually peeling off the walls. And that wasn't all – as I stood in front of the mirror to shave, water dripped onto my head from the light socket above. A moment later, the power in the entire hotel went off. I couldn't help but laugh to myself – I knew NASCAR's tolerance level for this country was already extremely low, and I was sure he was about to start throwing things around his room in frustration. My suspicion was confirmed ten minutes later when I met him in the lobby. I won't go into the details.

After a quick breakfast, we met with the hotel manager to square away our lodging requirements. Typically, we would handle only the CIA's travelers. In this case, there were more than 20 individuals, including our additional security team, traveling with General Gordon – but still nothing out of the ordinary for us.

What *was* out of the ordinary this time was that we were responsible for handling the air crew's hotel requirements as well. We decided to keep everyone at the same place, which meant we needed almost 40 rooms for our entire party. After *four painful hours* and several pencils and sheets of paper later, the front desk manager finally checked us in with proper room assignments.

Over the next few days, NASCAR and I had much to do in anticipation of General Gordon's arrival and brief visit. One of the major concerns was to get our five-car motorcade through a potentially dangerous route in an area called the "go slow," which was on the main road from the airport to the central part of town. It had this name due to the fact that *thousands* of Nigerians used this area – some just as a convenient walking route, others to take advantage of the slow-moving traffic to panhandle or to make money by selling anything to the "captive audience" of new arrivals. It was like a river of humans flowing over the airport road, with Nigerians (many in their vibrant African dress) *everywhere*.

It wasn't uncommon to see legless children sitting on homemade skateboards rolling alongside the road, looking for the kind of vehicle with passengers who would make eye contact with them and give them money. Sometimes these "skateboard children" would hold onto a moving car's fenders with one hand, knocking on the windows and reaching out for money with the other. Our local sources also warned us to beware of partially dressed individuals with open leprosy wounds oozing fluids who would lay their bodies on vehicle windows and beg for money. It was impossible not to be saddened by the worst of what we witnessed – but also amazed by these individuals' fortitude, ingenuity and ability to smile in spite of their daily challenges.

The "Go Slow" in Nigeria.

Overall, it was a motorcade security nightmare for protecting General Gordon, which required many motorcade dry runs to consider our risks and response options in the event of an accident, breakdown or attack. We looked at all route options to avoid this maelstrom, including alternate routes, helicopters and boats. However, we soon realized this was, in fact, the best route available at the time – and it was up to us to figure out how to work around the variety of challenging obstacles without things going horribly wrong.

One particular element of personal safety in a foreign country may be less obvious to most, yet still highly important: understanding and carrying local currencies. At the time of this advance, I wanted to exchange some U.S. dollars for local money. Through the bullet-resistant glass window at the hotel, I gave the teller $200 in U.S. currency and then waited for what seemed like an hour. When the teller finally returned, I initially thought the bank made a counting mistake, as the employee began to slide *stack after stack* of Nigerian dollars through the window. But there was no mistake – that was the exchange rate. Now, I just had to figure out how to carry this stack of cash without needing a large backpack.

As our luck would *not* have it, three hours prior to wheels down for General Gordon, a local group came together near the "go slow" area and started a riot against the local taxi union. This protest included burning some tires and other nearby debris. Shockingly, it was reported they added some unsupportive bystanders to the fire.

I had received news of the riot and was now making my way to meet the Regional Security Officer (RSO) at the embassy to get his assessment. The RSO had been around for a while – he was a Vietnam vet and had been stationed in Lagos for a couple of years. I asked about the riot and his thoughts on how to work around it. He responded very calmly that it happened almost weekly somewhere and normally the crowd would disperse within a few hours. He also said he would put several members of his local security team along the route and they would provide updates every 15 minutes.

I reminded him General Gordon's plane was less than three hours out, and if the riot was not over and the route was still obstructed at least one hour prior to landing, I would divert the plane to Abuja, the "new and improved" capital of Nigeria. The purpose of the visit was important to the U.S. ambassador and the embassy, and the RSO knew the ambassador would not like it if General Gordon had to be rerouted to Abuja. He felt it was very important General Gordon see the appalling environment and conditions in which the embassy employees had to work every day.

The ambassador wasn't minimizing the dangers: During this advance alone, one of our CIA communications employees and his wife survived an attempted carjacking while being driven home in an armored vehicle. The attackers fired multiple shots into the windows before speeding off.

Armed with what information I had, I immediately went to our secure communications office and asked them to put me in touch with General Gordon's plane. I spoke to the General's team, advising them of the current risks and conditions on the ground. The response: "You're on the ground; the DDCI will take your lead."

As we were leaving the embassy, we were contacted by the RSO, who said the ambassador would like to meet with us. We then had a very short but candid meeting with the ambassador. While the ambassador was rather insistent we ensure General Gordon make it to the embassy, I respectfully reminded him I worked for the CIA and my primary responsibility was the safety of the DDCI. With (polite) pressure from the ambassador and the weight of a potentially volatile situation on my shoulders, I proceeded to inform him if the road from the airport was not clear and determined safe to travel within 90 minutes of wheels down, I would divert General Gordon's plane to Abuja.

In other words, the protesters had an hour and a half to shut down their party and go home.

With the intelligence and experience at hand of those who knew the area and risks best, NASCAR and I continued to prepare as if the plane would land. We made one more stop by the RSO's office, picked up an embassy radio and reviewed our options for safe havens if we had to stop along the route to the embassy for any reason. We collected and assembled our motorcade vehicles, conducted sweeps of all of them, and double-checked the condition of the vehicles provided by the embassy. Both of us appreciated the professionalism of their drivers, fleet maintenance crews and support teams – especially in light of the challenges they faced every day. Our combined successes around the world often relied heavily on assistance from RSOs, other embassy support staff and our own offices located somewhere within the region.

Our standard operating procedure was to be at the airport at least one hour prior to landing. This time, I was anxious to see the route again. As we were leaving the embassy, we heard on the radio the riot was breaking up, just like the RSO had predicted. By the time we entered the area near the main bridge to the airport, the fire was just light smoke and most of the crowd had departed. We contacted our surveillance teams about the conditions and the chance of secondary riots or blockades and they agreed with the RSO the worst was over.

We made one final check with the embassy and our communications team to see if there were any local reports or news releases of our principal arriving in Lagos. After we conducted other security advance efforts and established certain precautions (which I will not discuss), we proceeded to contact the plane with a green light to land. It was one hour to wheels down.

General Gordon's plane landed like clockwork and our reduced motorcade navigated the "go slow" the best way possible throughout the chaotic streets of Lagos. The rest of the trip went well, and 36 hours later, everyone was safely on the plane on to the next African stop.

Many of those who have not experienced the behind-the-scenes of EP will not realize how much work goes into the "ease" and facilitation of daily activities to ensure our principals have a safe, on-time and successful experience. If it had not been for the protective intelligence we were able to derive from many sources over several days in advance of General Gordon's visit, we could have made critical and possibly life-threatening mistakes or errors in judgment.

I cannot overemphasize the importance of protective intelligence for high-profile and high-risk principals. The mechanism you create to receive and analyze this intelligence *while traveling* is even more critical. You may have to make decisions in minutes or even seconds regarding your principal's safety based on intelligence received.

Other Key Program Considerations

Now that we've reviewed the basic elements included in the "four pillars," let's look at a few other key components to most EP programs. As mentioned previously, there is no such thing as "EP in a box," but most programs will include consideration of the following elements:

1. Health Security for EP Programs
2. Weapons – To Arm or Not to Arm?
3. Office Security
4. Residential Security
5. Security Operations Centers (SOCs)

Health Security for EP Programs

Individuals or organizations routinely spend large sums on risk management activities including protective services, countersurveillance, armored vehicles, high-tech security systems and even safe rooms. But they focus very little attention on ensuring they are ready for the measurably predictable risk of a medical event. The bottom line is principals should make sure their security programs cover their most precious possession of all: their health.

What I'm about to say might sound shocking but, in my opinion, UHNW families sometimes receive some of the worst medical support money can buy. Their protection is so focused on outside physical risks, they neglect to attend to a more likely threat – a medical emergency or traumatic injury. The reality is anyone, even someone who is a potential security target, is more likely to be faced with a medical emergency or potentially fatal accident than they are a hostile attack. This means it is essential to spend time on the topic of health security.

Given the importance of this subject, I reached out to Drs. William L. Lang* and Robert G. Darling** to better understand the importance of medical preparedness for EP teams and their principals. Both Drs. Lang and Darling were physicians in the White House Medical Unit (WHMU) and assisted in its redesign during the Clinton administration. Dr. Lang was the Director of the WHMU and Dr. Darling was the first board-certified emergency medicine physician to serve the President of the United States. This section combines their insights and my own.

It goes without saying, but UHNW families and large organizational leaders can be potential targets for violence. These families and organizations often determine it is prudent to install security systems, hire security guards, travel in armored vehicles and so forth. The level of security typically varies by perceived risk, location, prominence of the individual and other factors determined by at least a basic analysis.

This same analysis also needs to be performed for health and medical considerations. In fact, health contingency planning *must* be integrated into the routine security preparedness analyses that prudent individuals and organizations execute on an ongoing basis.

This does not mean every health security modality must be fully developed for every situation – no more than comprehensive physical

---

* Dr. Lang is currently a vice president at a D.C.-area comprehensive healthcare system. He previously served as Associate Chief Medical Officer at the U.S. Department of Homeland Security and is considered among the world's foremost experts in medical contingency planning and organizational response to natural and man-made disasters – including threats from weapons of mass destruction. He has traveled to over 80 countries providing health systems assessment and/or advisory services, including health security consultation for heads of state and other senior leaders.

** Dr. Darling is a retired Navy captain who served over 25 years in uniform; he spent another three years in government service as a flight surgeon, emergency medicine physician and Director of Disaster Medical Services at the Uniformed Services University of the Health Sciences (USUHS) School of Medicine in Bethesda, Maryland. Today, he helps UHNW families and corporations address their medical readiness challenges – and is considered a respected subject-matter expert in this field.

security measures are required in every environment. What is important, however, is that planning for medical emergencies has at least as much importance as planning for traditional security contingencies, and a basic all-hazards security survey (which includes medical issues) is applied to all situations.

You may wonder: Why not simply rely on 911 and emergency department systems? Well, the same argument could be made for utilizing police services rather than having a well-developed and resourced emergency response plan of your own that includes EP. Those with means often don't feel police services can provide the immediate responsiveness and individual attention private security services can – nor are these municipal safety and police professionals trained, prepared or authorized to provide EP service at the individual, family or organizational level.

When you combine those considerations with the knowledge that retreats, country homes, yachts, aircraft and so forth are often intentionally located in remote areas, the need for comprehensive security and contingency-based planning including both physical and health security becomes obvious.

One important thing to realize in all this is that health security is not simply another take on "concierge medicine." Concierge health services help ensure access to top-notch physicians and hospitals and integrate the full spectrum of care for their subscribers. However, having the cell phone number for a concierge physician or clinic has limited utility for someone experiencing chest pain in a private plane over the Pacific, or who has been stung by an Irukandji jellyfish while swimming off a yacht near a secluded beach off Australia. Knowing your concierge hospital is near your Midtown office or apartment does little good in the case of a natural disaster, blackout, terrorist attack or any other catastrophic event that has disrupted systems near a country estate or rural operating location.

As with other security disciplines, health security requires planning and should address the possibility of urgent or emergency care at any time of the day or night. This plan should have protocols in place to protect principals wherever in the world they are located, and in whatever complicated situations that may arise.

Dr. Darling's medical practice, for instance, utilizes advanced technologies including telemedicine networks; it also employs the pre-positioning of diagnostic equipment, medical devices, pharmaceuticals, trauma supplies and advanced trained medical personnel (e.g., paramedics, nurse practitioners/physician assistants or physicians) as appropriate to the client's situation and the medical threat environment they face. This allows for effective planning and the ability to mitigate the impact of most medical emergencies before they occur. Dr. Darling and I have worked together for several years now to help clients integrate medical and health components into their broader safety and security programs.

Dr. Lang observes that principals often assume their emergency response team has the capability to address a medical or health issue, but this is not often the case for situations requiring much beyond first aid. While many security team members possess accredited certifications in the emergency medical field, Dr. Lang strongly recommends consulting with an experienced doctor with a background in international health and emergency medicine when planning for medical contingencies.

Dr. Darling advises principals to consider their medical conditions, activities and frequency of travel to locations with poor or inadequate medical services when deciding on the addition of more advanced medical support to their security team or a structured mechanism for accessing dedicated and trusted remote medical support.

The Drivers for Health Security Planning

Dr. Lang stated that, following the Cold War, contingency planning in general was relegated to the back burner. A decade later, the 9/11 attacks forced organizations to dust off their preparedness plans to be ready for terrorist events anywhere. The anthrax attacks (also in 2001) reminded us not all terrorist actions involve explosions or firearms. Barely two years later, New York City was sent back a century after a major blackout shut down just about all public services. In addition, the U.S. has always had to deal with a steady stream of wildfires, tornadoes, hurricanes and other natural disasters.

Bottom line: While some locations are more vulnerable than others, a disaster can strike anywhere, anytime. It can be widespread or even isolated to one person, family or organization. And even when the incident is not primarily medical, it can often have impacts that require a medical response.

In reaction to this steady baseline threat, the U.S. government has advocated an all-hazards approach to planning. For governments, this approach is encompassed in the National Response Framework (NRF). Recently, the NRF formally integrated health issues into its approach by establishing medical readiness and response as the primary goal of one of the fifteen Emergency Support Functions.

In many ways, this has caused individuals and organizations to develop a false sense of security. They believe that because our government has built-in ongoing planning for medical response to critical events, they do not need to address health preparedness issues themselves.

This way of thinking is extremely misguided. Even under ideal conditions with the most modern, streamlined systems in place, the quality of response depends on the availability of responders and on how well the caller was able to communicate the problem to the dispatcher.

And while there is no question governments have made great strides in emergency preparedness and emergency medical services, there are many areas where response systems are simply overwhelmed or inadequately skilled. You can find many examples across the U.S. and overseas where the local 911 systems are antiquated and overloaded.*[57]

The problem is even more challenging outside major metropolitan areas, where EMS stations and hospitals aren't as close by. In the early 1990s, the U.S. Congress's Office of Technology Assessment (now closed), detailed the challenges facing rural EMS. They reported (a)

---

* In fact, in 2016, the D.C. fire department medical director who was hired to reform the Agency's aging and failing systems and response resigned because she stated her proposals were being blocked and "people are dying needlessly because we are moving too slow." They say that major improvements have taken place in recent months, but this example of failing 911 systems can still be found in many major U.S. cities today.

long response and transport times, (b) low experience levels due to infrequent calls for major issues, (c) lack of training due to the typical volunteer and/or resource-poor operations of the emergency services organizations, and (d) lack of rapid access to specialized care centers for trauma, strokes, burns and so forth.

Although this report was made almost 30 years ago, Darling and Lang stress that not enough effort or progress has been made to address this critical deficiency – and many of the same problems remain today. They also highlighted the fact that many rural hospitals cannot generate enough revenue to acquire the critical technologies needed to perform modern medicine – or even to remain in operation. Since many UHNW individuals and families make it a point to escape to rural areas, many organizations now have contingency operations facilities in these remote locations.

In recent years, we've also seen instances where hackers have infiltrated 911 systems with denial-of-service cyberattacks.[58] In 2016, an 18-year-old Arizonan was arrested on charges he created such an attack on a local 911 system.[59] In March 2018, the Baltimore 911 dispatch system was a victim of ransomware that affected the system for 24 hours. Two weeks prior, a similar attack hit Atlanta.

Internationally, the problems are magnified enormously. While EMS services exist in most developed nations, the concept of highly-trained paramedics is limited to just a handful of countries. In most regions of the world, the primary role of EMS is simply to transport people to a hospital.

Knowledge of the caliber of nearby hospitals and how to access the best care (which may not always involve going to the nearest emergency room) is crucial when an emergency occurs. Health security preparedness planning is needed to ensure resources are known in advance and additional personnel or organizational resources are available when local resources are inadequate.

Even after the initial management of an event, once a person is stabilized, strategies must be addressed for any further care required. This could mean a conversation with a trusted provider at a major institution or involve transport on an air ambulance to a center of excellence or home. These activities can be more efficiently managed when they are considered ahead of time.

It is not only the EMS and hospital systems that drive the need for health preparedness planning tailored to the international environment. In addition to other concerns regarding developing nations, risk managers must look at the threat of political instability, communications difficulties (technical and language) and environmental hazards.

It is worth noting that emergency medical services systems are, for both good and bad, one of the great equalizers of our society. Once EMS is activated, the system applies the same basic principles and practices to all who enter it, poor or wealthy, influential or everyday citizen. EMS is based upon a standardized systematic approach to dealing with major illnesses and traumatic injuries and, in a life-or-death situation, this is the best approach. At least in major metropolitan areas of developed nations, it most effectively applies evidence-based, standardized practices that generally lead to the best outcomes.

For someone outside the medical field, however, it is hard to know when entering that standardized system is the best choice. For UHNW and other powerful individuals who are used to controlling every aspect of their lives, relinquishing their financial sovereignty and autonomy to enter the depersonalized emergency services system is difficult to do.

One notable case occurred in 2009, when actress Natasha Richardson fell during a beginner's skiing lesson in Quebec. She sustained what she believed was a minor head injury. After initially refusing medical attention, she later complained of a headache and was taken to a local hospital where she rapidly deteriorated. She was later transferred to Montreal and, in less than seven hours, was listed in critical condition. After being flown to New York's Lenox Hill Hospital the following day, Richardson tragically died from what may have otherwise been non-lethal injuries had she received immediate medical attention.

Of course, no one wants to think there will be a medical emergency or a life-threatening event just around the corner. But having a reasonable degree of medical preparedness (based upon the activity, travel destination and/or personal health considerations of the principals involved) with robust backup support from medical experts is crucial.

An instance in my own career illustrates this well. While working for several months on a security project in the Caribbean, my team received word in the middle of the night that an individual had suffered a potentially life-threatening head injury following a golf cart accident.

The paramedic assigned to the project determined the injuries were significant and local resources were not adequate to properly evaluate or treat the victim – immediate transfer to a trauma center was required. Without a moment's notice, our team now had to coordinate a Coast Guard helicopter response to our remote island.

Fortunately, only a couple months prior to this incident, our project had an unexpected visit by a former U.S. president for which we rehearsed the same type of medical transport response. Because of this rehearsal, our team was able to react quickly. First, we established a landing zone on a nearby soccer field lit up with golf cart lights and a strobe light. Then, using a UHF radio to communicate with the pilot on approach and landing, our injured patient was transferred safely and flown to a hospital with advanced care and he was able to make a full recovery.

Planning for medical emergencies is enormously proactive and will significantly reduce the risks of reliance on external resources or outside entities that can be variable and, in many situations, unreliable. In some cases, the very lack of planning might even lead to an unnecessary and escalating life-threatening scenario.

Weapons – To Arm or Not to Arm?

Once a decision has been made to use, hire or develop any level of close protection or to build an EP detail, one of the next questions you will need to answer is whether or not they should be armed. For many principals, like most people, the thought of having a weapon in your presence will elicit many different emotions. The only point I will make here is this: A weapon is a tool, and an important tool, for protecting a person from another person – who may have the same tool.

The decision to have an armed detail or close protection specialist is important and requires a well-thought-out plan of action. It will depend on many factors, but should start with determining the threat. To a professional close protection specialist, a weapon is like a surgical instrument to a surgeon, wrench to a mechanic, saw to a carpenter, or a vehicle to a race car driver – in the wrong hands, all these tools can kill someone.

Consideration must be given to the type of weapon(s) needed, training and certifications, and management must conduct additional background checks and psychological testing. You'll need to determine whether each person's weapon will be open-carry or concealed, what the rules of engagement are and whether your officers/agents will also have a less-than-lethal option. They will need to fully understand the *deadly force continuum* that provides the legal justification to use lethal force with any type of weapon.

You will also need to create policies and procedures for all aspects of the armed requirements, including associated equipment, holsters, bags, packs and types of ammunition, along with weapons policies surrounding when and how often to clear and clean them. You should also devise policies and procedures outlining if your agent(s) will store weapons on your property or keep them at home and bring them to work every day.

In addition, you may not need to arm your team across the board. For example, you might decide to have an armed detail at your residence but leave your office and close protection officers unarmed. Or you might decide to have an armed element at both your office and home, but not require your close protection to have weapons. In certain cases, you might decide all those providing protection should carry weapons – it all depends on the situation, need and your personal comfort level.

When ready, you and the person in charge of your protection should have comprehensive discussions regarding your EP team's armed status and weapons in general. Once a decision and a comprehensive plan have been agreed upon, the next essential element is ensuring your plan can be executed legally. This is a broad subject but includes city, state, country and cross-state/country carry laws, as well as the issues of certification and licensing. Ultimately, you must ensure your EP provider (whether in house or contracted) is *legally armed* and meets all requirements. Having an individual assigned to your protection who is illegally carrying a weapon can result in significant negative consequences and liabilities to both the principal and the agent.

Many details will hire current or former police officers because of their ability to carry legally, as well as their certifications and relationships with local law enforcement. Additionally, their off-duty status as badged police officers can be an important component to the overall plan for an armed detail.

If you decide to arm your detail, that doesn't mean you need to rely solely on former or current police officers. Your best or preferred EP agent may not have police credentials and may need to acquire open or concealed carry licenses (possibly in several states) to wield a firearm. Depending upon your local laws on carrying weapons, you should be able to arm your team if you meet the standards, training and legal requirements – even without using police officers.

Lastly, if you do decide to arm your protective staff, the individual(s) who will be armed must have significant previous experience with carrying similar weapons. Ongoing training and qualification must continue throughout the time they will be armed – no exceptions.

Office Security

Office buildings of all types and sizes require security planning and a full TVRA should be conducted on them to conceptualize and understand any of the potential risks facing the principal or staff members while at the workplace.

Because there are so many details that go into establishing EP programs for the wide variety of principals and lifestyles out there, this section cannot cover every possible office EP scenario in depth. Following are just a few examples of the *many* elements that need to be considered:

- Principal's arrival and departure locations
- Use of vehicles (with or without a driver)

- Use of parking lots and garages (and risk associated with identifying signage)
- Access to the office building by other tenants, elevator controls, security officers, vehicle barriers, visitor/employee access control, separate executive suite access, general building/office access control systems, emergency exits
- Panic alarm placement and procedures, safe room location(s), ballistic glass or doors
- All-hazards emergency procedures, training and drills – including fire evacuation, active violence, bomb threats and other 911 situations
- Comprehensive mail screening and delivery procedures
- Video and still camera locations

For the principals who require or request office EP coverage, we must consider all elements of securty from the moment they leave their residence to their return home at night – and all the time in between. While many best practices exist regarding office security, the culture of the business or the personality of the executive often drives what is acceptable. Without a doubt, there are ways to blend corporate culture, personality and security levels to be acceptable to all involved.

Residential Security

Your residence does not need to look like a fortress, but it should provide you with a level of confidence that you can feel safe within your home. With the help of today's security design subject-matter experts, a combination of technology, barriers and procedures will help you feel secure while still allowing you to enjoy your space as you should – no homeowner, principal or protectee ought to feel like a prisoner in his or her own living space.

Security design engineers will use the "layers of security" approach when developing the key elements for a residence. Residential programs are based on principals' risks, threats, lifestyle, size of home or property, and comfort level. The following are just a few of the considerations in a design plan:

- Distance from public roads or easy avenue of approach
- Comprehensive live video camera coverage
- Various levels and types of access control
- Buried ground sensors and property intrusion detection technology
- Night vision and thermal imagery
- Programmable unmanned aerial vehicle transmitting video coverage for large estates/properties (where legal)
- Trained K9 units
- Residential security officers
- Walls, fencing, hardscape (e.g., water features), impenetrable bushes, shrubs and other landscaping concepts to create obstacles or for use as a physical barrier – more commonly known as Crime Prevention Through Environmental Design (CPTED)
- Effective perimeter and residential lighting
- Physical structure upgrade of the home exterior, including highly secure doors and windows with ballistic-rated glass or film
- Interior hidden passages and safe rooms

Most importantly, you should design a plan of action and make sure the family knows it. The plan should include feedback from all key stakeholders to ensure the preplanning phase captures all the requirements – especially the owner's taste and appetite for utilizing creative concepts to provide less obvious layers of protection. These concepts should all work in unison and provide overlapping support.

I would recommend occasional testing of these precautions by an experienced and qualified Red Team to check for gaps and vulnerabilities in the plan. In most cases, a combination of design, technology and procedures will keep principals safe and provide them with a greater level of confidence.

While rare, a considerable percentage of premeditated kidnappings or attacks occur either at the victim's residence or around vehicles. Though both one's home and vehicle may seem to provide a physical barrier, vulnerabilities exist between the entering and exiting of each that can be exploited by bad actors. This means UHNW families should ensure the design layout of their residence does not invite opportunity, but rather portrays a deterrence to a potential kidnapper or someone looking to cause harm in any way.

The following is extreme, shocking and very disheartening to write about, but my hope is that readers will consider the unfortunate Savopoulos family tragedy I'm about to summarize and consider how we all can prevent something like it from ever happening again.

In May 2015, three members of the Savopoulos family, along with their housekeeper, were held hostage and brutally murdered in their home in upscale Washington, D.C. – just minutes from the U.S. Vice President's residence.

This crime was perpetrated by a former employee of Savvas Savopoulos, who was the CEO and owner of American Iron Works. Investigators believe the suspect entered the house without anyone being notified of the intrusion. He then proceeded to torture and kill this family in their own home. The suspect also set the house on fire and stole one of the family's vehicles. He was found guilty on multiple charges in the fall of 2018.

Out of respect for the Savopoulos family and their housekeeper, I will not comment on any specifics of what they might have done or tried to do during this horrific event. But, based on their financial means, perhaps a plan and utilization of technology and best practices could have allowed them to survive this horrible crime.

24/7 Security Operations Centers – Their EP Role

A security operations center (SOC) is a 24/7 nerve center for communications and funnels important information as required to EP teams in the field. Sometimes it's given another name (e.g., command post), but it generally serves the same function from program to program.

Not all EP programs have or will use a SOC. However, where

possible or necessary, even smaller but permanent EP family programs should have a manned 24/7 location with the responsibility to manage (among other things) CCTV monitoring, alarms, visitor and access control, news and weather updates, aircraft and vehicle movement tracking, emergency management and all the procedural aspects of family or office security.

SOCs can also often be a primary radio and telephone point of contact for the EP detail. Because of their 24-hour operational status, they can serve as on-call support for unique requests field agents may have. Any EP SOC should be an integral part of the EP program and a major part of the field team. A SOC can be incorporated and managed through the corporate security office, be a separate EP unit within the corporation, be outsourced through a vetted third party or even be a function of the residential team – which often already serves as the principal's EP SOC.

Regardless of the location or title given to any corporate or private family SOC or intelligence unit, it should be organized by functions and responsibilities with specific procedures and response plans to as many situations as the security management team can develop. Many corporate SOCs will create a type of "fusion center" to cover all the EP activities under their watch. Many corporate EP programs have a single seat in a SOC to concentrate on all things EP. They will monitor social media and other open-source platforms, including police and emergency updates for anything that might have a negative effect on the principal and detail, as well as just for general situational awareness. They may monitor key information regarding persons of interest presenting some form of concern or threat towards the company or principal and could be available to generate quick intel reports for the EP team while they are in the field.

EP Team

Protective Intelligence

SOC/CP

Security Technology

Policies, Procedures & Training

If part of a corporate SOC, the single EP seat there will reduce the amount of information shared among too many employees, which is preferable when dealing with the high level of confidentiality extended to certain executives and corporate activities.

If the corporate or family office SOC serves as a global center to provide broader worldwide assistance to employees and operations, it should have a multitude of capabilities including data management, intelligence processing and analysis, duress monitoring, a global crisis watch, an emergency communications plan, emergency travel assistance and tracking where applicable, and other functions critical to the company's success and operations or the family's safety and security. A SOC can be the backbone of a 24/7 EP program due to the immense capabilities at its disposal and can also provide a lifeline to all who have need of its services.

"IF YOU THINK HIRING A PROFESSIONAL IS EXPENSIVE TO DO THE JOB, WAIT UNTIL YOU HIRE AN AMATEUR."

– RED ADAIR

CHAPTER IV

EP Teams and What They Do

EARLIER IN THE BOOK, we looked at the threat and risk landscape of the 21st century, your own *personal why* for having executive protection, and how an effective EP program is established and managed. In this section, we'll look at the types of people in the EP profession, their jobs within your team, and some questions you'll have to sort out along the way as you embark on this journey.

Professional Backgrounds and EP Talent

Who is your average EP agent? Where does he or she come from? Thirty-plus years ago, a majority of EP agents came from the military, law enforcement or both. Today, the executive protection field includes more people with other backgrounds, educations, previous experiences and career paths – and I can say the profession is stronger as a result.

For instance, today you will find a larger share of former government agents in the EP environment. While some come from "three-letter" government agencies or departments (FBI, CIA, DOD, DEA, etc.), many are veterans of the U.S. Secret Service or the U.S. State Department. This is a result of the sheer numbers of people in these organizations with these skills and experiences who have transitioned to the private sector.

How do these people get their start without experience in the military or law enforcement? Well, the government trains them. The Secret Service, for example, has one of the largest (if not *the* largest) and most in-depth training academies in the world. This allows them to choose high-aptitude candidates – sometimes straight out of college – who can pass stringent background checks and meet pre-hiring qualifications, but who don't necessarily already have security or protection experience. The military and law enforcement also provide very successful transition programs into their organizations for those who possess the right aptitude, education and capabilities.

In other words, it's not necessarily what candidates already bring to the table – it's their potential to become what these organizations need.

It's not just the Secret Service, military and law enforcement that recruit and train this way. While I was at the CIA, our protective detail consisted of former military and special operations personnel, attorneys, pilots, former NFL players, former law enforcement officers and academics – and all underwent several months of classified specialized training with the Agency.

To be clear, former government experience in and of itself is not an automatic qualification for an EP candidate. Just because someone is retired from the police, armed forces, Special Forces, Secret Service or CIA does not mean they possess the necessary skills, training, experience, aptitude or personality to be a successful private-sector EP operator. Your dentist may be very skilled in his craft, but this does not mean you would want him treating you if you needed to remove a brain tumor.

This increase in training capacity has taken place outside the government as well. Just a few decades ago, there were only a few private-sector schools with a solid reputation for training individuals without any prior military, police or government experience in close protection and other related skills.

Fortunately, over the past 20 years, there has been a significant increase in the number of companies and private schools providing this type of hands-on education. In some cases, these schools have become outsourced educational institutions for organizations lacking their own internal training programs or academies. They are also often a vital resource for remedial or continuing education for all levels of EP professionals.

Within certain military or government organizations, you must qualify by completing and graduating from a rigorous and lengthy close protection course before providing this sort of protection. Of course, military and government organizations are not the only places with training requirements, but they normally have the most extensive courses due to the expense of operating them.

There has also been momentum in recent years to establish internationally recognized standards and qualifications for the EP field (as currently exists within the medical or legal professions, for example). While many of these efforts are still underway, and several training academies have gained approval for GI Bill, VA-funded and GSA-approved courses, the industry is not there yet.

Until we have national and international standards within the private EP industry, it can be difficult to verify if your EP provider has the level and depth of training to provide the protection and service you need or desire. To assist you or your organization with verifying potential new candidates for a full-time EP position, I would recommend contacting a professional EP advisor or employment consultant who has the specific experience necessary to evaluate your candidates.

Many companies and organizations will use a qualified outside third-party advisor to interview candidates and verify training, qualifications and experiences before you make an employment offer. Some groups will even take this to a higher level of testing by administering firearms, fitness and special skills tests as well as conducting an interview panel design to determine the suitability of the candidates.

Perhaps as important as anything else is the depth and quality of experience an EP practitioner has acquired throughout their career and in various environments. Like in most careers, it's not just a matter of getting a certificate or degree, but the experience you have gained since graduation. Since most protective details are for civilians, it is important your initial conversation is not only with someone who has been professionally trained, but also someone who has significant private-sector experience. This person should understand how to function with the subtlety and finesse necessary to be effective without being able to use a principal's powerful position or title as a point of leverage.

We have also seen and benefited greatly from the growth in the number of female close protection specialists over the past 20 years. I have dedicated a section to female agents up ahead to highlight the progress the industry has made – and the work we still need to do to fully incorporate women into the profession.

Another development in the field is the increasing "cross-pollination" of EP operators on an international level. Many EP specialists from around the world have now traveled and worked alongside their international counterparts. The U.S. and other developed countries have increasingly trained foreign military and government operators in close protection, especially in high-threat environments. There has also been a significant increase in the numbers of U.S. security companies setting up operations and business overseas – and vice versa.

Because of these international experiences, EP operators have been able to share and exchange their methods, procedures and experiences. The profession is better for it. Not only that, but operators and practitioners who have taken the time to develop a personal, vetted network of trusted international EP specialists can now reach out to their network when required. They are able to support their principals' and clients' international travel with a level of confidence that did not exist in the past.

This international network has personally served me and my clients tremendously over the years. I cannot count the number of times I have been called late at night by a client or colleague who frantically asked, "Do you have someone in Prague (or South Africa, Moscow, Casablanca, Rio, Beijing, Mumbai, Monterrey, Santiago, Halifax, Bangkok, Dubai or dozens of other locations around the world)?! I was just informed my principal is headed there tomorrow and I need assistance now!"

If it weren't for this great network of friendship and shared experiences with international and trusted operators, we would not be able to provide this type of assistance. I have always felt my personal contact list, professional relationships and, most importantly, friendships are by far the most important assets I possess. I have carefully and judiciously spent the past 30 years developing and maintaining these connections.

Ultimately, the evolution of the EP industry over the last few decades has created a more cohesive and cooperative environment that better serves protectees. It has led to improved consistency, accountability and professionalism in this industry throughout the world.

Kuwait – Dogs in the Desert

An example of the importance of networking and previous relationships is when, unexpectedly, the support comes from former associates at a time when it's needed the most. In this case, it came in the late 1990s when I was traveling with Director Tenet in the Middle East. We were in Kuwait City and the Director had an important meeting at an iconic high-rise building in the city. Dan ("Doc") O'Conner, our detail leader, was insisting on a K9 bomb sweep before he would let Tenet arrive at the meeting.

The only problem was the advance team had not been able to locate or secure dogs for the sweep. The Marines Security Guards at the U.S. Embassy said the only place to get certified bomb dogs on such short notice was at a nearby joint U.S./Kuwaiti air base. They explained the dogs belonged to the U.S. Air Force but came under the command and control of a retired Air Force colonel who served as the base security director and was a U.S. contractor.

They said they made a call the day prior to request the bomb dogs on behalf of the advance agents but this security director denied their request. They also said this civilian was known for being difficult – and considering we now needed the dogs in less than five hours, if he didn't give them to us yesterday, there was no way he was going to give them to us now.

Doc passed me on his way out of the embassy command post and said in his thick Irish New York accent, "Trott, do your Air Force thing and get me my dogs."

With total reluctance and a knowledge my efforts would probably result in failure, I asked the Marines for the civilian's name and contact number. They pulled out a card with the name "Ralph Beckett" and an Air Force command post number. I couldn't believe I was reading the name right. Could this be the same Ralph Beckett who, eight years prior, was my Air Force group commander in Germany and who, as I recalled, owed me a few favors?

I called the number and the command post transferred me to Ralph's home phone. As soon as he picked up, I knew it was former Colonel Ralph Beckett by the angry way he answered. Even though he was a civilian now, I said, "Colonel Beckett, this is Special Agent Trott with the CIA." He responded in true "Colonel Beckett style" with, "Is this Sergeant Mike Trott and are you with those Agency pukes requesting my dogs and handlers at the last fucking minute?"

I thought to myself, *Yup, that's my Colonel Beckett.* After I endured five minutes of reprimands (but this time with a smile on my face because neither of us were in the Air Force now), he ended his admonishment with, "The dogs and handlers should be there in 90 minutes."

We then caught up on old times and actually had a good chat, as we had previously had a good working relationship. Ralph could be a hard man to work with and most people and other senior officers despised his leadership style. I'd often needed his approval to accomplish a lot of things with my special teams, so I would always try to make him look good as the commander. Plus, as mentioned before, he did owe me a few favors, so my request had unfair leverage compared to the advance team.

I walked out of the command post to catch a ride to the hotel to change and gear up. As I walked past Doc and the team standing in the hall, I said, "Your dogs and handlers will meet our advance security team on site in 90 minutes to conduct their sweeps." Doc started to ask how, but I interrupted him and said, "Don't ask."

After this event, we began to travel to certain locations with our own K9 bomb dog and handler, who became a great addition to our team and our capability to protect the Director.

Unfortunately, Ralph never made it out of Kuwait. Just a few months later, he had a massive heart attack near the flight line. He was a force to be reckoned with and I know everyone who knew Ralph had their own stories to tell, good and "not so good." But on that day when I (and my principal) needed him in Kuwait, he came through for me and I was extremely grateful.

The importance of having a great network can't be stressed enough. Whether I've needed particular specialists, intelligence, armored vehicles, weapons, planes, boats, helicopters, support or favors to achieve the mission (whatever it took – around the world), the friends, former colleagues and key relationships I've developed and maintained have always come through for me – and ultimately for the principal.

Agents, Officers and Bodyguards

Often, there can be some confusion on the part of principals and others who may not know what to call "us." When it comes to various titles in the EP field, is there a difference between them?

An analogy I like to use for understanding all these different roles relates to the restaurant business. At any large restaurant, there are dozens of roles played by people working together to provide you with a great dining experience. Sometimes a variety of roles can be played by the same person, and sometimes roles are very clearly delineated – it is obvious the maître d' is not a bus person or server. And if you refer to an executive chef as a cook or prep cook, you may get more than an ugly look back. But all these roles are vital to the successful functioning of a good restaurant.

Similarly, a full-capacity and dynamic EP program can also have dozens of roles, responsibilities and related titles held by people working together to provide their principal(s) a safe, secure and private environment.

Not long after you, or someone for you, has chosen to pursue some level of personal or close protection, one of the next steps in the process is identifying and hiring/contracting the right people. To help conceptualize who these individuals are, let's break down their typical roles.

In most cases in this field, an EP agent will provide close protection, conduct travel advances, liaise with law enforcement, corporate executives and event planners, and have a variety of other specific roles. Depending on your risk and program needs, or how big your EP "kitchen" is, you may only have one or two EP agents. You may require a small security team who balances many roles. Or you may need a full-service program managed by a vice president, chief security officer (CSO) or director.

Another role may be filled by officers, whose job description and skillsets may be slightly different from agents. While both functions are equally important, in some cases both are not required. Officers are usually individuals whose responsibilities include manning residential gates or command posts, conducting foot or vehicle patrols of corporate or personal property, and controlling access to and monitoring executive suites and offices. They may be armed or unarmed and can be uniformed or plain-clothes.

Not to complicate these terms, but in some cases, especially in police organizations, there may be officers who serve in a close protective capacity for a governor or traveling dignitary; sometimes these officers are, in fact, serving as EP agents but are under a title of "special police officer." There can be variances to the actual titles, but the roles and responsibilities are similar and should be well defined.

Then there is the term "bodyguard," which has been associated with protection longer than the terms "agent" or "officer." Bodyguards today still have a role when the requirement is essentially about a physical presence designed to be a deterrent – usually in cases where a human shield or other immediate response is likely needed and highly expected.

Some in the security industry do not like the term bodyguard, but, in my opinion, the title and mindset play a vital role in today's personal protection. You might think of professional bodyguards when you see a fully-equipped specialist with weapon in hand as part of a protective team escorting a high-profile official in a high-threat area like Afghanistan or Iraq. You might also think of a team of individuals who resemble NFL linebackers or WWE wrestlers providing a "human wall" for a celebrity at a public function.

Outside of the United States, you will find the title of bodyguard used more than agent or even executive protection. Often, they may resemble what you think of when you see Secret Service agents.

As the field continues to evolve and becomes increasingly inclusive, bodyguard training schools are addressing more advanced protective skillsets. This additional training helps to blur the lines among skilled international close protection operators, their roles and titles.

I would not get hung up on the names and titles too much. All are an integral part of any fully fleshed-out EP program and form a team requiring static, patrol and close escort personnel, as well as armed and unarmed levels of close physical protection and travel facilitation. They may work together at special venues and events, corporate offices and residences to ensure the proper security umbrella is in place. Their roles can be passive in nature or a physical part of deterrence.

While all of these roles may overlap in some sense, bear this in mind: When you refer to your EP agent, close protection officer or bodyguard – who probably has gone through extensive training, has years of experience, is possibly a decorated military veteran or police officer, probably holds a couple of educational degrees and may speak multiple languages – as "my guard," you might get a similar look of disappointment as you would calling the executive chef a "cook."

Deciding Between Hiring EP Staff and/or EP Companies

Before we continue, I want to provide a word of caution regarding the use of security consultants and EP companies.

Over the past few decades, the use of private EP security companies and independent contractors has become more popular due to the number of firms and individuals specializing in this area.

There are lots of companies with highly experienced and respected security/executive protection practitioners and security management advisors. Many provide excellent service and can become an integral part of any EP program. In some cases, a blend or hybrid of contractors and permanent EP may in fact be the most suitable coverage and provide the most flexibility.

In previous roles and positions while serving in private companies, I have built, managed and sold these services. At other times, I have requested these services to support my own principals. Because I have been on both sides of the equation, I can tell you that, in the end, these companies are in business to provide a service and to make a profit.

At times, their legitimate advice might be to add personnel or services to your security detail to cover new risks and concerns, manage day-to-day requirements or support complicated travel itineraries. More EP coverage might be an appropriate recommendation and part of a greater mitigating strategy. However, in some instances, this move could actually be counterintuitive, creating more anxiety and needlessly increasing the profile of the principal – resulting in higher risks.

There is no way to represent each and every situation in this book, but when making the initial decision to employ or hire any level of security or personal protection, following a judicious approach will more than likely lead to what I like to refer to as, "What starts well, ends well."

If you ultimately decide to outsource portions of your protection, you must start the process by drafting a well-articulated and accurate request for proposal (RFP). An RFP is a document outlining your requirements and desired approach. You'll use it to solicit official bids from companies interested in providing you with protective services.*

Whomever you meet with should be well-vetted and have a diverse background involving various levels and types of high- and low-profile personal protection and protective intelligence. They should be able to confidently outline methods for implementing a risk-based protection program specifically designed for the individual (protectee), the company, and any family members or others who might fall under the protection umbrella.

In most cases, I also recommend you internally hire a qualified EP manager to supervise the contract team and operation. This person should report directly to the principal, senior corporate security manager, general counsel or possibly the family office and/or chief of staff. There should be a well-defined separation between them and any hired contractors. Many elements will need to be considered, including the state or country in which you reside and where the team is based, your family profile, asset liability considerations and other factors your legal counsel and a trusted security advisor can help you navigate.

Overwhelmingly, most corporate or family EP details hire and retain their own staff, whether under the parent company or a subsidiary under the parent company's umbrella. However, a professional security company who has a strong ethical reputation can be an excellent resource to help build and support your EP needs. There are legal and some potential liability disadvantages in creating a corporate or family EP program, and your general counsel or outside legal counsel should be consulted regarding the best structure for your program and company. When properly established and managed, a corporate or family EP detail or staff will serve you well; in many cases, your protection needs will include a combination of owned and contracted services.

Ultimately, employing your own security versus contractors has advantages and disadvantages. The following are elements to consider when making your decision:

---

* A third party and independent advisor can be helpful in crafting your RFP and evaluating your proposals.

Contractor	Hybrid	Employee
• Easier to evaluate before hiring full time • In some cases, reduces personal or family legal liabilities • No ownership of a security company, no associated legal requirements (assuming contractor is verified and in legal compliance) • Provides interchangeable agents assigned based on needs, frequent surges, foreign travel • Existing contractor can allow flexibility due to unforeseeable circumstances, scalability, new threats or risks, special events, etc. • Some companies can provide complete turn-key solutions for many principals and have robust capabilities to provide additional service support as needed	• In some cases, the contractor might support all travel, but local support is covered by employee(s) • Good in times of surges or when the need is less than full-time monthly support • Good way to augment existing team with more personnel • Can add certain language, technical or other skills as needed • Residential security teams and off-property patrols where armed personnel are required often use off-duty law enforcement officers under a contract company, but are managed by a principal's security manager or estate manager	• More often a higher comfort level between employee and principal • Direct supervision by company or employee detail manager without co-management issues that can occur with contractors • Agent/officer receives and reflects a mutual commitment to the principals, often creating longer employment and reducing frequent change of personnel • Employee compensation is generally greater than the contractor counterpart, resulting in less turnover and increased longevity and loyalty in most cases

Take the time to carefully consider this important step. It will define your approach and program and set the tone for what may eventually become an extension of your personal life and privacy.

Selecting an EP Program Manager

Before we get into staffing the entirety of your EP team, I'd like to go into more detail about selecting your program manager. Success or failure in choosing this person will have a ripple effect on the rest of your program – it's crucial to get this right.

Across most corporations, there will normally be one EP program manager whose sole responsibility is managing executive protection. It is highly recommended any program with a significant level of executive and employee travel have a single point of contact to manage all the integrated facets and to provide consistency, sustainability and responsiveness.

The ideal candidate will have a *strong EP background with previous global close protection and team mission support experience.* It is preferable the candidate has 10 or more years of EP experience, which may include a combination of military, law enforcement, government, private-sector and corporate experience.

Not all EP missions will require a manager to travel in support of their principal, as risk profiles, individual characteristics and protective details vary greatly among protectees. Program managers or EP leads must at least be available to monitor all missions effectively so they can make any adjustments as necessary on behalf of their principals. They should also be available to respond to regional managers, individual client managers, key stakeholders and team leaders to support ongoing assignments and address new EP initiatives as required. Again, based on the size of an EP program, the EP manager or director may need to travel with their principals as the lead EP provider and advisor.

A good candidate will have accumulated over time a list of trusted and vetted international third-party security vendors – i.e., a pool of EP providers and independent contractors they have utilized in their past and are able to contact in advance and on short notice.

This candidate should have previous experience identifying and writing EP policies and procedures as they relate to current and future operations. They should have experience with both corporate and private EP programs. They also should be able to provide advisory support on EP-related initiatives to corporate executives and client security managers.

While not always required, the ideal candidate should have some law enforcement or government/military intelligence experience, as well as the ability to draw from these professional relationships as missions require and to assist in creating a protective intelligence program. As mentioned before, if your candidate is transitioning from the military or a government organization, consider their total experience "package" and the possible need for a transition period before managing a private-sector program.

A broader list of general essential requirements and responsibilities appears in the Appendix. Ultimately, this person needs to be more than just a practitioner. He/she must be a "security/protection" architect with a diverse security background, a healthy level of experience, patience and a bag full of lessons learned.

Choosing the Right EP Professionals

Principals, I highly recommend you participate directly in the hiring of your protective management team and, when possible, your detail members. After HR, recruiters and/or security managers have narrowed down the search, it is important you interview at least two or three of the final candidates for each role.

So, who is the right person for a detail? Well, it depends on many factors. As a detail leader or manager assembling a new team, I always start by considering the profile of the principal. While this is not as important for a one-time protective mission or short assignment, when building a permanent or long-term team, you must start by considering the principal's personality, profession, activities, likes and dislikes. These factors are important, because the roles you're trying to fill will determine the people you're trying to attract to your team.

There are obvious testing and evaluation requirements new agents should have to go through before being hired. Obviously, all candidates should be tested on the basic requirements and skills necessary for the position. Depending on the mission, this could include testing for physical fitness, basic self-defense ability, firearms proficiency, and medical or first aid skills and knowledge.

Your team should also evaluate and confirm candidates' performance in past jobs. Testing for some of the above requirements might not be necessary if the candidate has copies of their training records, course certificates or verifiable recent employment involving relevant training, experience and qualifications. An old Russian proverb is important regarding this matter: "Trust but verify."

Before a potential candidate ever meets a principal, they should also complete a full background check regarding professional and personal worthiness, including reference checks. I also recommend a psychological background evaluation – especially if the individual may be armed while working with principals and children.

This is a sensitive subject in the personal protection industry, but I believe it is important to ensure candidates are not only physically capable but also mentally stable. The evaluating psychologists should have experience working with former military and police officers. (It should be noted in the case of current police officers that most departments conduct an annual psychological review of their officers to ensure they are fit for armed duty.)

When interviewing your EP team member(s), the following reference list includes some skills and resources you might be looking for, depending upon the principal, position, risks and EP mission:

- Professional training as an executive protection specialist (mandatory)
- International travel experience – i.e., more than two stamps in their passports (highly preferred)
- Experience as a liaison (very important)
- EMT/paramedic or advanced first responder training
- Professional training as a security driver
- Surveillance skills and experience
- Experience in operating in high-threat environments
- Weapons proficiency (advanced skills preferred)
- Self-defense skills (advanced preferred)
- "Maritime adventures" specialty – e.g., swimming, diving and other water activities (specific to client)

- Investigative skills or ability to apply basic investigative and analytical theories
- Protective intelligence specialty or basic practitioner experience
- IT security familiarity with above-average computer skills
- Security technology savviness with basic understanding of security design engineering and equipment
- Above-average physical fitness
- Knowledge of two or more languages (helpful but not always mandatory)
- Solid network of professionals

Character and personality matter too. Some important traits include:

- Psychological soundness (mandatory)
- Polished, professional demeanor
- Friendly and pleasant
- Sense of humor (helpful)
- Trustworthiness, loyalty
- Team-player mindset
- Ability to operate solo with confidence
- Blend of confidence and humility

For high-threat situations, you should find the highest-quality operator with practical experience as quickly as you can find them. But if you're establishing a full-time EP program with normal operations, it's worth spending the time to find the *right person*. Part of that equation means someone who will fit in with your corporate and family cultures as well as other lifestyle factors (e.g., sporting activities, principal's hobbies, foreign language requirements, etc.).

Along those lines, an important thing to consider is your own personal connection with your security professionals. Some members of full-time security teams may be with principals and their families in close proximity for extended periods of time. Some principals may even spend more time with their security personnel or EP team than any other member of their staff – in some cases, even their own family.

For this reason, I recommend principals consider security personnel whose company and personality they enjoy. It may seem trivial, but if you don't enjoy their company, an important part of the partnership can already begin to break down: effective communication.

You should also look at how these people will come across to those outside your own circle. These individuals will represent you (principals) and your families, and often will be intimately involved in many aspects of your family's life. They'll frequently serve as your "ambassadors" while conducting travel security advances, attending special events and at many other occasions. Your security detail may greet guests at your residences and offices, may pick up your children at school, and may conduct meetings on your behalf with officials regarding certain security issues.

All this means is you have to consider the *whole person* when evaluating an agent. Unfortunately, I have seen many principals make their decision solely based on appearance, but you should never "judge a book by its cover." I've even seen principals make superficial judgments based on hair, or the lack thereof.

Sometimes, corporate principals and security managers also make the mistake of thinking "bigger is better," but that's not always the case. Yes, in some scenarios, a large-framed person can be necessary – especially if physical deterrence is the goal. But good security officers and protective agents come in all shapes, sizes and packages with varied backgrounds. I have worked with highly capable, confident and skilled men and women who were shorter than 5'6" with an average build who have performed brilliantly.

Most CEOs and principals have developed a keen "sixth sense" when it comes to reading people. In addition to the obvious required skillsets and experiences of a potential EP hire, I would recommend looking for someone who possesses a good balance of personality, confidence, intelligence, flexibility, patience and humility. A successful candidate would also be someone who takes charge when needed. They should be polished, trustworthy, ethical, and able to anticipate and solve problems. They should be team-oriented yet able to operate as an individual with limited direction when necessary. Finally, and perhaps most helpful, they should have a decent sense of humor.

It comes down to the people themselves and their attitude, aptitude, skills, experience, mindset, fitness, personality and ability to assimilate into the principal's environment comfortably and confidently. The rest will come in time.

What I Learned from My CIA Interview

I had been at the CIA for less than a year when I interviewed for a position as a special agent on the Director's security staff in 1997.

While my career at the Agency had been brief at the time of the interview, I had spent the previous decade in the military, including six years overseas. I had served in various roles as a security specialist and was on many close protection details. I'd been a team leader and field supervisor for tactical operations and an anti-terrorism team. I had served as an instructor at the Air Force Security Forces Academy and an undercover narcotics investigator in Europe.

As for academic qualifications, I had gone through many months of advanced professional training and coursework, obtaining college degrees in Instructor Technology/Military Science and Security Administration/Industrial Security. I was also a recent graduate of the Federal Law Enforcement Training Center.

I was confident I had what it took to be on the Director's protective staff. I believed my previous training and experience had prepared me for this interview. In many ways it did, but in some ways it had not.

I was interviewed by three individuals serving on the Director's security staff, including the deputy chief of the detail, Scott Kafer. After the introduction and a few softball questions, Scott asked me a question I still recall today: "Do you consider yourself to be an 'expert' in the field of protection?"

I was completely taken aback. I thought, *What kind of answer was he looking for? What would be his follow-up question? Am I an expert? Do I look arrogant if I answer 'Yes, of course' with confidence? This is, after all, an interview for a position with immense responsibility protecting the director of the CIA... On the other hand, would it be better to answer humbly with a 'no?' Would he then turn me away on account of my professed lack of expertise?*

I had probably less than five seconds to begin my answer, but it seemed like eternity as I quickly processed my response. After I replied with a cautious "Yes," he began to drill me with several follow-up questions. I struggled to formulate an intelligent response and quickly realized I had answered his initial question incorrectly.

I desperately wanted a do-over.

His question helped me to shape my approach to executive protection and security in general. I learned something during that interview that I continue to think about after more than 30 years in the industry. The EP field is so enormous that no one – not the generalists, the specific practitioners nor subject-matter experts (SMEs) – can know everything on their own. There are no true experts in the field of security and protection, and no one person has all the answers. Just when you think you do, someone or something will often prove otherwise.

To practitioners, my takeaway from that interview is to be humble but confident in your capabilities and knowledge, always be open-minded, and constantly strive to put more tools in your toolbox. This includes admitting where you might fall short. This attitude will take you further and is more palatable to principals and colleagues than overconfidence and arrogance.

This experience also helped me to break down the areas of my profession on which I wanted to concentrate. I was then able to accelerate my progress as an SME in certain subfields. To this day, when I lack the answers on a particular topic, I seek out the proper SME to assist me or the program I am responsible for managing.

I'll leave it up to the interviewer if you think the "security expert" question is appropriate for your candidates. If you ask the question, it should cause the interviewee to pause and consider how they want to best answer. It might give you good insight into their mindset.

By the way, I did pass the interview and became a special agent on the Director's protective detail after several months of intense and advanced protective operations training.

Before concluding this discussion, practitioners, this section is for you. Every close protection agent will eventually need to determine what kind of principal personality type is best for them as a professional. That's not always an easy decision. Just as it's important for principals to have the right agents, for long-term protective assignments, it can be as important that an EP agent is able to work for the right protectee.

EP professionals also have to decide what their preferred operational "comfort zone" looks like. It might be for corporate C-suite executives or government officials that require structure, schedules, business suits and attending meetings at high levels. Other agents may prefer the travel, engagement with large crowds and the "rock star" lifestyle that all comes with protecting high-profile celebrities. (For agents protecting musicians, some are lucky enough to already be fans.) Of course, there are many environments that fall somewhere in between these two extremes.

For both the principal and the agent, the right combination of respect and lifestyle factors can mean the difference between a long-term relationship and one that is short-lived.

Former Military Members in EP

A somewhat delicate issue I would also like to address is the role of former military members, both men and women, who want to explore the EP profession. Former military operators (especially those from our Special

Forces) can quite often be the right person for an EP team if the principal frequently ventures into possibly dangerous areas or participates in high-risk activities (e.g., skydiving, scuba diving, adventure travel, etc.).

As a veteran myself, you'll receive no argument from me that, generally speaking, former members of our armed forces have a certain advantage when it comes to the world of security, if only based on the level of training, experience and discipline acquired during their years of service.

At the same time, a former special operator might not be the right person to "suit up" and conduct an advance to the White House for a state dinner or take the children to school with the nanny. In my experience, very few special operators make this transition successfully – and perhaps more important is whether or not they are *satisfied* with what they are doing in their new role.

Our Special Forces brethren, regardless of branch or special unit, undergo months and even years of advanced training to be successful. For many special operators, the military spends millions of dollars on their training and then subjects them to high-risk missions.

In the EP world, however, former Special Forces operators need to fully understand some of the less challenging, less exhilarating aspects of their new roles – e.g., standing outside the door of a conference room most of the day, driving kids to play dates or taking a principal's spouse to yoga class. I'm not implying these aren't important tasks or that they should be taken lightly. I'm only saying this transition can be challenging, particularly for those who have just completed a military career as a special operator.

As such, a principal must holistically weigh the primary responsibilities of a role against the skills, traits and experience a candidate brings to the table. If you are filling a permanent EP position, you should consider aptitude, attitude, personality and other unique characteristics along with your core requirements before making a decision.

Think of it this way: If a surgeon spent 10–15 years training and perfecting their skills, you would not recruit them to be a chef, gardener or chauffeur. The same consideration should be applied when you're recruiting a highly trained military or security professional and then assigning them duties not commensurate with their skills or expectations.

You can't expect them to remain motivated and satisfied – *unless that individual has a genuine desire for change.*

I had to deal with this kind of change in my own career. Much of my early military training, mindset and skills were more in line with *taking* a life rather than *protecting* one. Over time, my focus became all about *avoiding any situation that could jeopardize the life or safety of my principals.* This required a shift in mindset. Yet as a former veteran who transitioned to a new life as an EP specialist (especially having operated in hostile environments), I felt I needed to keep that warrior spirit at the ready – but the goal was to never actually need it.

I was very fortunate with my own career transitions. After 10 years of military service in environments and with teams that were very serious in nature, I made my first transition to the CIA. Even though it had its challenges, finding myself overseas in small teams once again brought me back to my military days and allowed for better assimilation into my new career.

Not long after completing all my training and accepting my assignment on the Director's security detail, I found myself behind the wheel of his primary vehicle. On one particular day, the Director was delayed in leaving his office for a meeting with the President at the White House – a meeting you don't want to be late to, though that was not totally out of the norm for our beloved Director. Once we exited HQ and merged onto the G.W. Parkway, we realized it was going to require a little heavier foot on the gas to make it to the White House on time. I'll admit I had a "lead foot" after my years living in Germany and driving on the autobahn at speeds much higher than what's acceptable in most parts of the United States.

After arriving at the White House and delivering

the Director to the West Wing, one of our senior agents made a beeline for me. I could tell by the look on his face this wasn't going to be good. He calmly but confidently began "schooling" me on my excessive speed. While still complimenting me on my driving skills, he reminded me we were not in Germany on the autobahn, nor were we being chased by some terrorist group – and I should "slow the fuck down." His point was taken – although I must admit it still took a few months to make this transition fully.

Many years later, when I accepted a position as senior security advisor for a major international corporation, my transition was again not so difficult since the CIA fit somewhere between the military and a corporation. Regardless, I still had another period of making a mental adjustment where I had to remind myself I wasn't still in the CIA protecting a principal who had a much higher risk profile and was part of our country's national security apparatus and a Cabinet-level official.

A few years later, I made further interesting transitions, first as an embedded advisor in the Middle East and later as Director of Security for a UHNW family. All of the other incremental transitions readied me for these new roles, but if I had gone straight from the military or CIA to this private family, I might have appeared more like the proverbial "bull in a china shop."

You might recall the Hollywood movie *The Pacifier* with Vin Diesel, who played a Navy SEAL who is handed a new assignment to protect five kids whose father (a government scientist) has been assassinated. To have a SEAL take on the role of "manny" (male version of a nanny) might seem crazy and highly unlikely to most. I'm not sure, but I must believe somewhere on the set of this movie there must have been a former SEAL turned "manny" as an advisor, because many parts of this film were *very accurate*.

I want to highlight a very important caveat on this topic. If you find a former special operator whom you feel has the right mindset, they should be put at or close to the top of the list of candidates if they possess the other requirements I have mentioned. This person will bring skills, training and experiences most will never have, simply based on the amount of time, exposure, money and commitment our government has invested in the careers of most special operators. Remember, make it a whole-person decision.

This perspective on career transitions is not mine alone, but is shared by many friends and former colleagues who have served with various Special Forces teams. Without exception, they all agreed and experienced the same similar difficulty in transitioning themselves.

A SEAL with a Diaper Backpack

Trevor (protecting his name so he won't be shamed by this story) and I worked together for a UHNW family protective detail I was managing as Director of Security. As a bit of background, Trevor was a former SEAL team officer and served on another very high-profile detail for several years after his transition from the Navy. He was a graduate of a prestigious university and had earned a master's degree. In his career, he had undergone extensive military and special operations training.

Because of his previous operational tempo, after a routine trip with our principals or weeks of day-to-day coverage close to our principals' home, I would cut Trevor free for a week or two so he could attend some kind of training or take part in other unique activities – all so he wouldn't suffer "death by a thousand cuts" from normal day after normal day. When he went off for training, it was like freeing a bird from a cage.

Later, he took another position working for a different

UHNW family. After several years, we caught up in New York while he was providing cover security for (i.e., escorting) the nanny and toddler (principals in this case).

We met at a local establishment which catered to moms and nannies taking their little ones out for playtime. The two of us sat at a small wooden table on little chairs, and each of us had our own juice box as we caught up on life. Trevor was keeping a keen eye on his principal, a toddler less than a year old. At one point, the toddler picked up something very small on the floor and put it in his mouth, as Trevor mumbled, "Damn nanny, I wish she would do her job."

We stood up to depart the rendezvous location we had chosen for our clandestine meeting, whereupon he reached under the table and picked up the nanny's grey and pink striped diaper bag. With baby bottles, diapers and a couple very important toys protruding from its flaps, he slung it over his shoulder as if it were a 75-pound rucksack filled with weapons and SpecOps equipment.

He then moved closer to the door in a key position of advantage to follow his principal, who was now securely snuggled in his nanny's chest baby carrier. I will never forget the look Trevor had on his face that silently implied, *I'll f-ing kill you if you tell anyone about this*, as he turned to follow behind his little principal.

After several years now, Trevor's new employer has finally recognized his skills and appropriately selected him to oversee and manage a new humanitarian quick-response rescue team that has the ability to launch just hours after a disaster with critical resources to assist in initial recovery efforts.

Not long after assuming his new role, we met again and I had never seen him more satisfied.

The transition period is critical for many who are leaving the military, not just for special operators. While I've known and worked with many who struggled to make the transition, I have also known and worked with those who have successfully made it with honor and distinction – and have become irreplaceable members of EP teams. These examples are not meant to discount former military personnel or special operators, but to emphasize that when you find the right one who is ready for the transition or whom your management team is capable of assisting, you should consider them highly but include the "whole person" concept in your decisions.

The Female Agent

No doubt, executive protection is still a male-dominated field with some longstanding prejudices. Today, while we can find many examples of women who are extremely valuable contributors in the EP field, they are unfortunately still overlooked and suffer the disparities inherent in a male-centric profession.

Because of this, I continue to support changing attitudes and want to stress to all principals and practitioners the importance of the positions female agents and officers occupy. There is a growing appreciation for women in the field, and they are more frequently viewed as equals to their male counterparts – often providing a principal or detail a unique operational advantage. I look forward to the day when this view becomes universal.

Throughout the centuries, women have been warriors, served as bodyguards and occupied other key roles in protecting their principals. The Chinese military has trained women for years as highly skilled and disciplined bodyguards with tremendous success. Various countries and regions of the world with cultural and religious sensitivity regarding women and children have also trained and used female bodyguards to protect members of elite and royal families.

In 1997, the Israeli domestic security service Shin Bet opened its ranks to female close protection agents. In recent years, the United Arab Emirates and other Middle Eastern countries have provided advanced training to female guards for royal families. During my travels and operations in Europe and elsewhere, I've worked with many impressive female officers, security drivers and close protection agents.

America's experience with female officers begins earlier than most are aware. In 1856, a woman named Kate Warne went to the Chicago-based Pinkerton Detective Agency to answer an ad in a local newspaper. Company records state:

> [Pinkerton] was surprised to learn Kate was not look-ing for clerical work but was actually answering an ad-vertisement for detectives he had placed in a Chicago newspaper. At the time, such a concept was almost un-heard of. Pinkerton said, "It is not the custom to employ women detectives!" Kate argued her point of view elo-quently – pointing out that women could be "most useful in worming out secrets in many places which would be impossible for a male detective."[60]

Kate won the argument and became the first female investigator for Pinkerton – and possibly the first woman doing such work in the United States. She became very successful as an investigator and reports even suggest she was often put into tough situations where she was quite capable of physically handling herself.

In 1861, Kate was part of a team sent to Baltimore to provide security for President-elect Abraham Lincoln on his way to Washington, D.C., for his first inauguration. Kate was instrumental in her undercover role while in Baltimore and discovered key parts of an assassination plan, including the exact location and time it was to take place. Kate then assisted with an alternative plan to get Lincoln to Washington, which included an elaborate scheme of involving disguises, decoys and unique tradecraft that could still be used. Kate and several agents rode with Lincoln and positioned themselves in his train cars so as to be able to respond to attacks and protect their principal.

In 2015, only hours after accepting a position as vice president for a security company based in the Washington, D.C., area, I was preparing to make a quick flight to Los Angeles to meet with the senior risk officer and our CEO, both of whom I had known since my time at the CIA.

As I was boarding, our CEO called and said, "So, do you think you can assemble 30 armed female agents for a 30-day royal family EP detail?"

I paused, waiting for him to start laughing and say, "Just kidding!" He did not.

I said, "Well, I'm sure I can, but how long do we have before they arrive?"

He replied, "They're on the ground now."

In short, we had 48 hours to assemble over 60 officers and agents to provide 30 days of protection for a visiting royal family consisting mostly of women and children from an important U.S. ally in the Middle East. For religious and cultural reasons, this team needed to consist primarily of women providing their close protection.

Throughout my career I have trained, supervised, been supervised by, worked alongside and admired many extremely capable female military officers and special agents, but this was the first time I had worked with such a large number of female agents at once. I was highly impressed with the level of talent, professionalism and dedication this team exhibited. At much personal sacrifice, they worked to ensure the royal family's privacy and security was maintained until their departure. This protective detail gave me new perspective and much greater appreciation for all the female agents and officers who answered the call on short notice and performed professionally over this very long month.

While managing this royal visit, I had the opportunity to meet and work alongside Doriane, a French female EP manager for the family. For many years, Doriane had been providing coverage and EP management for the women and children principals of this family at various locations around the globe. Doriane explained that in her principal's region of the world, male EP agents are generally prohibited from being in close proximity to women and the children of principals due to their religious and cultural sensitivities.

She also went on to explain that, for many reasons, many female executives *prefer* a female agent, even in Western contexts. For example, a male agent cannot walk into a women's lavatory first to make sure it is safe for the principal. She also described occasions where she was able to step in and defuse a conflict at a venue between event security and her male EP counterparts due to her being perceived as less hostile.

Cheryl was another EP agent assisting on this detail. She was retired from the U.S. Secret Service and one of the Service's first black female agents during the '80s and '90s. Cheryl said she and other female colleagues had been faced with many challenges and stereotypes during their careers, including dealing with some male agents who still believe women "cannot handle the job" in the presence of wealthy and powerful male clients or protectees. She disagreed, saying properly trained agents of any gender who understand the ethical and professional responsibilities that come with the job do not have such issues.

Cheryl, Doriane and many other female specialists with whom I have worked and exchanged conversation frequently mentioned another interesting point of view I had not fully considered. They said women can provide certain "mental" tactical advantages because, at times, they can think from a different perspective than their male counterparts – for instance, paying more attention to details. As Kate Warne argued to Pinkerton in 1856:

> *A woman would be able to befriend the wives and girl-friends of suspected criminals and gain their confidence. Men become braggarts when they are around women*

who encourage them to boast. Kate also noted, women
have an eye for detail and are excellent observers.[61]

As Doriane commented, female agents are generally better at multitasking and can focus longer on specifics and the fine details of a complicated advance or special protective event. And if your detail or program requires a level of protective surveillance, a female agent can blend in far easier than a male agent can. As another female agent told me, "When I'm in a surveillance role and I need to get close or make eye contact with a POI or suspicious person, especially if he's a male, they'll look at me like I'm interested in them for personal reasons – not a security threat."

As an EP manager, I have assigned female EP agents to accompany female and male principals in shopping locations. I'm not implying only females shop or can carry shopping bags, but in certain circumstances we might utilize covert EP and need to provide the best "cover for EP actions" for our principal.

In the same situation, male agents might walk around awkwardly and could look like they are stalking the principal – or worse, look just like "bodyguards," in which case people would pay unwanted attention, realize the person is a VIP and try to identify them. Of course, if the principal is already highly recognizable, they will require a more obvious level of protection or deterrence, but a good female agent can easily assist with this role as well.

Cheryl commented that female EP agents are still typically not given due credit for being able to work in all of the environments and challenges with which they are presented. Times are changing and society is becoming more accepting of women in these types of professions, but she believes the industry still continues to lag behind. In addition, women still have to work harder than their male counterparts to be recognized for their contributions. Regardless of their qualifications, women are often placed at desk jobs answering phone calls, given positions deemed "not that dangerous or important," or only assigned to protectees who may have children.

Many people simply believe women can't handle the physical demands of being in this business. But if you think a highly trained female agent can't protect you or herself, you should step into the ring with mixed martial arts fighters Joanna Jedrzejczyk, Amanda Nunes, Holly Holm or Ronda Rousey and see how you fare. I'm not implying female agents need a higher level of self-defense training than their male counterparts in order to be effective – just that all agents can benefit from advanced training.

Whether male or female, EP professionals rarely, if ever, are required to turn into anything like the Incredible Hulk, Bruce Lee, Wonder Woman or La Femme Nikita to protect their principals. The vast majority of EP situations require soft skills, not brute force, which is why EP professionals specifically train to *avoid* confrontation but will have a set of well-practiced defensive skills if needed. Most of our work requires extensive planning and sometimes choreographed movements to ensure we have the tactical and strategic advantage.

If an EP agent has dozens of stories of how they've had to fight off attackers or use their weapons and defensive skills to protect their principals' lives, you might want to think twice about the person to whom you are talking. In most cases, a strict reliance on physical presence is not enough to protect principals. Agents, male or female, must possess *all* of the necessary skills to handle a variety of situations.

Final point: As mentioned before, do not underestimate anyone, regardless of gender. It's about the whole person, their abilities, attitude, mission and – maybe most importantly – their ability to do the job with professional integrity.

Security Drivers

Every principal/client could benefit from a professional, dedicated executive driver. A driver who has also been professionally trained as a security agent could sometimes be the only level of protection a principal may have or need.

I have a definite level of connection with and appreciation, admiration and respect for professional security drivers, given my own past as a protective driver. Throughout my career, I have never shied away from getting behind the wheel in a security detail – as I got my start in the EP profession in Germany driving a 5,800-pound (nearly 3 tons) Level B7 armored Mercedes-Benz.

As soon as the principal steps into the vehicle, the most important person in the entire team is the driver. They must maintain a high level of concentration, preparedness, attention to detail and, most importantly, the right mindset. This need for focus has led to a common mantra in our profession: "Drivers drive."

In the world of personal protection, we often focus much of our attention and security efforts on what we perceive to be the obvious threats against our protectees. No one can deny the need to defend against armed attackers, potential kidnappers, hostile surveillance, extortionists, terrorists, paparazzi, slips and falls, and other security risks. As protection specialists, we receive initial and continuous training in firearms, surveillance and countersurveillance, self-defense, tactical and defensive driving, counterterrorism, first aid and many other skills generally associated with personal protection.

But in our industry, when we look at the probabilities, risks and events that actually occur most often which affect our principals' well-being, one risk stands out: *motor vehicle accidents*. Wealth or having a well-trained detail doesn't provide ultimate protection from this risk. Whether principals are driving themselves or being driven by others (including security drivers), motor vehicle accidents have killed or seriously injured protectees at higher rates than all other threats.

We advise our clients and principals about known dangers, risks of travel, potentially disgruntled individuals and insider threats, but sometimes we avoid bringing up one of the most obvious risks due to the "embarrassment" factor: their potentially unsafe driving habits. We often feel we are intruding on their privacy or insulting them and thus avoid being persistent regarding the risks associated with their driving routines.

But as Tony Scotti, one of the world's most respected and trusted professionals in the driving and training industry for over 40 years, will tell you, "Transportation by vehicles is the most dangerous period in the principal's day." Many principals have unskilled chauffeurs or drivers, don't always wear seatbelts (especially in the back seat, which is just as dangerous), and drive or are frequently driven under poor road or weather conditions.

Some can succumb to the "sports car" factor, where the principal or someone driving them operates a vehicle they're not completely trained to drive – e.g., a high-performance sports car – at high speeds. I have also followed many principals as they are driving alone in their own cars who are emailing, texting and talking on their cell phones and/or weaving in and out of lanes.

In the cases of young protectees, these risks are tripled. We often are assigned to teenagers learning how to drive, and it is well documented that vehicle accidents are the leading cause of death among young adults aged 15–20. When teenage drivers take passengers with them, their risk of being in a fatal car crash doubles as teens who already underestimate or are unable to recognize hazardous driving conditions are distracted by their passengers.

As security specialists, very often we drive the principals ourselves – which, in most situations, is the preferred method of protection and security. Often, the biggest risks are encountered when we travel and use local drivers in foreign countries where defensive driving skills are not always taught or practiced.

In the best of scenarios, we send an advance security person or team to identify and evaluate qualified drivers. These will be drivers we have used before or who come highly recommended by other details. If we know in advance that we may not have the type of driver we'll need, we may bring our own driver who is capable and familiar with driving in a particular location.

In the worst-case (or even perhaps the usual) scenario, we get off the plane with our principals and into a waiting car with a driver we just hope is skilled, trustworthy and driving a well-maintained vehicle. In my tenure, of all the things that could go wrong, the *most dangerous situations* I have encountered occurred when I and/or my protectee were in a vehicle with a *relatively untested driver.*

I have had to change foreign and domestic chauffeurs and even federal agent drivers several times during travels due to risky or unsafe driving habits. In one such case, I made the driver stop the vehicle and switch with another driver to finish our route because he had committed serious judgmental errors while the principals were in the vehicle. That was a very unpleasant, but necessary, decision.

While in a vehicle in the front right seat, I've had to tell drivers:

- Don't use a cell phone while driving (and they still would).
- Slow down and/or don't drive aggressively in traffic (using my own hand signals to communicate this to the driver as a principal sat in the back seat).
- Don't slow down rapidly while on highways to avoid dips or bumps, since this maneuver can cause traffic behind us to slam on their brakes in order to avoid our vehicle.
- Don't drive too fast on poor road conditions (e.g., rain, snow or dirt roads).

In 2010, while traveling with a family in one of my favorite countries, we had drivers assigned to us from a royal guard I had worked with many times during my days with the CIA. I was accompanying my principal's child and the nanny late one evening to rejoin the group when our driver decided to drive in the oncoming lane as he prepared to turn left.

Suddenly, a car traveling very fast came around the curve ahead of us. This car was on a collision path with us – and we were on the wrong side of the road. Immediately, I yelled to our driver to get back in his lane. While his driving skills were generally very good, his overconfident attitude (probably from working as a royal driver), nearly caused a head-on collision that almost had a devastating outcome for all of us. I had the driver replaced minutes later after another unpleasant but necessary conversation with the King's detail leader.

When traveling in places such as China, India, Africa, Latin America, etc., many local drivers are relatively new and have not had any formal driving instruction. This may be our biggest risk of all. And in many countries, roads are crowded with pedestrians, scooters and bicyclists, making local driving conditions very precarious. The last thing our principals need is to be injured in an accident in another country – especially if a local resident is also injured or killed.

If your principal is required to travel to a high-threat area, a local driver may or may not meet your "security driver" needs. While it has only happened to me under extreme circumstances, one question I might ask when looking for a driver in a high-risk situation is, "If I order you to push a vehicle in front of you or jump a curb to avoid a dangerous situation, or I need you to be aggressive/defensive and require you to possibly damage this vehicle, could you do this?" Often, I get heavy hesitation or a flat-out "no."

Of course, many of these drivers appreciate and need their jobs and enjoy driving a very nice vehicle in some of these regions of the world (it is viewed as a status symbol among their family and peers). This is even true in the United States. It is admirable and understandable drivers take very good care of their vehicles and have a great deal of pride in them, keeping them very clean and without a scratch. In many cases, if they should be involved in a "fender bender" (no matter how minor), they could lose their position or vehicle. But from an EP perspective, that does not outweigh the well-being of a principal.

EP professionals, if you observed an agent sleeping on the job or unsafe weapon handling, you would probably correct that dangerous activity immediately. Poor or unsafe driving risks should be handled with the same level of attention and concern, if not more.

For more evidence on the risk car accidents in general pose to our principals, consider the following:

- General George S. Patton was killed in a car accident in Germany shortly after World War II had concluded.
- Actress Jayne Mansfield, her lawyer and her three children were in a chauffeured car when the driver plowed into the back of a truck. Mansfield, her driver and lawyer were all killed.
- Princess Diana and boyfriend Dodi Fayed were being driven by a known chauffeur when he crashed in a Paris tunnel, fleeing from paparazzi. Princess Diana's bodyguard was the only survivor.
- Lisa ("Left Eye") Lopes, singer with the popular group TLC, was driving a rental car in Honduras and tried to pass a vehicle

when a truck approached from the other lane. She swerved to avoid a crash, but her car flipped over and she was killed.

- Famed fashion photographer Helmut Newton died when he lost control of the car he was driving after he left the Chateau Marmont Hotel in Los Angeles and slammed into a wall. He was rushed to the hospital, but died a short time later.

- David Murdock Jr., son of billionaire David Murdock, Sr., died at the age of 36 while driving his Ferrari too fast on a curve when exiting the Santa Monica Freeway in Los Angeles.

- Former New Jersey governor Jon Corzine sustained chest injuries and multiple fractures when his sports utility vehicle, driven by a New Jersey state trooper, slammed into a guardrail at high speed. He was not wearing his seatbelt.

- Vietnam War critic and Pulitzer-winning reporter David Halberstam was a passenger in a car when it was struck by another car and knocked into a third vehicle. He was pronounced dead at the scene at the age of 73.

- British oil magnate Charles Ward's son, Lee, died in a crash after losing control of his Lamborghini and plummeting off a 250-foot cliff in Spain.

- Paul Walker, star actor of the *Fast and Furious* movie franchise, and his friend Roger Rodas both died when Rodas lost control of a Porsche Carrera GT and they collided into a pole and trees which resulted in the car exploding.

- John Nash (the mathematician whose life inspired the film *A Beautiful Mind*) and his wife died in an accident when their taxi driver lost control trying to pass another vehicle.

- Bob Simon, veteran news correspondent for CBS and *60 Minutes*, died after suffering head and neck trauma, two broken legs and two broken arms. He was being driven in a Lincoln Town Car in New York City. In this case, high speed was believed to be a factor. He also was not wearing a seatbelt.

I could go on and on listing vehicle accidents that were the cause of death or serious injuries for high-profile and UHNW individuals.

While we still must be prepared for the numerous threats which may come our way, we all need to be reminded that the greatest threat to a protectee's life and well-being may at times be closer than we think: the vehicle and underqualified or reckless drivers.

Retaining Your EP Team Members

As a principal, you do not want your detail to be a revolving door of mixed security personnel – or any staff for that matter. Frequent turnover can be disruptive and creates security and privacy risks, not to mention a negative impact on operational effectiveness.

How can you minimize turnover? Appreciation, training, advance opportunity, additional duties, education, proper pay, benefits and work-life balance are all key elements of keeping most employees happy. EP types are no different. Typical agents/officers are just like anyone else and need the same basics and essentials to be happy employees. They should:

- Feel respected and appreciated
- Be compensated fairly and competitively
- Be given adequate time off
- Be provided the opportunity to be promoted or be involved with other professional challenges
- Have opportunities for training and continued education

It should really be the job of your EP manager or director to ensure these things happen for team members, but these topics should also be discussed at least annually (preferably more often) depending on the size and dynamics of a protective detail.

A simple example of the appreciation I refer to occurred once when I was with my principal in a Middle Eastern country. During my advance a few days earlier, I'd fortuitously managed to arrange a high-level last-minute meeting for my principal with a member of this country's royal family who was also an important executive.

This meeting was to take place just prior to my principal's final departure for the airport. His pilot had advised we had a tight window of departure, as they had already submitted a request to enter and land at the next country – and their landing time there was now set.

After escorting my principal to the office in the iconic high-rise where the meeting would take place, I waited for him in the (very ostentatious) lobby on the 63rd floor. In the distance, you could see a massive shamal (dust storm) beginning to approach the city.

My principal's meeting was already running past his airport departure time, so I contacted our pilots, who were nervously tracking the storm. They said if they were delayed because of it, they would miss their slot for landing at the next destination. If that happened, the boss would have to decide between staying another night or flying to a new destination and missing his next scheduled dinner meeting. Neither option was good.

I first tried to advise the male executive assistant working for the royal family member that I needed to interrupt their meeting to speak to my principal about the situation. He said, "Please, please – let's give them five more minutes." (They don't like to interrupt the royals.)

Looking westward, you could now see the wall of dust coming closer – and heading directly for the airport. Suddenly, I received an urgent text from the pilot telling me we had less than 20 minutes to get airborne or they'd be stuck for the night. I now advised the executive assistant that either he could politely interrupt the meeting, or I would.

With great reluctance, he softly tapped on the door and advised the royal executive that I needed to see my principal – though his request was a moot point, since I was standing right behind him. I stepped into the doorway and advised my principal of the situation and our urgent need to depart. My principal quickly got up and apologized for the sudden departure, but the royal executive totally understood. Fortunately, their meeting had been successful, so they said their goodbyes and we immediately headed out.

On our way to the airport, I was in constant contact with the pilot, who was urging us to get there as fast as possible now that the shamal was closing in. In addition, the control tower was advising they would be closing the airport soon. To expedite my principal's departure, the aircraft's engines were running and ready for an immediate takeoff, and an immigration officer was standing by at the plane to authorize his boarding.

The dust storm was approaching rapidly behind us. At one point, my principal said, "We're not going to make it, we should plan for other options." But my job was to get him to the plane as quickly as possible – I would need to let him and the pilot make that final call.

During my advance, I had arranged special ramp access to the plane for our vehicle. I called five minutes out and we were met at the gate and escorted directly to the aircraft. We stopped at the bottom of the stairs leading up to the plane door and the principal sprinted up as I grabbed his bags for a quick handoff to the copilot.

They closed the door and were taxiing in less than five minutes. At this point, based on the massive cloud of dust approaching, I didn't believe it was possible to take off – I assumed they would need to either return to the terminal or wait out the storm in the plane. Exposing the plane's engines to this amount of dust wasn't good – it was going to be close.

I returned to the VIP lounge prepared to stay put for a few hours as the storm passed over, since I was scheduled to head to another city later that evening. As I stood at the large window overlooking the runway, I watched the shamal approach the west end of the tarmac where my principal's plane sat ready for departure. When the plane began to taxi, it was like a scene from a movie as they took off with the shamal at their heels. Once they were finally airborne, I exhaled a huge sigh of relief – just as the dust storm consumed the airport.

My principal's plane was the very last aircraft allowed to depart before the airport shut down. Seconds after takeoff, I received a text from him: "Fantastic meeting, thanks for setting this up – great job!"

Principals, it's those little moments that only take a few shared words of appreciation which will keep your EP staff motivated – and ready to do just about anything for you.

The Highly Important EP Advance

While this section may be last in the chapter on EP teams and what they do, ultimately, out of the many EP functions that practitioners need to know and perform well, few are as important as the security "advance."

The primary purpose of any advance is to remove the *unknown* in as many as areas as possible (time, resources and conditions allowing). An advance should be conducted whenever a principal is engaged in movement, whether to known or unknown areas, at home and abroad. A properly conducted advance can help avoid what I like to refer to as "UFOs" – i.e., unidentified future occurrences. To do the job right, you have to be thorough and flexible. You have to prioritize and be all of these clichés: Think on your feet, always have the answers, and expect the unexpected.

It's my opinion the advance is also where many EP operators can become the most complacent. After several successful advances where all goes well, sometimes agents begin to cut corners and make more assumptions than they should when conducting a true "eyes on" advance.

Disciplined operators and effective EP management require a checklist to be completed before the arrival of their principal – much as a pilot does before take-offs, landings or inflight emergencies. A well-developed checklist keeps us from forgetting or eliminating an important step in our advances.

Just like Red Team activity, an advance begins with gathering as much information as possible about the event or trip itself from various sources. Principals with EP support who have traveled extensively over the years should already have "post-trip reports" filed and retrievable. This information will generally involve hotels, persons of interest, previous security and drivers, airports, forward operating bases, hospitals and many other important data points. EP agents will pull from these very valuable resources to begin the next trip.

Most principals have no idea of the amount of preparation necessary to ensure everything goes smoothly upon their arrival -- sometimes just minutes prior, EP details can still be fielding multiple calls to finalize logistics and facilitation requirements. If you are a lucky practitioner, you have two or more advance agents with you but, for probably at least half of my professional career, I have gone solo.

Many times we pull off the impossible and they may greet us asking if everything is okay. We smile and say, "Yes, everything is just fine." If they only knew.

Not long ago, I had lunch with a former CEO and principal with whom I had circled the globe several times. He had since taken a new position that no longer included a security detail. Even though his level of wealth would have allowed him to continue his security support, he did not do so.

However, he still admitted how much he missed his security team.

On his first trip solo, he stepped off his plane overseas and was greeted by his driver (prearranged by someone else), who said, "Where to, sir?" He said he actually had no idea of the specific location for the meeting and began to frantically look through emails and for the trip folder his executive assistant had provided him, which he couldn't easily locate now. Unfortunately, he had wanted to stop by his hotel before his meeting, but wasn't sure he would have the time – during our advances, we would always pre-check him in and simply hand him the key.

It's the little *and* the big things we do prior to arrival to ensure we have all the answers we can, allowing our principals to focus on the purpose of their travel. And we also know our principal will sometimes play the "stump the advance agent" game. I have given up my own cuff links, ties and sport coat to many a principal getting off his plane who needed to go directly to a meeting but realized he did not have an item on him or it was packed, wrinkled or just inaccessible.

As a result, many of us get used to traveling and dressing like Inspector Gadget, pulling items from God knows where when asked for things by our principals – e.g., "Do you happen to have a Vitamin B12 on you?" or "Have you got a charging cable for my [name random phone or laptop]?" or "Can you get me a Diet Sunkist, grape flavor?" What is even stranger, most of the time we are able to provide what they ask for because we have come to know our principals so well.

The *art* of the EP advance is an "advanced" learned and practiced skill in itself – and one too many EP teams can take for granted. As mentioned before, technology has become as much a vulnerability as an asset in certain situations regarding EP, and professionals need to keep current on these risks. In most schools and training academies, the EP advance is covered and even practiced, but rarely do they go into the level of knowledge and detail that should be recommended in today's environment.

Recently, a report I read stated that when all a CEO's logistical needs are handled by an EP team coordinating with the administrative staff, the executive's effectiveness can be elevated by as much as 20 percent per day. With all we do, I believe that number could actually be higher. The following story might help to illustrate all that can occur before your plane even touches down and you see the face of your calm, smiling EP agent.

It's a long story – for a reason.

An Advance to Remember

Everyone in this profession has their own "war" story of the advance they'll never forget. I've had many challenging and interesting advances around the world over the years, but one in particular comes to mind that required me to be imaginative, think outside the box and bring all my resources together to pull it off.

It was the spring of 1999 and another special agent (also named Mike) and I were advancing Aviano, Italy, for John Gordon, a four-star Air Force general and the CIA's deputy director (DDCI). This particular journey was also unusual for the CIA, as he was traveling with a U.S. senator and a few staff members. This particular senator was not necessarily known for his support of the CIA, making this trip even more interesting.

From the time they departed Andrews Air Force Base, this trip was already not going well. The senator was attempting to dictate and change the travel locations and itineraries, creating some frustration for General Gordon, his staff and our protective detail.

Mike and I had prepared all the typical elements for the arrival of General Gordon (our primary principal), the senator and several staff members. We had planned for events, contingencies and schedules on Aviano Air Base, as well as meetings in the city of Aviano. We also had to contend with a large protest outside the base, as usually took place in Europe when the U.S. military was involved with any conflicts in the region. Much of this visit was to include meetings regarding the ongoing conflict in Kosovo.

One day prior to arrival, we received word the Aviano portion of the trip would probably be canceled. We were instructed to stand down and to prepare to be redirected to another as-yet-unknown location. We awaited further instructions but, considering we had some down time and less than a two-hour train ride to Venice, Mike and I decided to visit.

At about 7:00 pm local time, we were preparing to head back from Venice when I received a phone call from our Ops Group at Langley (CIA headquarters) advising me that General Gordon and the senator's new destination would be Ramstein Air Base in Germany – and they would be arriving tomorrow morning.

They also told me I needed to get to Ramstein *tonight* to prepare. In addition, I was also told to conduct my advance and prepare for the arrival without using General Gordon's name. (He was becoming so aggravated with this trip he wanted no association with the senator's requests.)

They advised they were looking for commercial flight options to get me there, but they were coming up empty-handed. My next call was to Isabella in one of our European offices to see if she could work her magic on any last-minute flights.

Like most staff at CIA stations, Isabella had many roles, and one of them was logistics. By the time we were on the train back to Aviano, Isabella called to say there was nothing available until the morning, and whatever we got would probably arrive over in Frankfurt – 90 minutes away from Ramstein.* Normally that would be fine, but the General would be arriving mid-morning and we needed all the time we could get.

---

* Commercial flights don't fly into Ramstein, and Frankfurt was the closest commercial airport.

Isabella had always been very resourceful but she, too, was coming up empty-handed. We looked at buses, trains and even considered my renting a car to drive all night over the Alps up to Ramstein (arriving around 6:00 am), assuming I could consume enough espresso to stay awake. Even at that, I would only be arriving a few hours before the General. Not the best option – but it was now looking like my only option.

During this time, it was decided the other Mike would remain in Aviano in the event they changed their minds again. Normally, a new location is never a problem – usually just a quick flight. But having such short notice, lots of moving parts, unique requests and very few transportation options at that time of night were all factors that conspired against my ability to get to Ramstein in time to prepare for their arrival.

That's when I was told I also needed to *quietly* arrange a C-130 aircraft to take the senator and several staff members on a small congressional delegation downrange to a base where much of the air combat operations for Kosovo were being managed. Again, I was reminded to do so *without mentioning General Gordon*.

This entire trip was becoming what felt like a boondoggle (or what we sometimes referred to as "FUBAR"), but it was my boondoggle to advance. We soon exhausted all options for getting into Ramstein that night – including driving, which would simply get me there too late.

Then I recalled an airman I met at Aviano Air Base Operations earlier who was very helpful with coordinating some of our requirements for the (now-canceled) landing of General Gordon's aircraft. Even though she was a junior enlisted airman, she appeared to be the kind of person who liked challenges, so I was going to give her one.

It was getting close to 8:00 pm local time when I called her and told her I needed to get to Ramstein Air Base *tonight*. "How can you get me there or anywhere close?" I could hear her wheels turning and, as I expected, her first comment was, "Let me work it and get back to you." As Mike and I arrived at the Aviano train station, she called and asked, "Could you be at base ops in 30 minutes?"

I ran to the hotel, picked up my bags, jumped into our waiting van and headed to Aviano Air Base, where I met my new best friend as she took me to an Air Force Gulfstream IV on the tarmac preparing for departure to Ramstein. As my (lack of) luck would have it, it was also an absolutely terrible night for flying, with heavy winds and rain – I was even doubtful the plane would be able to take off.

When we arrived at the aircraft, there seemed to be some confusion as to my presence. The crew members were told little about who I was, so they challenged me and wanted to see my identification. Understandably, it was their aircraft and they needed to know who would be on board. The pilots had been briefed they would have another passenger, but they were surprised I was a civilian. Because I was instructed not to mention that General Gordon might be going to Ramstein, I didn't want to show my CIA credentials. (We didn't always carry our credentials on overseas trips for obvious reasons, but I did have them for this particular one.)

With the advance preparation from the airman and a commonly used alias background, fortunately, I was now on board for Ramstein. However, given that I was sitting on an Air Force Gulfstream IV, it was obvious we were waiting for a high-ranking officer to arrive for this flight. A few minutes later, a staff car pulled up and a brigadier general (one-star) in his Air

Force flight suit stepped out and boarded the plane. Extremely irritated, he yelled to the pilots, "Close the door, boys, and let's get the hell out of here!" He was obviously not having a good day, and I wondered if he would ask the obvious question: *Who are you and what are you doing on my plane?*

Instead, he quickly sat down facing the rear of the aircraft, propped his feet up on the seat in front of him, tipped his flight cap over his eyes and crossed his arms with a heavy sigh. Now sitting just ten feet away from him, I promptly did the same and tipped my baseball cap over my eyes, crossed my legs and pretended to sleep as I ran through my mental checklist and prioritized what I needed to do before the General arrived in Ramstein.

Fortunately, the weather broke briefly and it was a less than 90-minute flight as we crossed north over the Alps. As we descended and prepared for our landing at Ramstein Air Base, the brigadier general suddenly pushed back his flight cap, looked at me and popped the question I had been waiting for: "Son, what are you doing on my aircraft?" I thought, *Shit, I knew I should have served him a bag of nuts and a Coke.*

During the flight I had prepared various responses to evade the specific reason I was on board. But I also realized I had a lot to do in just a few hours and I needed an ally on the base to help – I knew I could really use his authority if I got into a jam. And while I was officially not to tell anyone that General Gordon might be coming to Ramstein, I also knew that most generals don't become generals by being stupid. Since we'd just left Aviano, where General Gordon was to be, there was a good chance that this brigadier general sitting in front of me might already know or have inferred our new plans.

I started with my typical cover story, but the brigadier general was very astute. He quickly asked again what I was doing on his aircraft and why was I coming to Ramstein: "For General Gordon?" I decided to tell him the truth, including that I was from the CIA. I also explained the request for the C-130 that had been laid upon me. I also relayed General Gordon's instructions not to disclose his arrival just yet to Ramstein. I did play up his discontent with the senator traveling with him – I figured that couldn't hurt. Most military officers I know really don't like it when members of Congress show up, interrupt their operations, ask silly questions and want their pictures taken for all of eight minutes before heading back to Washington with their mementos.

He confirmed he believed General Gordon was coming and he would look into the senator's request for the C-130 but expressed that probably wasn't going to happen – not what I wanted to hear.

As we landed, the rain was coming down hard and it was close to midnight. I thanked the brigadier general for giving me a ride on his aircraft and gave him a quick overview of my time on the base nearly 10 years prior. He stepped off the plane and got into his waiting car.

After all of my other thoughts and planning for General Gordon, I realized I had no plan as to where I was staying the night and had just landed on a military base with no real authorization or supporting documents to be there. I ran over and tapped on his window: "Sir, may I ask for another favor? Could you get me a room at the base temporary lodging (hotel)?"

I jumped in and he took me on a three-minute drive to the base hotel: the Ramstein Inn. When the night manager asked for my identification or military orders, I tilted my eyes to the brigadier general and, without saying a word, gave him a look that said, *You know I don't have what he's asking for.* The brigadier general stepped up to the counter and instructed the manager to just provide me a room.

Unfortunately, the Ramstein Inn had no rooms available, but they were able to get me a room 20 minutes away in Vogelweh, an Army and Air Force community off base. The brigadier general waited until I had my information for the room, gave me his card and told me to call him if I needed anything else. *I could really use your car,* I thought, but I felt I had exhausted my requests for the evening.

It was midnight and my advance was just getting started, with my principal only a few hours out and most people on the base now asleep. I called our ops office in Langley and updated them on my arrival at Ramstein. They responded with, "How in the world did you get there in less than three hours since we last talked?!" Then, they confirmed General Gordon and the senator would be there in the morning and I did, in fact, still need to arrange a C-130 for the congressional delegation. This was going to be fun.

As I was still on base and had worked and lived there, I knew exactly where Air Division Headquarters was – just a five-minute walk from the billeting office. I stored my bags at billeting and started making phone calls. I did need a car, so my first call was to the AFOSI Protective Service Detail. Fortunately, I'd had this number in my contacts for more than eight years. I called their 24-hour ops line and identified myself, who I was with and why I was there – and dropped names from my time at Ramstein and OSI I knew they would still know. Fifteen minutes later, I had an OSI sedan delivered to me, which included a few extra "essentials." Because the rain was still pouring down, I drove over to the Air Division Headquarters while thinking to myself, *This is where the real fun begins.*

I reached out to Diane, General Gordon's executive assistant, who was traveling with him. It was late where they were too, but I knew she would be awake and in the traveling command post.* She said the request for the C-130 had been made through the senator's Washington, D.C., channels, but had not been confirmed. She told me to do whatever I could to make it happen, because when they landed at Ramstein, the General wanted the senator to be able to walk straight to the waiting C-130. General Gordon also had other meetings I needed to facilitate on his behalf.

I then drove to the Air Division Ops building. Before entering, I made a quick call to the Cannon Hotel, a small hotel designed for visiting high-ranking officers, located behind the small secure enclave of homes occupied by U.S. Air Forces in Europe (USAFE) and NATO general officers. I needed most of their rooms for General Gordon, the senator, his staff and our security. *Now I'm really going to stir the hornet's nest.*

The night manager answered the phone. I identified myself, said I was traveling in advance of a four-star general and gave him my wish list. I told him I was going into a meeting at the Air Division Ops building but would visit him later that night to follow up. I advised him the General was scheduled to arrive mid-morning and I needed to take him and his staff straight to the hotel. I "recommended" he might want to wake up his boss with this news.

When I arrived at Air Division Ops (which hadn't changed locations since I left Ramstein in 1992), it was

---

* Any time the Director or General Gordon traveled, a command post with a communication specialist would accompany them to ensure they had secure communications with the Agency HQs, White House and all other essential offices.

after midnight. I rang a call box outside the back door and, after suspiciously articulating my reason for being at their door unannounced in the middle of the night, they agreed to meet with me – but probably only to see if I was for real. At that point, I did have to drop the three letters that often opened doors: CIA.

After showing my CIA credentials to the captain who greeted me and, again, giving a brief synopsis of why I was there, I was escorted inside to a room where the Ops team was plotting certain bombing information from their F-16 aircraft downrange in Kosovo and Serbia on a large clear board. As I sat there listening to the aircraft radio traffic and watching several Air Force enlisted members updating their sortie board, a major walked into the room, but he didn't notice me initially. After addressing his men, he looked at me sitting at a small round bar top table in the back and said to the captain in a very disapproving voice: "What the hell is this civilian doing in my command post?" *This just kept getting better...*

Over the next three hours, through many phone calls with Diane, the senator's office, the White House and several pots of coffee, the major, captain and I re-hashed my requests, with a long progression from "No way in hell this is going to happen" to "This is not going to happen with such short notice" to "This probably will not happen tomorrow."

At one point in our conversations I was getting the impression they felt my request was just for some personal use by a rogue CIA agent. I must admit, it was a reasonable concern, since I did just appear without warning in the middle of the night with this peculiar request.

Finally, out of pure exhaustion and frustration, I paused our negotiations and took a moment to remind them of a very small but important piece of information they might want to consider: "When you look at me sitting here, you shouldn't see a tired, hungry and aggravated special agent who would rather be having a few Bitburger beers and schnitzel while catching up with my German friends.

What you *should* see in front of you is a four-star U.S. Air Force general who happens to be the Deputy Director of the Central Intelligence Agency operating on behalf of the President of the United States while traveling with a very senior U.S. senator. So, when you tell me 'this is not going to happen' or 'not possible,' realize that when I walk out of here, my first call will be to the General's traveling command post adjoining his hotel room. When the General walks into the command post first thing this morning, roughly three hours from now, this will be the first news he receives. I personally have no rank in this situation and, while I understand and totally respect your positions, I have previously served here at Ramstein longer than both of you combined. I know very well how things work around here – and in the military the one thing that does happen very effectively is 'shit rolls downhill.' While I don't know who General Gordon is going to call first, I *can* tell you who will receive the second call. Any thoughts?"

It wasn't long after this conversation that we received notice that the request had been approved. With a big handshake, I thanked the major and captain for their efforts and cooperation with my unusual requests at such an odd hour with no advance warning. As a former member of the Air Force assigned to Ramstein, I departed the Ops Center with a degree of pride and nostalgia for my earlier days in Germany and working together as a team to complete the mission. After all, we *were* on the same team.

The Agency has a few European offices that might support a trip like this one and other activities throughout the continent. One particular office had been alerted through calls and secure written communications earlier in the evening of General Gordon's impending arrival. I had worked with this office before and, as always, they were very responsive with all of our requests and they would be sending certain resources and support in the morning before he landed.

While I still needed to coordinate a few other urgent issues, hotels were always at the top of the list to ensure all would go well. There's nothing worse than having dozens of exhausted and frustrated travelers looking at the advance agent and asking why they don't have hotel rooms. No matter who was supposed to arrange them, it would always be the advance agent's fault if all wasn't in order.

I had time to kill from 4:00–6:00 am until the others I needed to talk to would be awake, so I decided to drive off base to the billeting (hotel) location in Vogelweh, where I was given my room. I figured a shower and change of clothes were earned.

Of course, *leaving* a base is never a problem, but trying to return without an ID or pass is a little harder, so at 6:00 am, I reached out to Lieutenant Colonel George Yochum, the German military police commander assigned to Ramstein, whose number I still had in my contacts.* When George answered, I said, "Guess who?"

---

* The Kaiserslautern Military Community, which includes Ramstein, is a large population of U.S. service members working alongside many local German civilians supporting all the U.S. Army and Air Force operations there. The American military police were supported by the German civilian military police under the control of George Yochum – a good guy and a great friend.

It may have been eight years since I had last seen him, but some people's habits never change and I knew he would be on his way to the base at that early hour. George met me at the Ramstein visitor's office located just outside the main entrance. We took a few minutes to catch up and I promised to stop by his office before leaving Germany. He secured my base pass for the week and, as always, told me to reach out for whatever else I needed while I was there.

Next stop was the Cannon Hotel, where I met with my new friend, the day manager, and was able to secure the rooms required for the next couple days – they only had to move four high-ranking officers out of their rooms to another hotel. One thing the military does do well, especially on Ramstein, is recognizing the principal's rank and RHIP ("rank has its privileges").

I began preparing our initial command post and started making calls, setting up meetings and arranging additional resources. I secured a few cars, including one armored car from the OSI fleet supporting HQ USAFE for any of our off-base movements when deemed necessary. Diane had a few other requests by the general I needed to address before "wheels down."

After all schedules were finalized, I stopped by the base clinic, ensured all my other "base essentials" were still located where I remembered, and confirmed all the phone contacts I would need. I generated a quick two-day schedule and faxed it off to our ops in Langley who forwarded it to Diane so they could review this portion of the trip.

The team at the last location notified me that the general was "wheels up" and should be on time. I quickly advanced two last-minute locations for meetings. (With any principal's advance, we want to know exactly where they're going and be prepared with all the pertinent information about that location, including safety and security concerns.)

By now, our European support team had arrived at the base and I escorted them to the Cannon Hotel so the they could continue assisting with setting up the General's command post and ensure he had secure communications with Langley.

Back at base ops, I met with the host team, briefed drivers and other support staff, and had a much-needed cup of coffee while I reviewed the schedule, trying to anticipate where "Murphy's Law" might come into play on this trip – as if it hadn't already.

Just 14 hours prior, I was casually sipping a cappuccino in Venice when I received the instructions from Langley to find my way to Ramstein and prepare for the arrival of the DDCI and his nemesis, the senator. Now I was in Ramstein and hadn't slept in more than 30 hours – which was not atypical for the advance security agent or any EP agent while traveling.

At approximately 10:00 am, the Air Force cargo plane landed at Ramstein. Parked just three planes over was a C-130 and crew ready for departure to take the senator downrange for his congressional delegation trip. As I walked up the steps of the military aircraft, I met General Gordon just inside the door. He smiled, put his hand on my shoulder and said, "Hello, Michael. Any problems? Is everything okay?"

I smiled back, took a deep breath and said, "Yes, sir – everything is fine."

"FAMILY IS NOT AN IMPORTANT
THING. IT'S EVERYTHING."

- MICHAEL J. FOX

CHAPTER V

FAMILY PROTECTION

O NE DAY YOU are being interviewed about your military service, executive protection background, shooting skills, martial arts and self-defense proficiency. The very next day, after you are hired, the principal (or perhaps the nanny) tells you not to forget the diaper bag, or maybe, "Can you please take the dog for a walk and pick up his droppings before heading to the FBO to board the plane?"

Welcome to family executive protection.

Most of the concepts, methods and requirements pertaining to executive protection are similar whether in the corporate or family environments. But there are some important differences that need to be considered when developing a private/family program.

Before we begin, I want to reiterate something I mentioned earlier: the misuse of fear by practitioners. We all know fear can be a motivating factor for establishing a family or personal security program. But as I said before, I have a strong aversion to those in the profession who use fear to influence principals to achieve certain program goals without legitimate reasons (e.g., budget, staffing, equipment, control, proximity, etc.). Beware of these kinds of practitioners and vendors.

With that in our minds, let's begin our look at this unique type of program.

I've mentioned it before and you'll hear this same sentiment from others: Executive protection is often more of an art than a science. This is especially the case with protection programs for families. These require a great deal of patience, communication and finesse, since they are usually much more personal and dynamic than a corporate EP environment.

Because EP programs for families are so unique, there are many factors you should consider when approaching one. At its core, such a program is a very delicate balancing act of security requirements versus the principal's risk appetite. In many cases, a family security program may be established because of a level of corporate risk, legacy protection and/or family social profile with related risk factors.

As time passes and the coverage requirement grows and extends to family members, the program often shifts or expands. Most commonly, though, the corporate coverage and the family program completely split. The separation is often requested by the board of directors or the principals themselves (e.g., CEOs) or comes at the recommendation of corporate general counsel. It may become necessary to separate the corporate from family protection to ensure compliance with the Securities and Exchange Commission and the Sarbanes-Oxley Act, as well as to avoid any shareholder concerns or allegations of corporate financial abuse (if a publicly traded company).

I highly recommend taking a programmatic approach to any request for personal protection, whether it will be a short-term, long-term or permanent program. A programmatic approach allows the "architect" to outline their recommendations based on a particular well-thought-out methodology. Principals and key stakeholders can then ask the hard questions and prioritize stability, consistency and confidence in the level of protection required or desired. This approach might include a plan for implementing a security program in phases (based on the identified risks).

No program can truly be built effectively without a thorough understanding of the issues at hand. It bears repeating: It is essential to conduct a Threat, Vulnerability and Risk Assessment (TVRA) that also includes lifestyle activities to understand all a principal's needs and their prioritization before getting started. If you leave this assessment out, the protection program will be like throwing darts at a board. Such an oversight can leave principals confused, uncertain and apprehensive regarding their security coverage. The TVRA should continue to be updated throughout an ongoing program – it's not a "once and done" event.

Purpose of a Family EP Program

As we've been reviewing, there are many reasons an individual or family may believe they require personal protection. The following list contains a few examples to help determine *why* personal protection might be needed, as well as *what* is needed to ensure the protection is properly in place for the appropriate *when* and *where*.

- A real/perceived threat has been received against you or your family.
- You or a family member holds an executive title within a high-profile organization.
- Your career or profession draws undesired negative attention that is a cause of personal concern regarding your safety and security.
- You have a high-profile family name and/or wealth and attract a great deal of public attention.
- You're a very outspoken and high-profile person who sometimes draws negative attention.
- The type of business you're involved in comes with inherent risks or threats.
- You desire or need a level of security facilitation due to your public profile and frequent travel.

- You and/or your family routinely travel to high-risk foreign or domestic areas.
- You're welcoming the birth of a new child as a wealthy and high-profile family.
- You have major assets that need an adequate level of protection (e.g., estates, collectibles, yachts, airplanes).

What complicates the above profile is the composition and lifestyles of the family who may fall under the EP umbrella. Points to consider include:

- Results of your TVRA
- Frequency of travel, including international
- Use of private or commercial travel
- Number of residences
- Lifestyle activities (e.g., skiing, golfing, biking, motorcycling, boating, sailing, hunting, exotic travel, or other high-risk sports or activities)
- Number and ages of children, their activities and their schooling (especially abroad)
- Use of nannies or extended family to support children
- Medical health issues or concerns of any principals
- Number of extended family or friends who fall under the security umbrella
- Expectations of principals
- Privacy issues or concerns
- Religious or cultural practices and concerns

As previously mentioned, there must be a financial source and budget to provide a level of family protection to the degree discussed in this book; in most cases, personal wealth along with perceived and actual risk will determine the acceptable level of resources that will be applied.

Children and EP Details

Programs involving children can often lead to unnecessary anxiety, embarrassment and trust issues among security, staff and the family. Let's face it, raising children has enough challenges without adding close protection to their little lives and development.

Family and children EP details might be the most important program for which policies and procedures *will* be needed to define proper limitations and expectations. Many family EP professionals become very close to their protective families, so it's natural and even usual they would hear and see things that might be a potential problem for their young principals. This is a delicate subject, but in some cases EP agents (male and female) can become surrogate parents or older "siblings" – whether realized, acknowledged or not.

This often creates a complicated balance between "protector" and "surrogate parent," and will lead to some difficult decision-making – especially whether or not to report certain behaviors. I've had my team members enter a bar or club to check on their young (legal-age) principals who have consumed too much alcohol with friends, only to carry them out and help pull their hair back as they vomit. This unfortunate scenario may have been followed by the young protectee thinking or saying, "Please don't tell my mom and dad I was drinking" or maybe … "with that guy."

I could give you a dozen other examples, but I think you get the point. Just like with any child, children of wealth and privilege can very often get themselves into serious trouble. The difference is there may be an armed EP agent in the car behind them, two tables away in a restaurant, escorting them overseas to a sporting event or even living in the flat above them while the young principal is attending university abroad.

The family dynamics of a very successful mother and father can sometimes bring unique psychological challenges to their children; it goes beyond my professional ability or training to speak on this subject with any authority. What I can say with *some* experience in this area (and as a father myself) is that the merging of two responsibilities by the EP agent needs to be addressed – and all parties need to agree upon rules, roles and expectations beforehand. I highly recommend that if a program is being built for families with children, it should be built on *specific* policies and procedures which are reviewed and agreed upon by the parents and the security detail managers. Without this, it will be more difficult to create the consistency necessary for a successful program and for our young principals.

I have worked for a few principals and estate managers who did not believe it was important to develop key policies and procedures; they felt it just was not in the family's personality or culture to be so rigid. Many new details and families avoid this important step in the process for various reasons – they worry policies and procedures are excessively regimented or may be too time-consuming to write, review and discuss. But in the end, if you have or are developing a full-time program involving EP, family and children, this might be the single most important part of your program's success, sustained continuity and consistency.

Even more important is understanding the need to continually update the program (and staff) as needs and requirements evolve. As the young principals grow and mature, so will their protective requirements. Without this approach or something similar, it will be a source of frustration and anxiety – and might increase the risks for everyone.

In most cases, there are considerable changes to security programs over time. If these changes are handled correctly with subtle adjustments, it will be less disruptive during transition periods for the children involved.

Normally, there will be substantial changes affecting security coverage every three to five years. The following are some occurrences or factors that could result in changes (both positive and negative) to the principals, security detail and program as a whole:

- Confidence level over time as a factor of performance
- Level of trust and comfort with the detail and its members (i.e., inappropriate action by one member of the detail can affect confidence in all of them)
- Birth of another child

- Divorce or separation of principals or protectees
- Evolving child and nanny activities
- Significant health change of a principal requiring more security support or facilitation
- Child attending preschool
- Child and parent separation anxiety regarding security concerns (e.g., overnight stays with friends)
- Increase in foreign travel and benefit of pre-advance travel agent and facilitation support
- Children starting to drive and travel with peers, including internationally
- Assistance with and facilitation of certain family lifestyle activities
- Proper or improper handling of a security incident
- Positive or negative public attention for one of the principals
- Discovery of a new threat to the family
- Emergence of a new person of interest (or change in the status of an existing one)
- Personal or family stress (which often has repercussions on the security detail)
- Improper balance of security, confidentiality and privacy

As close protection specialists assigned to families, especially on travel, things can get out of hand very quickly. On a moment's notice a dynamic family can push the capability and capacity limits of any team. Throw in the typical "can do" attitude of most EP teams with a last-minute request involving complex movements, and your best hope is your team is able to adapt to the situation adequately while keeping everyone safe and secure.

Tuk-Tuks and Another Lesson Learned

If you have ever traveled to India, you surely have your own interesting stories to tell. I find India to be both fascinating and exhausting – but somehow, it has a way of getting in your blood and leaving you wanting to experience more of this part of the world. I have been fortunate to have traveled to New Delhi, Agra, Hyderabad, Chennai and Mumbai several times; just a few of the many amazing places to explore in India.

Life there constantly challenges your senses. You try, but cannot make complete sense of the semi-controlled chaos and perpetual unpredictability of what you see, smell, hear, taste and touch: the motorcycle with, impossibly, a family of six on it; the heartrending sight of a small naked child bathing in a dirty puddle in the middle of the street in front of a five-star hotel; the unexpected and surreal appearance of sacred cows roaming freely or comfortably lying on busy streets; the enticing aromas from the spices used by street food vendors that compete with the acrid smell of raw sewage on a warm summer day. By the evening, you are left with a sensory hangover, begging for a quiet, dark hotel room to recover – and maybe a cold Kingfisher or two.

As they said in the movie *The Best Exotic Marigold Hotel* (which is appropriate given this movie took place in India): "Everything will be all right in the end. If it's not all right, then it's not yet the end." One thing you quickly learn when working in places like India is you *must* adapt, have patience and expect the unexpected. Somehow, things always seem to come together when you least expect it. As the late Secret Service agent Jerry Parr used to say (and I always felt he must be talking about India), "Everything is collapsing into place perfectly."

I had been to Agra a few times in my career to advance the Taj Mahal, both as an agent for the Agency and for corporate executives and UHNW families. The Taj Mahal is magnificent and no matter how many times I have seen it, I am still in awe of its splendor. On almost every one of these occasions, I had been driven or flown into Agra.

This time, for reasons I can't recall, I had to take the train along with another agent (our medic) to Agra in advance of our principals, a family of six. We pushed and shoved our way through the station as we tried to identify our particular train's platform, bypassing the hordes of travelers (some carrying what appeared to be everything they owned, including small farm animals).

After getting on three wrong trains, it was like a scene from *Indiana Jones* as we ran to and literally flung ourselves onto what we hoped was the right one as it was pulling away from the station. However, we quickly realized it wasn't the right train *car* – it appeared everyone here would be standing for the entire ride. We pushed through, and with my best attempts at "mujhe maaph karen" ("excuse me" in Hindi), we finally made it to our correct car and found our seats.

India has some of the most beautiful and luxurious trains in the world. They have a long history of providing exquisite experiences that take you through the enchanting countryside. You only have to think of the Maharajas' Express to be transported to another place in India's rich history.

However, that was not the train experience we were about to have. Our supposed business-class seats were no more than a straight-backed bench with a sideways view out the window. I had the middle seat and what was either a small goat or strange dog was lying between my feet. This train was not fast, and we stopped at a couple dozen small stations and road crossings along the way. At each stop, more and more people got *on,* but no one ever seemed to get *off.*

With headphones on and relaxing music in my ears, I tried to find my "happy place." Out the window, I witnessed a rolling dreamscape: a cow casually walking out of a house; an elephant crossing the train tracks; a group of half-naked men standing around a fire in a drum and cooking meat; the magnificent and breathtaking architecture of an ancient Hindu temple; a Hindu wedding lit by thousands of brilliant lights, with people dressed in their colorful very best attire and the captivating rhythm of music playing right out of a Bollywood movie.

The images in my mind from that three-hour train ride were truly unforgettable. But while it can be beautiful and heartrending at the same time, I do believe it is important to remember that viewing the lives of Indians from a distance is not a movie. There is true suffering every day there on a vast scale, with overwhelming numbers living at a level of poverty not commonly seen in most countries.

It was on this same trip I thought I almost lost my entire family of principals in a sea of "tuk-tuks" and that my EP career might be over – or, at a minimum, it would be another valuable lesson learned. As my colleague on that trip said to me, quoting from the movie *Top Gun,* "Trott, do you have the name of that truck driving school? I think I'm gonna need it."

At the time, my principals wanted to open the minds of their children to the challenges of other countries and cultures with a trip to India. We visited a local school this family had sponsored and built through their foundation. At one point, four agents and I took dad and the children (ranging from pre-teens to teens) on a tour of a local historical building in New Delhi. While it was interesting, teens are teens, no matter their wealth. They were beginning to complain to dad that they were bored. Dad tried to keep them interested in this ancient site, but they had endured all the culture they could take in one day.

Earlier that day, the kids had asked if they could ride in a tuk-tuk. They are a very common form of transportation in the congested cities throughout India, consisting of a thin metal shell around the frame of a motorized three-wheeled rickshaw or tricycle. They are generally designed for three or four people, but you can often see them packed with six passengers or more.

Being a dad myself, I noticed the look of desperation on dad's (my principal's) face, so I asked him, "If I could make it happen safely, would you want to take tuk-tuks back to the hotel instead of our vans?" With the slightly sheepish grin my principal showed sometimes, he said yes.

While they continued their walk through the ruins, I hurried back to where we parked the vans and told the guides assisting us, "Go out on the street and pick three of the best tuk-tuks you can and ensure they appear as safe as possible. And talk to the drivers – if you don't like them, I will not like them."

I then went back to dad and told him we had a plan and should be ready in 10 minutes. He informed the kids of the idea and you would have thought we were going to Disneyland. The next thing I thought was, *I'm so screwed.*

I hurried back to meet with the team, who had three tuk-tuks lined up, and briefed them on how we were going to do this. I said, "Okay, our lead van is going to pull out on the main street and each tuk-tuk will pull out, driving one behind the other." I stressed, "*Do not pass one another and do not pass the van.*"

"The van is going to lead you back to the Taj Palace. There will be another van behind all of you and you are not to fall behind this van. The first tuk-tuk will have dad and one of the children, the second tuk-tuk will have two children and one EP agent, and the third tuk-tuk will have the fourth child and our EP/medic agent."

I was going to ride in the follow van and I assigned one agent to the front van. I had a small roll of black tape in my backpack and quickly placed an "X" on the top corner of the rear of each green and yellow tuk-tuk to help me visually keep up with them.

We each got into our respective vehicles and began to drive slowly out onto the main road. This is where my "best laid plans" went completely out the window. Each tuk-tuk driver took off as if it were in the Indy 500. My brilliant plan to keep tabs on the group by tracking each black "X" quickly proved to be insufficient. In a matter of seconds, they all disappeared into a sea of dozens – then hundreds – of identical tuk-tuks. From the rear, it was like trying to focus on following one salmon swimming upstream among thousands.

(iStock Photo)

I began to imagine at least three ways this was going to go, and none of them were good. I was in communication with the front van and asked him if he had a visual on all three tuk-tuks. He replied, "I have one, no wait two, no, wait. I don't have any, no wait, there's one … nope, lost him."

This lost-and-found pattern continued for what felt like hours. I had sent five high-profile principals, members of one of the wealthiest families on Earth, off in tuk-tuks in the middle of midday New Delhi traffic. A little part in the back of my brain called common sense began to weigh in and was pounding between my eyes, yelling, *What the hell were you thinking, Trott*? I had no answer; I just hoped it would end well.

In reality, the trip only lasted four or five minutes. As we approached the curve for the entrance to the Taj Palace (where, by the way, tuk-tuks were not allowed), the lead van pulled through the gate and gave the hotel guard a forceful instruction to allow three tuk-tuks in behind him. I watched and counted … one … two … and then three tuk-tuks, and we followed them on the long winding driveway through the hotel property. At the entrance, I did a rolling dismount from the van to see if we had, in fact, the *right* tuk-tuks and all principals were safe and accounted for.

The kids and dad jumped out laughing and comparing rides like they just got off the best roller coaster ride at Magic Mountain. As we walked into the hotel, I wiped sweat from my forehead and told their dad, "You know, if this had gone horribly wrong, it was all your idea."

EP Programs For School-Age Children

Though still rare, mass shootings have become an increasing part of public life. Very often, these unspeakable incidents occur at schools – places we once considered safe enough to send our kids every day without a second's hesitation.

Hundreds of school shootings have taken place in America since the 1999 Columbine massacre, and we must understand these incidents will continue to be a fact of life for the foreseeable future.

As with any program, you should start a school-centered EP component with a TVRA focused on the school environment itself. This will help you to become more familiar with *all* the associated risks – yes, gun violence but also possibly chemical spills, natural disasters, fires and so forth.

When you have little principals in school, take the same approach as if they were a CEO at their office or headquarters. Providing protection requires planning, communication, procedures, rehearsing actions (by EP and the child) and much more. Most importantly, it requires consideration, respect and tact when working with schools and teachers.

Just as with our daily response to the threat of terrorism, we also must be reasonable with our approaches and considerations – and, most importantly, not increase our little principals' anxiety about school by immersing them in a heavy-handed EP program. Whether centered on preschoolers or college-age children studying abroad, all school programs require a great deal of discretion.

As EP professionals, you'll need to work with school administrators and often school security resource officers (sworn law enforcement officers). You'll need to gain support and cooperation for your involvement at their school, and you must realize you are representing the family on a very sensitive level. Parents will also need to be involved (if only initially) regarding the formal request for cooperation between the school and the EP team.

Principals and EP managers: Set aside a specific time to have a very open and informed discussion regarding the risks and your combined considerations on the security of your children while attending and traveling to and from school. Agree on the approach, review the procedures and work together to formulate the plan that is best for the child's physical and emotional safety.

I'd also like to say something relevant to EP programs engaging in protective intelligence and threat management. Each of these horrible school shooting events is different, but many seem to follow a similar pattern: A child who is suffering from some sort of mental health condition and/or is the victim of bullying resorts to taking a weapon to school and doing what was once considered unthinkable but has become sadly familiar – or is even, in some instances, predictable.

This was the case in Parkland, Florida, where the 19-year-old shooter practically provided all the warning signals *right out in public* before the day of his rampage. These overt reports and signs were the reason the FBI and many others admitted their own bureaucratic/procedural failures after not properly following up on reports that might have stopped this horrific event.

This tragic lesson learned is just as important for EP teams with a robust protective intelligence and threat management program. Despite all the sophisticated software and algorithms for tracking threat messages on social media, "see something, say something" campaigns and call-in tip lines, our response and follow-up must still be swift, judicious and effective. If it isn't, the system has a big hole that needs to be repaired before the next warning signs are missed, leading to another tragic ending. This is one disturbing trend I know we all would like to see vanish before the next potential shooting.

The Nanny Connection

In recent decades, there has been a major increase in "new wealth" associated with many professional couples waiting until later in life to start a family. Therefore, the subject of professional childcare providers (nannies and/or mannies) helping to raise children is perhaps more of interest now than it has been in previous years. (For simplicity, I will reference them only as "nannies" in this section.)

I didn't put this topic last in this chapter because it's the least important consideration in a family EP program – far from it. In fact, the proper relationship between nannies and security will be one of the most dynamic components of your family's protective environment – it's so important, you cannot discuss family protection without it. (And for both the security professionals as well as nannies, it is hard not to become attached to our little principals!)

Nannies to UHNW families should receive training for proper responses, countersurveillance, anti-kidnapping measures, situational awareness, driving, first aid and more. They must also be educated on effective/appropriate communication with any security staff; confidentiality considerations should be noted and explained. In most cases, nannies and the EP assigned to the family work together, but this is not always the case; when they do not, it can be the cause of unnecessary stress for all.

In addition, respectful treatment of nannies by the principals is important. Providing proper sleeping accommodations, working hours for the nannies and staff, etc., is crucial for them to give children the best care possible. Unfortunately, I have witnessed too many instances of exploitation of nannies, especially those working extremely long days under intense stress while caring for newborn babies.

As for confidentiality, this might present the most delicate balancing act of a career for a close protection officer. We protective agents must be cognizant that, because of their necessary proximity to the principals/parents, nannies are privy to an enormous amount of confidential information (either overheard or from conversations they're a part of). The nannies need to understand this is *privileged* information – and, in many cases, is not to be shared with security.

Security professionals, especially close protection types, like information – e.g., "What time are we leaving the house for the airport?" "Is everyone leaving together?" "Do we know when the family is returning?" "Are other people joining us on the trip?" I could go on and on with examples. Because nannies might often have heard this information, security will sometimes try to elicit answers from nannies as if they're undercover sources.

Sometimes, principals encourage this level of teamwork between the nannies and security, and sometimes they don't want it to take place. Either way, it is up to the principals to set the tone and give examples as to what can be shared and what should not be. It should never be assumed by principals that nannies or security will do what you consider is acceptable, even with the best of their intentions.

To illustrate some more of the challenging dynamics regarding nannies and security working together, I reached out to a good friend who has been a nanny for more than 15 years for several UHNW and high-profile families. Paige* has traveled the world with her little clients

---

* Because of the confidentiality and sensitivity of her position (and out of respect for her current and former clients), I am not going to use her real name. "Paige" holds a master's degree in Marital and Family Therapy with a specialization in Children's Alternative Treatment Modalities with an emphasis in expressive arts therapeutics. She is also an active member of the Association for Prenatal and Perinatal Psychology and Health (APPNPAH).

and I have witnessed her skills in action, seeing firsthand why she is sought after as a professional nanny. This woman is much more than just a nanny to the children and principals she works with – she is the very essence of a childcare professional.

When I sat down with Paige, one of the first things we talked about was both the negative and positive effects on a young child of having security and nannies working together to provide them care.

She explained it can definitely be difficult (if not impossible at very young ages) for small children to understand the differences between caregivers and family members. Children are bundles of excitement and unbridled affection; as a result, they may struggle with understanding the "time and place" for certain behaviors in the relationship between families and staff. Further complicating things is the fact that staff are likely present in the household and other intimate environments such as hotels, yachts and private aircraft.

In general, most families are warm and receptive to the staff members who care for them and their precious children. In fact, for small children, nannies and security teams can easily be required to take on the role of a sort of extended family in their daily lives. While the attachment that may develop with hired providers is learned rather than innate, these caregivers do become a source of security and comfort for youngsters – they're the ones who often meet their needs more frequently in a parent-child manner.

In Paige's experience, a positive relationship between a nanny and the security can assist in providing a seamless and consistent environment for the child to thrive under circumstances that could otherwise induce strain – e.g., travel to very exotic and unfamiliar locales.

Paige stresses children thrive on consistency and familiarity – particularly small children and infants who learn about their world and express their needs through cues. For instance, Paige said she has seen children who refrain from going to the bathroom or limit their eating as signs of distress during travel because familiar components of life are missing. The needs of the parents and the children can sometimes be at odds in these circumstances, which is how the consistency of the nanny and even EP can play a crucial role in their sense of safety and security in an unfamiliar world.

Paige explained this can be further studied in the works of psychologist Erik Erikson, where the first years (newborn to three) are based on a trust/mistrust schema on the consistency of care provided to them. The easiest example of this can be seen in an infant or toddler who recognizes normal sleep time because of dim lighting, a warm bath and the familiar sound of their beloved lullaby.

This trust can even simply come out of a caregiver recognizing the infant's nonverbal cues that they are hungry (e.g., bringing their fists to their mouth and sucking, turning their cheek). Seamless interaction of staff members and parents will facilitate appropriate responses to those cues – e.g., providing favorite toys, snacks, car seats, play equipment or even medicine when the need arises. This will ensure peace of mind for the parents and foster the overall health of the child by making them feel safe and secure.

Paige could not reiterate enough the need for cues of familiarity. As children grow up (starting at around ages five to seven years old), their needs can change depending on their gender. Boys around this age still often seek the nurturance of a female provider but become most interested in young men they can look up to. It is not uncommon for boys around age seven to be drawn toward engaging with security professionals in sports talk or learning about those with military or security backgrounds. Parents should welcome this even if it seems to come from a place of infatuation.

Many fathers in the corporate world may feel threatened by this dynamic. I've even seen our little principals get off the family plane and run over to say hello to their EP agent before hugging their dads. However, young boys are likely to pass through this stage; it in no way undermines the parent-child relationship (unless the child feels the need to defend their interest in other male examples in the family EP circle). Paige stated it is important to know that, according to Jean Piaget's theory of developmental psychology, the years between two and seven are considered "preoperational" and are egocentric – though this egocentrism may not be what you are thinking. Children at this stage are simply unable to grasp a worldview outside of their own. They may not realize their attachment and expressions of endearment toward staff – a tender and nurtured bond with non-biological caregivers rather than a nature-based attachment with a relative (e.g., mother and child) – can cause discomfort to their parents.

Children in general are fun to watch grow up, regardless of economic wealth or status. Paige told a story of a toddler who, oddly enough, was beginning to understand the staff support around him. This young child would pick up a toy phone and pretend to call the family driver (named John) while at hotels or in the park – or even at his preschool. She would watch from the observation room at times, seeing he did not have the verbal skills or symbolic thinking to grasp John's exact role when his teachers would ask him who he was. The parents were fuzzy on what the response should be as well, so the nannies always called him a family friend.

Information sharing is another key topic in the relationship between nannies, security and families. I will admit this is a delicate balance sometimes and doesn't always go off without a hitch. In my positions where I have managed EP agents working with nannies, I would often consider this zone of information sharing to be difficult.

Paige described an occasion where a lack of communication led to an embarrassing situation. While tending to her infant charge in New York City, a nurse-nanny noticed someone was following her. Unbeknownst to her, multiple security teams from the family's office had been tasked to loosely shadow her and the CEO that day. At some point, they lost coverage of the CEO, so they then placed more coverage on the nurse-nanny, anticipating the CEO (father) would soon join his family.

The EP detail shadowed her from a distance, but the observant nanny grew nervous because she didn't recognize the men following her, so she led them on foot to a nearby police station.

This made for a bit of a fiasco with the police. She had signed an NDA and did not want to say she was working for someone that was high profile. But her situation did require some explanation: She was an

African-American with a small, blonde-haired, blue-eyed baby saying she would not answer questions about her child – but kept demanding the two men outside be questioned. The police eventually questioned the two EP agents, only to find out they were there to assist her.

All of this took place because the parents had not communicated with security and nanny staff, and therefore laid a faulty foundation that resulted in a day of chaos while the parents were attending a very important event in the city.

I asked Paige to describe a few more pitfalls that security and nanny combinations should avoid during a child's early developmental years. She explained that all stages of childhood benefit from self-sufficiency. Children's growth occurs because of their struggles and the opportunity to overcome setbacks and challenges. The ages of one-and-a-half to five, in particular, revolve around autonomy and initiative versus shame or guilt. As a result, it is vital to impart flexibility as a life skill in the daily activity of a normal child, as children can learn to embrace change. Having staff should not deny children the opportunity to grow in these ways. Paige recommended an excellent read for further information regarding these concepts in the book *The Price of Privilege* by Madeleine Levine.

For families who have staff to assist them with the dynamic world in which they live, it can take a small or large "village." When it comes to a child's or several children's well-being, those hired to help with the responsibility of their care have a specific role and must work in unison together – but perhaps, more importantly, understand what that means and looks like for all involved.

Inevitably, a child who is raised with the care of a nanny and/or protective services may see those closest to them through their young lives come and go. When a unique bond has been formed between the caregiver and child, separation may feel no different than a divorce to the child and can be sad and confusing. I have been in the unfortunate position of having to write a letter to a young teenage principal explaining why I was no longer able to be supporting him or her because I took a new position, but I wanted to provide some clarity on my departure so the child did not take my leaving personally.

In these unique cases, the parents and nanny or EP member should discuss the method for delivering this news and any follow-up communication between the two if both sides believe it would be helpful and appropriate. While many nannies, EP agents and little principals have all shed some tears when saying their final goodbyes, ideally, the relationships can and should have a beneficial lifelong effect on the children.

Me climbing over one of several obstacles we had to navigate during a military competition held near the Air Force Academy in Colorado Springs. This obstacle was eventually eliminated because of its height and the many severe injuries sustained from falls.

After attending the U.S. Army's Survival, Evasion, Resistance and Escape (SERE) training in Germany, I returned to assist another class as part of a team using U.S. Army Black Hawk helicopters to search for trainees during their multi-day escape and evasion exercise in the German forest.

Our EST using explosive breaching methods to blow doors during live fire assault exercises.

Our Air Force Emergency Service Team (EST) at a French commando school on the French/German border. Third from the right is our head German SEK instructor and my good friend, Horst Mehlinger. (I'm sixth from the left.)

A USAF ground defense graduation class in Germany. SSgt. Garth Freund (far left), Sgt. Tony Weatherholt (far right) and I were instructors. Tony and I were also the first two instructors for the newly created Air Force Ground Defense Readiness and Evaluation Center (GDREC) headquartered in Germany.

After the military and with the CIA, on occasion I would be back in Germany on protective missions and reconnect with my friend, Horst Mehlinger (formerly of the German SEK).

(Photo courtesy of Marc Heesters)

On August 28, 1988, planes from the Italian Air Force collided during an air show (Flugtag) at Ramstein Air Base in Germany where I was assigned. Approximately 70 spectators were killed and hundreds were seriously injured.

The solo plane flown by lead pilot Lt. Col. Ivo Nutarelli takes a path directly into the crowd of spectators. It was determined that he died instantly when he collided with the other planes before crashing to the ground.

(Photo courtesy of Mannie Garcia)

(Sipa Press/Arnaud Beinat)

This photo captured either me or Garth Freund running toward the crash site. As part of the EST, we were dressed in our black tactical uniforms and were well-prepared for our counterterrorism role – but we didn't expect anything like this.

The solo plane left a path of carnage and destruction before striking a refrigerator trailer – which probably prevented even further injuries and fatalities.

(Photo courtesy of Mannie Garcia)

I was the primary security driver for the brigadier general who commanded the 316th Air Division and Kaiserslautern Military Community. Kevin was our backup driver and together we put man autobahn miles on this armored Mercedes. This photo was taken in front of portions of the recentl torn-down Berlin Wall.

Receiving an Air Force Commendation Medal from Colonel Dieter Heinz, OSI District 70 Commander, for my undercover efforts while assigned to the Joint Drug Enforcement Team (JDET) in Europe.

Preparing to return to the U.S. after six years in Europe. After my last assignment as an undercover narcotics investigator, I had to lose my long mustache and hair – back under military regulations.

Me and a colleague at a U.S. Army base in southwestern Europe to resupply while on a protective mission.

Driving through bombed-out portions of Kosovo on a protective mission with our principal shortly after the 1999 U.S. air campaign had stopped – most Serbian forces had fled the area.

Taking off in Black Hawk helicopters with the CIA's Director and several senior officials during a trip to Asia.

In southwestern Europe while on an extended tour of duty with our CIA overseas protection team.

In Amman, Jordan, with the CIA's director after King Hussein died following a battle with cancer.

King Hussein's body was placed on the back of an open military vehicle and driven through the city Amman on the day of his burial so all Jordanians could say goodbye to their beloved King.

Crossing the Elisabeth Bridge in Budapest with the CIA's director and our protective detail.

In Germany with our local police escorts for the CIA's director. After being assigned to the country with the USAF for many years, it was always good to return.

Agent Mike Chang and I are looking into North Korea from an outpost along the Korean DMZ.

Being briefed by a U.S. Army commander inside the famous "blue hut" at the DMZ with CIA Directo͏ Tenet, his wife Stephanie (far right) and CIA Deputy Director John McLaughlin. A North Korea͏ soldier looks through the window trying to identify who was in the room with all the extra security I'm standing behind the commander. Agent Dan O'Conner (Doc) is standing behind the Director an͏ Agent Warren Stembridge is in the white coat in the back.

When the CIA Director or Deputy Director would travel overseas, we would sometimes use cargo aircraft to support our missions.

On a "shadow boat" in the Red Sea following the CIA Director.

Just a few of the many fascinating and historical places I've had the honor and privilege to visit with my principals or before their arrival.

(Above) The Taj Mahal in Agra, (right) the Kremlin and Red Square in Moscow, and (below) Pyramids of Giza in Egypt.

During one of my trips to Jordon, the CIA Director visited the historic site of Petra. Our protective detail is coming out of "The Treasury" (Al-Khazneh).

Preparing to go to work while in a Middle East location. Often, we would wear a suit but still carried the other tools of our protective trade.

This photo was taken during the 1999 ceremony for the renaming of the CIA headquarters compound in Langley to the George Bush Center for Intelligence. Included in this photo is former President Bush (41), who passed away in 2018. This ceremony included many former directors of central intelligence, including then-serving Director George Tenet.

Back row: (L to R) former Director Robert Gates, Director George Tenet, Special Agent Larry Nissen, former Director William Webster, Special Agent John Barchett, former President George H.W. Bush, Special Agent Joe Kuzel (Chief of the DCI's Protective Staff), Special Agent Dan ("Doc") O'Conne and Lynda Webster (wife of William Webster).

Front row: Special Agent Mike Trott and Special Agent Mike Chang.

The faces of the other individuals are required to be redacted, but they were all special agents on th DCI's protective staff.

George H. W. Bush

June 12, 1924 – November 30, 2018

George H. W. Bush was the only director of the CIA
to ever become President of the United States.

His Secret Service detail continued their duty after his death
as pallbearers at certain services. They remained with him
until he was laid to rest at the George Bush Library in College
Station, Texas. His protective detail tweeted this last message at
the end of their coverage, using his Secret Service call sign:

*Timberwolf's Detail concluded at 0600 hours on December 7, 2018
with no incidents to report at the George Bush Presidential Library –
College, Station, Texas.
God speed former
President George H.W. Bush –
you will be missed by all of us.*

-Bush Protective Division

Receiving an "Exceptional Performance" award from Director Tenet. (This is one of the few pictures that would ever capture the Director sporting a goatee. Rumor was neither Mrs. Tenet nor President Clinton liked it. It didn't last long.)

After the military and CIA, I transitioned to corporate and private sectors. Travels and missions continued to encompass immense variety, including this high profile wedding my principals attended at a castle in northern Scotland.

Below: I took this picture from the rooftop of the Taj Mahal Palace hotel in Mumbai of the famous waterfront around the Gateway of India monument. We received a briefing from a hotel employee describing his account of the 2008 terrorist attack on the hotel and the city of Mumbai.

Ten Pakistani men associated with the terror group Lashkar-e-Taiba seized the city for four days and killed more than 160 people. Reportedly, some of the terrorists came ashore from small boats near this waterfront.

From 2008 to 2010, Cheryl and I lived in Abu Dhabi, UAE. One of their most beautiful structures (completed while we were there) was the Sheikh Zayed Grand Mosque. This truly magnificent architectural design lights up the Abu Dhabi skyline at night.

While I had traveled throughout the Middle East region for many years, it was a unique experience to share it with Cheryl while living in the UAE. Above we're enjoying true local hospitality in the middle of the Wadi Rum desert in Jordan as a Bedouin invited us into his tent and served us hot tea.

Reassigned to Texas from Germany, I would often assist in my son Jonathan's Taekwondo school as an instructor. This promotion class included Jonathan (front row, center frame with American flag patch) who was nine years old at that time.

Jonathan and me in Washington D.C., at the same time as I was preparing to relocate to Abu Dhabi. He was returning to Iraq the next day after being home on military leave.

After the military, Jonathan continued serving as a contractor in the various Middle East locations. This picture was taken just hours before his base came under attack.

Mom and dad having
a little impromptu
fun and fulfilling
my dad's childhood
nickname – Trouble.

My wife Cheryl
and I after being
married in Aspen,
Colorado in 2004.

When you think of writers who might have drink or two (or more) while finishing their manuscripts, you might think of Ernest Hemingway sitting at his typewriter in Key West with a glass of whiskey, or John le Carré sipping his favorite spirit as he crafted The Spy Who Came in from the Cold.

Former CIA employees who decide to write a book (fiction or non-fiction), or publish a manuscript or paper are legally bound to submit and receive approval from the CIA Publication Review Board (PRB) before going to print. This process can often delay a publication from a few months to a few years or longer.

As a former employee, I understand the reasons behind not disclosing information that may still be considered classified. While I know not all authors drink, I do recall sitting down with a shot of tequila after receiving the first round of redactions in my manuscript from the PRB.

I might have had a couple more before finishing the book.

"ETHICS IS KNOWING THE
DIFFERENCE BETWEEN WHAT
YOU HAVE A RIGHT TO DO
AND WHAT IS RIGHT TO DO."

- POTTER STEWART

CHAPTER VI

HUMAN COMPLEXITIES OF
CLOSE PROTECTION

O NCE YOUR EXECUTIVE PROTECTION program has been established, you will no doubt run into issues along the way – some of which you would never have anticipated. Because EP is such a human and intensely personal service, many conflicts or challenges can be magnified with full-time programs. Following are a few of the complexities you may encounter as your EP program develops, grows and evolves.

Operational Threat Transference and Overprotection

In most cases, a good EP or risk specialist has done their own Red Team effort against their principal (even if just conceptually) in order to provide a snapshot of concerns they need to address. This should be done at various times throughout the lifecycle of a permanent program.

When these mini-assessments are conducted or a new concern surfaces, it is very important for principals to know the motives or experiences behind these concerns. After all, many EP specialists themselves possess (or are at least very familiar with) the same skillsets as the threatening actors they're defending against. Many also have access to and have reviewed real accounts of successful and attempted attacks, kidnappings, assassinations, extortions and other associated risks – and very possibly have had their own close calls and survived attacks while protecting someone else.

Enter the EP dynamic and potential pitfall of what I call the "over-protected" – a situation where principals are protected against threats that may not reach the level of a true risk. This can be a difficult balance between being proactive or prepared to be responsive on the one hand and overprotected on the other. In many (but not all) cases, this "inflation" of perceived threats comes from the EP specialists themselves, not the protectee.

For example, if an EP specialist's primary experience is operating in high-risk areas and being ready for an attack every time they leave their safe haven, they may struggle with providing their principals the appropriate level of security in the normal world. This is what I refer to as "operational threat transference." Since September 11, 2001, many brave men and women who have deployed to high-threat regions of the world (or have been assigned to high-profile, high-risk principals) have returned to civilian positions but still carry with them the need to operate at a level that may not be in line with the actual risks or threats faced by their new principal.

I recall being caught in this trap myself in the early 1990s after returning from serving six years in Germany. In those days, I was always on guard protecting my principals from Red Army Faction terrorists, leading a tactical unit and serving as an undercover narcotics agent. This lifestyle often included daily checks of my car for potential explosive devices and consistently checking my mirror for hostile surveillance.

When I returned to the U.S., I had to readjust – and realize there was not a bad guy behind every dark pair of sunglasses or a sophisticated roadside bomb near every bicycle or parked car, and sometimes that car behind me with two guys was really just a car with two guys traveling in the same direction. Paranoia, when tempered and controlled, can be a very valuable and human emotion and a personal survival skill. But when fear is out of control, so too is the chaos and anxiety that can follow.

When an EP operator or security manager expresses a level of concern regarding a possible risk, take a moment for an honest discussion. Be aware that, in most cases, they just want to protect you and your family and not let something happen to you which perhaps they previously experienced.

Mutual Trust and Respect

What can make or break any full-time EP program is a low level of trust and respect between the principal and the provider or team. Principals, you have to trust the capabilities, judgment and confidentiality of your EP providers. EP professionals, you have to trust the access and accuracy of information you receive in order to provide the appropriate level of protection. Your relationship with the principal, or even their staff and executive assistant, will be crucial in your ability to fulfill your duties successfully.

There are many levels of trust and respect to be found between principals and EP providers. I've seen these qualities grow over time, even in cases where both have been previously thrown into question. Through the years, the best experiences I've had with my principals were the result of an honest level of mutual trust and respect. Because of that, our teams were able to provide what I felt was the best security possible for our principals.

A loss of trust can significantly reduce the effectiveness of a program and even become a major vulnerability, jeopardizing the safety of not only the principals, but the EP provider(s) themselves. For example, when trust is lost or damaged, a principal might not give the EP provider all the information needed to advance a meeting, travel location or activity. This is ultimately harmful to both sides – the principal doesn't get the assistance needed and the provider may make errors due to lack of information.

As with any relationship, business or personal, when trust is lost and can't be renewed, a change is often needed. For the principal, it might mean finding a new EP team leader; in some cases, I've seen an entire team replaced.

Poor decisions or personal conflicts may not be the only causes of loss of trust; a general lack of confidence or observation of poor EP habits will also factor in greatly. In some cases, principals may believe a member of their EP team may have inappropriately divulged personal information. In other cases, poor or unsafe driving skills make the principal uncomfortable. At times, it may just come down to personality differences or clashes, which can be the hardest to overcome.

Whatever factor causes a rift in the relationship between principal and provider, open communication may help to resolve the conflict and rebuild the loss of trust – or simply reinforce the fact the professional relationship is beyond repair and changes need to be made.

Crossing the Line and Professional Ethics

Practitioners – this part is for you: *Think twice, act once.* As a carpenter's apprentice in my teens, I learned very early the valuable lesson of "measure twice, cut once." This is a rule I've tried to utilize in my personal and professional life. (Of course, thinking twice but still coming up with the same wrong answer isn't helpful either.)

The very nature of a job in executive protection often includes invading personal spaces – and is where both the principal and the agents can "blur the lines," so to speak. Crossing these lines of professional ethics will always be one of the most difficult issues to navigate and balance between you, your protective family and your EP detail. Why? Because it is human nature. We are not computers or robots. It is a delicate balance between professional and personal – and if you're not careful, you can step over but can never step back.

We've seen this play out in some extremely high-profile and public cases involving lawsuits, settlements and agents being blacklisted. I've seen all types of security and EP agents abuse their titles, positions and privileged authority. Many corporate and private EP agents have taken certain liberties of utilizing their principal's resources for their own purposes. Some officers and agents indulge in unethical behaviors alongside or in the presence of their principals. This behavior may also extend to contract EP agents.

As for relationships that cross the line: It is natural for people to care about one another, especially when they spend so much time together – often in circumstances where the protectee feels vulnerable.

(All you have to do is look at how many agents have either dated or married their principals.) From the Secret Service and other government agents to Hollywood bodyguards to international royalty, it happens. When it does, it is the fault of both the principal and the agent and is difficult to navigate appropriately. In most cases, it's time for a reassignment, career change or retirement for the EP agent if the relationship is that important and both sides want it to continue.

However, I must hold the agent primarily responsible for crossing that line. Agents are most aware of the vulnerabilities of their principals and should be very careful not to take advantage of this knowledge. This does not only apply to improper relationships between principals and their protectors, but extends to their family, friends and inappropriate corporate relationships as well.

Some EP details and agents can also be guilty of entitlement. Just because the principals are most often UHNW individuals or families, this does not mean their success, advantages or privilege transfer to the agent or detail. It can be a difficult trap to avoid, and often many principals are very generous. But the individual agent or security contractor must resist this snare – I've seen it happen too many times.

I must admit I have mumbled words of frustration when I've put my principal on his large private jet in a foreign country, only to watch it take off to fly them directly home to the same city where I live – while I must make my way back to the hotel and wait another day to catch my multiple flights before getting home 36 hours later.

The bottom line: It is not our jet, our yacht or our Ferrari. EP professionals need to keep proper perspective and stay focused on their jobs and performance. And if you are invited to fly with them on their private airplane, consider it a privilege, not an obligation on the part of the principal.

Maintaining the Right Operational Mindset

You'll notice I have frequently used the term "mindset" in this book. Whether you are the protector or protectee, mindset is a very important element of close protection. For the protectee, appropriate mindset can also apply to how you conduct yourself around your protectors, in private and public. Some principals are very engaging and even entertaining with their EP teams. Sometimes this might be a healthy way to reduce stress or, in some cases, for the principal to let their guard down in a safe and friendly environment.

While many principals can quickly make the transition from friendly talk/bantering back to business, I've seen several instances where one or more members of a security team miss the cue and continue this "privileged banter." Worse yet is when this relaxed mindset continues in a public arena where the principal has already made the transition.

While I'm not trying to make this complicated, the delicate balance requires mindfulness and discipline on the part of all members of the EP team. These lapses in judgment and behavior will be noticed and can spell the end of an agent's tenure, and sometimes even that of the entire team.

Another mindset challenge I have observed through the years is that former military members, special operations professionals and law enforcement officers (as well as those from other "serious mindset" occupations) will at times possess a certain rigid posture. Individuals with this kind of intense professional focus can have difficulty adjusting to times when a more relaxed attitude is more appropriate.

During my first few years in the military, even when dressed in civilian clothing while flying on a commercial flight or sitting in a restaurant or public place, people would often ask me what branch of the military I was in. I wasn't in uniform or carrying anything related, but my haircut and demeanor would immediately make my "mindset" evident.

In the years since, I've learned to adjust. One of the ways I've learned to utilize a more "casual" mindset without drawing attention has been by pretending to talk on my cell phone; this allows me to walk or stand where I need to be or conduct surveillance without being questioned about my presence (for some reason, if you're making a cell phone call, you somehow belong wherever you are).

Other times, I've sat in hotel lobbies with a newspaper and a cup of coffee while waiting for my principal to exit an elevator or meeting room. Then, through a radio click or text advising a driver or team member that we were coming out, I would slowly join my principal by leading or following him/her out the door at an appropriate distance depending on the situation or environment in order to avoid attracting attention. My principal was always informed of this tactic so they would never think I was being lazy or inattentive. I was simply blending into the environment and not drawing attention to them or myself.

Though it can be difficult to fully develop this ability, it is *essential* to be able to shift mindsets regarding a specific task or transition from one set of skills to another in seconds. Some law enforcement or military people who haven't had the time to make the transition into EP can find it difficult to oscillate between mindsets in this way.

Take, for example, an extreme low-profile protection situation where an EP team member needs to completely blend into an environment and not draw attention (as a security person or a suspicious person) to themselves, their principal(s) and/or other detail members. This takes a specific chameleon mindset and sometimes training to perfect, which can be challenging for many serious-minded individuals, as their demeanors can broadcast a certain professional persona. While you may think you have everyone around you fooled about who you are, most of the time you don't.

Obviously, the chameleon mindset isn't appropriate for every situation. In the event a dangerous situation occurs and you need to respond quickly, your game face has to change to reveal the serious person you've been trying to conceal. You must immediately perform using a very different mindset which might require aggression and deliberate action.

Another mindset example relates to conducting surveillance. Some current or former law enforcement officers have extensive training in surveillance techniques and are extremely good at adapting to their environments or achieving a certain "cover of action" mindset. Not all have this skill. Law enforcement and military professionals without this training or the proper mindset can simply look like a police officer or soldier in plain clothes when they're trying to blend in. It's often their dress and demeanor, an intense stare or scanning motion, purposeful movement, crossing of arms, etc., that will make people take notice.

I've managed large surveillance operations requiring dozens of surveillance teams; for some officers, breaking the law enforcement or military persona can be difficult, which is completely understandable. If you've spent the majority of your years in a uniform, interacting with the public from an authoritative or investigative position, this mindset can be a hard habit to break.

Please understand, I'm *not* implying most former law enforcement or military individuals are not capable of providing physical protection, detecting a person of interest, having a good sense of situational awareness or evacuating their principals from harm's way. But if you're trying to develop a low-profile detail using low-profile tradecraft, some additional training might be required to take the right people with great skills to the next level.

Of course, if the protective detail, principal and/or environment require a deterrent posture because of risk or threat, the "stand-out" mindset is more appropriate than a lethargic or docile demeanor trying to conceal your true purpose. In some cases, a hybrid approach or having more than one team member in various positions may be the best solution.

Every situation is different. As an EP specialist, you must be able to adjust your persona but always retain the same underlying mindset of awareness, reaction and protection. If you don't fit into the environment, you'll stick out like the only red lemon on a lemon tree – but, depending on the mission, maybe that's okay too.

The Facilitation Factor

Any EP program not derived from a threat, vulnerability or risk and which might be mainly seen as a convenience or facilitation (e.g., driving, travel support, equipment and asset management, special projects) should be recognized for what it is, as well as what it is not.

In many cases, the risk assessment recommendations will include some of these support activities as part of the mitigation strategies. In other cases, the risk (or lack thereof) might not necessarily warrant all the levels of support under an EP banner but are still requested by the principals as a level of service and an ease of facilitation. To receive levels of assistance that may fall under the EP purview without overt risk is perfectly acceptable – as long as the principal is clear they are there primarily for facilitation and peace of mind.

Discussing these expectations will help both sides understand what is protection-related and what is service-related. Yes, an element can fit into both categories. But, for instance, hiring an extremely qualified EP professional with years of experience who is converted to a principal's driver or asked daily to run errands will generally not result in a long-lasting professional relationship – unless the EP professional is committed to the reduced level of EP service.

Sometimes this can be confusing on both sides and results in inadequate performance by EP providers and dissatisfaction on the part of the principals. Having an honest discussion and coming to agreement beforehand about expectations will eliminate high staff turnover and increase job satisfaction for your EP personnel – and should ultimately provide better satisfaction for the principal.

I have only addressed a few of the many complexities you might encounter in a close protection environment. I'm sure principals, operators and managers could all weigh in with the situations they have encountered, which may have required policy changes and/or the dismissal of personnel. The best tactic is to address circumstances or concerns when they arise instead of allowing any negative situation to get worse when it permeates the entire program.

Taking a Deep Breath

Our exploration of the EP world has just taken us through a very wide range of topics. While I can't sum it all up in just a few takeaway points, I can tell you this: For full-time protection, an EP program is a highly evolutionary process and requires a healthy understanding of everyone's roles and expectations – which takes some time and effort to develop.

And I'll reiterate: This level of personalized service normally goes beyond just protecting another person's body. The true goal is to weave protective services seamlessly into the fabric of the principal's life, giving them peace of mind with a minimal amount of compromise to their normal lifestyle.

In most cases, it isn't necessary to have all the answers all at once, but you will need a methodology regarding the process – and you can certainly make changes along the way (whether you're the principal or the practitioner). Communication, trust and confidence are the keys to establishing any relationship, just as they are in forming an EP program. In addition, if the SAFE approach is missing one of the four elements, you'll be constantly trying to address inefficiencies and deficiencies, which will hinder your efforts.

In the next chapter, I'll share reflections (as much as I can) on some of the most memorable times of my life and career. My intention is to give readers of all levels of interest in EP a bit of insight into the people that put their lives on the line for others every day.

As I mentioned before, these are not just my stories alone. They are also those of the many men and women I've had the honor and privilege to work with through the years. Through these accounts, I hope to provide some insight on how we gain our own perspectives – and ultimately the events and decisions that have influenced our paths in this unique profession.

"TRAVELING – FIRST, IT LEAVES
YOU SPEECHLESS, THEN TURNS
YOU INTO A STORYTELLER."

– IBN BATTUTA

CHAPTER VII

REFLECTIONS, TRAVELS
AND EXPERIENCES

ANYONE IN THE EP field who has had the unique opportunity and privilege to travel while protecting others will surely have their own unique stories to tell. In some cases, many of our experiences will have similarities and parallel one another.

During my time as a military and government instructor, I came to understand and utilize a very valuable tool for conceptual training. If you can relate a story or symbolic event to the subject you are teaching, in many cases there is no greater method by which to create "ah-ha moments" for your audience and underscore a lesson.

It's for this very reason I have carefully recounted a few events (both here and previously in the book) that I hope will educate, motivate, inform and possibly just entertain. Most of all, these stories involve many of my good friends and colleagues who have walked the same path.

I feel blessed that, in addition to being able to serve my country, my employers and my protectees, this career path has allowed me to live overseas for nearly 10 years in total. As a security professional, I've had the unique opportunity to operate in over 90 countries, and in some cases many times over. Traveling in foreign countries is when I feel most engaged in life; anytime you're out of your comfort zone and taking in unfamiliar sights, sounds and smells, your senses are all on high alert.

Having worked alongside so many colleagues, associates and international counterparts around the world, it can sometimes feel like my last 30 years have been akin to the late, great Anthony Bourdain's *Parts Unknown* (one of my favorite travel shows), sprinkled with images from movies and series like *The Bodyguard, James Bond, Jason Bourne, Rush, Ocean's Eleven* (long story), *In the Line of Fire* and sometimes even *Driving Miss Daisy* and *Guarding Tess.* If you're in this profession long enough and experience various protective environments, you've had many starring roles and stories to tell – or not to tell.

EP operators can have the opportunity to explore and experience the world in many unique ways. We sit at the tables of our host nation advisors and local counterparts as we define and/or negotiate (or, at times, demand) our security needs and requirements for our soon-arriving principals. During lunches and often late-night dinners, we share local food while having discussions about security, intelligence, tactics and guns – which often then lead to conversations on history, religion, politics and, in some cases, the telling of a few stories (and maybe, here and there, a few white lies).

The list of what we do can be long and varied: We work with local resources and assets, review intelligence, drive multiple advance routes our principals will be traveling, identify hospitals and other important locations, and rehearse arrivals and departures at airports, hotels and other venues to ensure we know our directions and associated risks or concerns. We review motorcade lineups, conduct preregistration at hotels, do technical sweeps and secure rooms from hostile technologies. We obtain additional equipment and resources we feel are essential to our success and our principals' security. In many cases, we receive the opportunity to preview special event locations where our principals will be during their trips – all the time identifying any threats, risks and vulnerabilities along the way.

In some cases, we meet with the local U.S. Embassy's Regional Security Officer (RSO) to let them know we're in their area and get updates about the local threat and risk climate. Sometimes, we might have coffee or lunch with former security or intelligence contacts or colleagues who have taken positions overseas in order to elicit any additional color on the local risks of which we should be aware.

Throughout my career, I have never taken for granted the incredibly rare opportunities I have been fortunate to have experienced – being allowed inside the walls of the Kremlin, seeing under the floor of the Taj Mahal, viewing rarely seen tunnels of great Egyptian pyramids and going on African safaris. I have been inside presidential palaces and retreats, aboard yachts and have flown on private jets. I've walked along the Korean demilitarized zone (DMZ), slept in true castles that were previously occupied by kings, and have seen some of the world's most expensive real estate and greatest historical sites.

I have also seen some of the most deplorable conditions in refugee camps, war zones and some of the poorest countries on Earth. The stark contrast has always left me shaking my head. As a human with even an ounce of compassion for another human, you can't help but be affected by the disparity between the two worlds, which should leave you thinking, *Where can I make a difference and how do I help a village?*

While living in Abu Dhabi in the United Arab Emirates in 2009, my wife and I were sitting on the beach behind the Emirates Palace under the desert stars, watching a documentary on a large outdoor movie screen. It was narrated by Ben Kingsley and was about Ibn Battuta, the Moroccan scholar, explorer and world traveler who said: "Traveling – first, it leaves you speechless, then turns you into a storyteller." How right he was.

I am going to take some time now to share reflections as to where I got my start and what has shaped me as a security professional in my career. Some of these events and experiences formed my personal perspectives I still draw upon today. Perhaps most importantly, these experiences illustrate how I developed my fondness, enthusiasm and passion for helping to protect others, even when principals don't know just how far we go.

Where It All Began

I was born in Knoxville, Tennessee, in the foothills of the Great Smoky Mountains, and spent a great deal of my youth with my family camping and exploring the outdoors. I have two older brothers (John and Jeff) and was raised by two very loving and dedicated parents, Vernon and Wanda. In a strong and composed, yet undeniable manner, my father was effective in ensuring the boys respected our mother, our elders, our military, our country and our flag. It was Mom who ensured we knew God and His love and taught us about faith. I am eternally grateful to them both for instilling these life lessons.

My father was injured while working as a government employee and, at age 39, was medically retired on a low pension in the early 1970s. While we would not have even been considered "middle class" due to my father's pension, my parents never made us feel like we were living paycheck to paycheck. They always managed to support our needs as young children and led us to believe anything was possible if we worked hard. All three of us brothers have fond childhood memories.

My life was rich with experiences and the love of my parents. When you enter the military and are fortunate enough to travel the world, you soon see how rare it can be to have such an upbringing. I lived in a rural area where, from the time I stepped off the school bus until I came home for dinner, I was on my bike or later my motorcycle. On other days, I could be found playing football and basketball with friends, shooting our guns in the woods and sometimes getting into adolescent mischief – which created lifelong friendships and bonds.

The little school in the foothills of the Smoky Mountains I attended didn't produce famous athletes, scholars, inventors or business tycoons, but my high school takes great pride in its alumnus country singer Kenny Chesney, who graduated a few years after me. Anyone who has listened to Kenny's music and lyrics will have a good idea of the wonderful values and simple life we had during those years, learning, playing and growing up on old dirt roads in the country.

I knew at an early age, without even being told, I had a responsibility to help my family financially by making my own spending money. When it came time to buy my first car, it was with money I had earned myself. Mom and Dad always pitched in where they could – but they taught me, without a doubt, "money doesn't grow on trees." So, I mowed yards, washed cars and did all kinds of odd jobs. At 16, I was able to get a job at a neighborhood grocery store, where I worked for two years before becoming a carpenter's apprentice. I have many great memories of those days.

Early Days in the Military

As we mature, we all pass through several formative years where life begins to form a pattern. Along the way, we meet individuals and experience life-altering moments that begin shaping our professional career choices. While we all develop our personalities and interests to some degree before we leave our homes, it's often during this early time of adulthood those experiences influence the path our lives ultimately take.

Our parents or other close family members can greatly inspire our occupational directions – there are many lawyers, doctors, musicians, actors, pilots, accountants, mechanics, athletes, carpenters, etc., whose children have followed in their footsteps. I may have been subconsciously following in my own family's footsteps as I enlisted in the military when I was 21 years old.

My great-great-grandfather fought in the American Civil War for the Union and was a sergeant assigned to Company A, 3rd East Tennessee Cavalry. On April 27, 1865, just days after being released from a Confederate prisoner-of-war camp, he was on board the (very overloaded) steamboat Sultana, headed for home, when a boiler exploded. The Sultana incident has been referred to as "the worst maritime disaster in U.S. history." It's estimated more than 1,700 Union prisoners died on their way home after months – even years – in Confederate captivity. To put this in perspective, around 1,500 people died in the Titanic disaster, and the Sultana was a fraction of its size. Unfortunately, this tragedy was overshadowed in the news and soon forgotten as it occurred at the end of the Civil War and only days after President Lincoln was assassinated.

I'm fortunate to have one of the original letters my great-great-grandfather wrote to my great-great-grandmother and their children, dated March 24, 1864. Their youngest son was my mother's grandfather. This letter, along with the original letter from the Record and Pension Office of the War Department confirming his death on board the Sultana, are all framed together and hang on the wall across from my desk. They are a powerful reminder of both the sacrifices made and just how far our country has come in 150 short years.

My grandfather on my father's side fought in France in World War I and returned home. Three uncles (my father's brothers) served during World War II, and my father served in the Korean War. I served in the Air Force from 1984 to 1994, and during the first Gulf War. My son followed in this military tradition and served his country and the U.S. Army honorably, returning safely after 17 months in the more recent Iraq War with several years of follow-on assignments in other high-risk environments on our nation's behalf. I am a very proud father.

Somewhat serendipitously, my son served all of his first enlistment in 2006 stationed overseas at Baumholder, Germany, assigned to the 1st Armored Division (Patton's "Big Red One"). Twenty years before this time, when I was assigned to nearby Ramstein Air Base, we would visit Baumholder often. After all, they had a better military clothing and equipment store there – and, more importantly for a young family with a three-year-old, a Burger King.

In early 1985, after basic training, I entered the Air Force Security Specialists training and career field. After months of specialized security training, I was selected to attend heavy weapons and Air Base Ground Defense (ABGD) training – an Air Force version of combat infantry school.

After graduating with Honors from ABGD, it didn't take long for me to realize I had a thirst and desire for something with more tactical or operational tempo than the normal day-to-day work as a security specialist. I realized I enjoyed and seemed to excel in the areas of physical endurance, tactics, self-defense and marksmanship, factors which played a major role in shaping my career and the opportunities unknown to me at the time.

During my first duty station at Carswell Air Force Base in Ft. Worth, Texas, I was part of a security force assigned to protect and control access to multiple weaponized aircraft always on high-alert status. The '80s and early '90s were transitional periods for the U.S. Air Force's physical security program due to new and emerging technology. Until that transition was complete, security was virtually the same as it was in the 1950s (i.e., it relied more on physical presence than technological monitoring). It is a rather astounding fact to consider: A group of people (mostly) in their twenties were protecting enough B-52s equipped with WMDs to obliterate most of the Earth as we know it. Quite an enormous responsibility.

While I was given a tremendous responsibility, it was incredibly tedious to me and I was quickly looking for other directions that were more operationally demanding and could match my young energy. For me, this came in the way of military competitions. During most of my 15 months at my first duty station, my tactical, physical fitness and marksmanship skills provided me the edge needed to be selected to participate in two national military competitions. I would spend approximately five to six months per competition, training and preparing along with a few other team members, and we competed at various locations across the country.

For both teams, we were assigned a master sergeant to prepare us for our competitions. Master Sergeant Marion Ross transferred to the Air Force in the late '70s after serving more than 10 years in the Army and three combat tours in Vietnam. At the time, I thought he was a cantankerous, crusty old man; he would smoke a pack of cigarettes a day and we never really believed it was always just coffee in his thermos. And even though he never smiled or laughed and seemed bent on breaking us every day like we were wild mustangs, none of that mattered to us because of the positive influence he had on each member of our team of young, impressionable airmen. Nor did his poor health habits prevent him from physically smokin' us on the obstacle course or during tactical patrolling.

We started out each day at 5:00 am with one hour of calisthenics and early versions of a CrossFit workout. During this time, he would always find a way to speak to us about our responsibilities as non-commissioned officers (NCOs) and read highlights from his NCO handbook. But, as he would always say, "All you really need to remember are the first three words that precede your instructions and duties: 'All NCOs *must*...'" What Master Sergeant Ross was trying to instill in his young airmen was that we should *follow orders without fail*.

He ran us hard and pushed us harder every day in ways we all dreaded. But 30 years later, those are some of my fondest memories.

After our warmup exercises, we would train and run the obstacle course, which included 19 different obstacles (like the modern-day *American Ninja Warrior* competition) along with a sprint of over 1.5 miles. We ran the course twice each day – sometimes three times – trying to shave minutes and seconds off our times. We would run at different times to ensure we were ready for any weather conditions. Upon sprinting to the finish line of the second or third run, we would continue without stopping for a run of another five to 15 miles, depending on our performance and Sergeant Ross's mood that day.

Almost every day we also loaded up and headed to the range, where each of us would shoot 1,000–2,000 rounds with various weapons. After the range, we would travel to an area off base which probably reminded Sergeant Ross of his days in Vietnam. This training area included open fields, dry and wet creek beds, high points, valleys, a ridiculous number of large Texas ants and venomous snakes, and many great places to conduct ambushes and raids. We would spend the rest of the afternoons rehearsing combat patrols, conducting ambushes and counterambushes, and practicing assault and recovery tactics on foot and in vehicles utilizing MILES (Multiple Integrated Laser Engagement System) gear. A couple afternoons a week, we would spend time in a classroom reviewing our technical data for the written test portion of the competitions.

After completing my first individual competition and taking a few weeks of needed physical recovery, I began training and preparing for the next one. Shortly after my second competition in Spokane, Washington, I received orders for reassignment to Ramstein Air Base in Germany. After several more months of training, building upon the last competition and enduring Sergeant Ross's wrath, I entered my final competition in October 1986. In November, I departed for Germany, where I spent the next six years.

Serving in Germany

My years in Germany would undoubtedly be my most formative. They greatly influenced my career, as they were where I developed my initial skills and interest in the profession of close protection.

In 1986, I began serving at Ramstein, one of the largest air bases in Europe (built in the 1950s), with three air combat wings and one of the largest Military Airlift Command (MAC) units and facilities. It was and still is the Headquarters for U.S. Air Forces in Europe (USAFE) and a North Atlantic Treaty Organization (NATO) installation. We also had numerous other small European allied units on the base as well as a large U.S. Army Air Defense battalion. As an HQ base, we also had one of the largest officer's clubs, a commissary and one of the best golf courses in Europe.

Ramstein had also seen its share of all types of activities over the years. The base participated in numerous NATO tactical and readiness exercises to ensure our operational preparedness during the Cold War. These resources and their devastating capabilities played a vital role in maintaining peace through deterrence, which contributed to the ending of the Cold War in 1991. Today, Ramstein is still considered one of the most important and strategic air bases in the world.

We also supported air ops for sick and wounded soldiers and civilians throughout Europe, the Middle East and Africa at Landstuhl Regional Medical Center, located just 15 minutes from the base.*

Not long after arriving at Ramstein, I again got a taste of protection for high-alert combat-ready aircraft and a major U.S./European weapons storage area. We also had squadrons of F-4 Phantoms and the new F-16 fighter aircraft, along with all the large cargo and troop aircraft that were part of the Military Airlift Command.

I quickly realized I couldn't spend the next four to six years as just a security specialist, so, again, I used my appetite and drive to explore other opportunities. I discovered my security group (one of the Air Force's largest in Europe) had a small but robust ABGD training section consisting of only a few full-time ground combat instructors. At this

---

* Landstuhl was and still is today one of the first stops for many newly released U.S. hostages, American POWs or military members killed or wounded in action. Once reaching Landstuhl, wounded soldiers, former hostages and POWs receive needed medical attention, psychological counseling and debriefing as they are prepared for repatriation and return to the U.S. and their families. For the deceased, their bodies are prepared for return to their Gold Star families and friends.

time, they were in need of a temporary instructor while one of their teachers would be away attending U.S. Army Ranger School.

My wife at the time (Angie) was pregnant with our son in Knoxville and she wasn't due for a few more months, so I volunteered to support the team before and after my normal duties. The other instructors quickly recognized my hunger for this training, not minding the long days, and willingness to do whatever it took to help.

What started out as a two-month temporary duty assignment, turned into a four-year permanent assignment as a ground combat and special weapons and tactics instructor. This included months of advanced and bilateral training with German special police units; the U.S. Army 10th Special Forces Group at Bad Tolz near the Bavarian Alps; Company E, 51st Infantry, Long Range Surveillance company attached to the 165th Military Intelligence Battalion; and others.

As a member of the Air Force, having the privilege then to receive training from these units only continued to fuel my desire for more challenging career opportunities. Those who represent the best in what they do will always leave their mark upon you, allowing you to develop additional skillsets, gain new perspectives and add depth to your life and career.

Those were some of the toughest weeks and months of training I have ever gone through – but are also some of my most memorable experiences (along with the pain of my aching joints).

My six years at Ramstein taught me one very important and intangible skill – networking. If any young readers of this book should take away anything from my experience and stories, it's the importance of building a strong professional network. Develop your networking skills early; most importantly, learn how to use them effectively and ethically. If you're honest, sincere and humble in your efforts, you will develop professional relationships, friends and a network of individuals who can help you – and you them – throughout your career and life.

I had no idea at that time I would one day be working for the CIA and would have to call upon many of the individuals I knew during those years – Americans, Germans, French, Italians, British, Irish and many others – to help me when I needed it most nearly a decade later.

Developing My Professional EP DNA

Somewhere along the way and very early in our careers, after universities, training and mentoring, we begin to acquire and sharpen our new skills, eventually formulating the mindsets that become the basis for our professional "DNA." For me, like the "wake-up call" after Herrhausen's assassination, the following stories represent the start of my professional security development and the early stages of developing my "EP DNA."

As mentioned before, EP specialists have diverse backgrounds and experiences. In no other profession will you find the need to perform flawlessly in a team *and* solo setting to be more fluid. Many EP specialists have military experience – a career in which operating as a team is the very foundation of the job. In some environments, life and death depend on each member pulling his/her weight, and you learn to operate at times and places without saying a word but with just a look, slight movement of the hand or nod of the head.

In my time with the CIA, teamwork and adrenaline rushes came with the territory. My colleagues and I could experience them as we escorted a person on foot through a hostile area – all the while knowing that if the crowds around us realized who we were, there would have been huge flashing dollar signs above our heads.

On other occasions, adrenaline would also begin pumping after an extremely long international flight of 12 hours or more on a military aircraft involving midair refueling to extend our flying time. As the air crew gave us the thumbs-up for our final descent, we would be finishing our preparations, briefings and reviews of roles and responsibilities. It was always slightly unnerving as a high-profile and high-risk protective detail to land in a foreign country with known threats and to disembark from a large U.S. aircraft with "unknowns" around the airport.

If we were using a cargo aircraft, we would untether vehicles and drop the ramp halfway right after touchdown as we readied for deplaning. Depending upon the plane type, a counter-sniper might take a position from the open hatch as we taxied. After we stopped, we would quickly unload our gear and conduct weapons checks. All our senses would be on high alert as we got our first whiff of the local air; everyone would quickly down water and sports drinks and stash energy bars and snacks in every pocket as we prepared physically and mentally for what was ahead. It was a "rush" – in every sense of the word.

Whether with the CIA or in the private sector, a similar adrenaline rush could occur if we were required to operate as a solo agent. Granted, it's not always the preferred method of close protection, but many smaller family or extremely low-profile details may use a single agent or solo practitioner. A solo agent might conduct and orchestrate difficult missions, calling on all resources and knowledge available (and sometimes going beyond) to do what some individuals might actually consider resigning over. Still, they accomplished the mission, all the while thinking, *You want me to do what?!*

Whether a solo agent or part of a larger team, most EP specialists hone their abilities to perform in either situation long before becoming an agent. The following stories are personal reflections on how my experiences played a major role in developing my "teamwork DNA" in areas of special services involving weapons, tactics and the life-and-death decisions that come with our profession.

All Before Lunch

It was 5:30 am and I was still waking up as I poured my second cup of coffee to take with me to my office at Ramstein. As I did almost every morning, I went into my two-year-old son Jonathan's bedroom to check on him – he was sound asleep.

These were my early years in Germany. When we first arrived in the late 1980s, no base housing was available, so my wife, newborn son and I had no other option other than to live off base. While we first believed we would prefer this unique experience to living on base,* it proved to be difficult for my wife, who spent many hours at home alone with our new baby in a small village far from the air base where very few people spoke English. This isolation for a young, new mother explained the many inter-

---

* When we were able to move to the base later, it was more like living in "little America" – and very convenient, with a five-minute drive to the office. If I jogged the long route, it would be a nice 30-minute run to work.

national phone bills that could easily be $800 a month (half my military pay at the time) – another reason we should convey a great deal of respect and appreciation to our military families who support their deployed spouses.

That day, about two years into our time in Germany, my pager went off with a "911" as I was heading out the door – which meant "call the operations desk immediately." The desk officer responded there was an emergency off base and the Emergency Services Team (EST) I belonged to had been activated.

I raced out the door and met up with my team members, all of us arriving around the same time at our base armory. We collected our assigned weapons and gear and assembled next door with our field supervisor, Technical Sergeant Higgins, to receive our briefing.

Our EST in Germany rehearsing a bus hostage rescue assault, utilizing tactics learned from the Israelis. I'm on the far right – armed with a sledgehammer to assist in breaching the bus windshield during the assault.

Our team was one of the few American military SWAT-style forces in Germany. Since we were assigned to Ramstein Air Base, one of the largest and most important operational bases in Europe, our EST assumed a more active Air Force role than most teams around the world. We'd been called for a lot of incidents before and had often been assigned to provide tactical support for a variety of special events and missions. In our time together, our team had supported visits to the base by President George H. W. Bush and Prime Minister Margaret Thatcher, a multinational celebration for the birthday of Queen Elizabeth II, U.S. Marshals transporting a captured terrorist to testify at The Hague, a high-risk joint German and American operation to capture a wanted fugitive, and many other special operations.

And while we routinely underwent intense training for hostage situations, we had never received a call like this one. The initial reports indicated a possible attempted kidnapping of a U.S. Army major general's teenage daughter and his wife on an Army base near Kaiserslautern, a small city just 30 minutes away. That brief initial description was all the information we had to go on at the time, so we quickly loaded up our tactical response vehicles with weapons, gear and equipment. Only 30 minutes after receiving our page, 16 members of our EST were en route to Kaiserslautern.

Once arriving at the base, we were escorted by a military police (MP) vehicle to their incident scene command post. This had been quickly established just three blocks away from (and out of sight of) the general's residence building, where the possible kidnappers were believed to still be holed up.

We were then told more of the situation: A neighbor had apparently heard a woman scream and called the base MP to report her concern. The responding MP personnel had arrived at this large three-story apartment building with two entrances. Each entrance led to six apartments on three floors. The building had a total of 12 large apartments built for high-ranking military officers and their families.

That wasn't all. When an MP serviceman started up the building's eastern stairwell toward the general's apartment, one of the suspects appeared over the railing on the third floor – and shot him before he could draw his weapon.

Other MP personnel immediately responded to calls of "shots fired" and set up a perimeter around the building. They could see the entrance of the stairwell where the MP serviceman went in and was shot, but no other communication or movements had been reported.

When we reached the command post, our field supervisor and Team 1 leader, Staff Sergeant Garth ("Ziggy") Freund met with members of the MP and the Army Criminal Investigation Division (CID) for a briefing as we prepared our equipment. The Army CID had command and control, and we were there to take their lead. Our part was to assist in containing and isolating the situation and prepare a quick tactical assault response plan in the event things went badly.

The fate of the potential hostages in the general's unit was unknown, and the MP serviceman who had been shot had been rushed to the hospital by the time we arrived. As for the building, two apartments were completely vacant and four families were out of town on vacation, leaving five other families possibly still inside their residences.

We then received more details from the neighbor directly across the hall from the general. She had looked through her door peephole and saw one or two men scuffling in front of the general's door with either his wife or daughter – but she said she couldn't be sure. She also reported seeing several men entering the general's apartment and the door shutting behind them. This was the only eyewitness information we had to go on at the time.

Several attempts had been made to contact the general or his family via their home phone, but there was no answer. His office confirmed he had not arrived yet – even so, we could still see his car in front of the apartment. As a result, the command post could not rule out anything from a domestic situation to even a hostage situation resulting from a failed kidnapping attempt. None of the scenarios were good.

We quickly sent out two-man spotter and sniper teams (Casper 1 and 2) to opposite sides of the building to provide visual intelligence. They would also hopefully be in a position to provide cover fire for our assault teams or take a kill shot at a bad guy or "tango" (terrorist) if the opportunity presented itself and was authorized per our rules of engagement.

I was a member of one of those assault teams. Our assault teams (Team 1 and 2) trained and normally operated as five-man groups, only broken into three- and two-man sub-teams when tactically needed. We in Team 1 and our counterparts in Team 2 remained at our tactical command post reviewing plans and available intelligence in order to design an assault plan we could continue to build upon until needed or until negotiations could prove successful.

A decision was made to use the base housing roster (our version of a telephone book) to call all apartments in the building and instruct the occupants to remain in their units behind locked doors and away from windows. Residents were also told to call the command post if they had anything to report, and otherwise to stay off their phones but remain close for further instructions.

We got the radio call from Caspers 1 and 2 (the spotter and sniper teams) indicating they were in place in two buildings across from the front and back of our apartments. While Team 1 (my team) stayed back, Team 2 proceeded to the northwest corner of the building, moving as close to the outside wall as possible as they did so. Because we wanted to utilize a surprise approach, they entered the building from the western stairwell. Just like the eastern stairwell where the MP serviceman had been shot, the western stairwell led upstairs to six apartments and downstairs to the basement hallway. The basement hallway went under the entire building, connected to both stairwells and contained laundry machines and storage lockers.

The five members of Team 2 moved through the basement hallway toward the eastern stairwell in a close stacked formation: one behind the other with each member pointing their weapon in a predetermined direction, and one team member walking backwards to catch a surprise from behind. Soon enough, Team 2 reached the eastern stairwell and held this position. At this point, we still hadn't seen or encountered any movement from the general's apartment or the building – it was eerily quiet.

Only moments later, an unidentified suspect (Tango 1) yelled out of a window in the general's apartment facing the command post in front of the building. He wanted to talk to someone in charge but didn't have a phone. We later found out one of the tangos pulled the phone from the wall during a struggle with the general during their botched kidnapping attempt. They were holding what we believed to be one hostage inside the apartment, but there could have been more.

Our snipers continued to report activity or shadows of movement from within the apartment (as all curtains were drawn). The on-scene commander, a major with the Army CID, decided to run a field telephone from the command post up to the eastern stairwell, which led to the general's unit. The other three members of Team 1 proceeded to unroll a couple hundred yards of communication wire in that direction, but intentionally left too little wire for the suspects to pull the phone back up the stairs to the third-floor apartment. Assuming this guy wasn't alone, our goal was to separate the suspects by bringing at least one to the front door of the ground-level entry.

Moments later, Casper 1 reported one male suspect exiting cautiously down the stairs to the field phone. He soon reached it, and at that moment the scene commander gave it a quick crank to make it ring. The man picked up the phone, began giving his demands and explained the fate of his *three* hostages if they were not met.

We now had a tense negotiation on our hands, but we were also beginning to get a better picture of what we were dealing with and how many people were involved.

By now, it was 9:30 am – approximately four hours since the situation had begun. Team 2 continued to maintain the valuable ground that had been gained in the basement hallway. Team 1 was still back with Sergeant Higgins in the tactical command post going over the building plans we had requested from the base civil engineers. We also continued reviewing what tactical intelligence we had. Our snipers were continuing to report shadow movements from within the apartment by using a grid matrix commonly used at this time for these types of operations. We recorded everything on a whiteboard in the command post.

Without being in the apartment, we couldn't confirm if any of our hostages were alive or even uninjured. But based on the hostile action of the tangos, it was safe to say our hostages were not allowed to move freely.

Tango 1 was sitting at the bottom of the steps, but just inside the building; he was doing most of the talking with the CID negotiator.

Our Team 2 in the basement was so close they could hear him swearing and getting frustrated with the negotiator; he was speaking English but with a German accent.

And while we knew we had Tango 1 running back and forth between the field phone and the apartment, we could only assume there was at least one more terrorist in the general's apartment – giving us two definite hostiles to consider in our assault plan. We thought, *If they were trying to kidnap a general on a military base, it was unlikely they would only use two people to attempt such an operation. There had to be more somewhere, but where?*

We knew the tangos probably never intended on barricading themselves in the apartment. And because of the stress of a failed plan and being surrounded by hostile soldiers on an American military base, it did not bode well for them – nor did it portend a happy ending for our hostages.

Just then, we were informed the investigating MP serviceman had died from his wounds. Additional intelligence was delivered to us that German authorities now believed the suspects might be members of the Red Army Faction – a terrorist group whose tactics were very familiar to many of us.* Because of the information and the nature of this situation, we were told the members of the Spezialeinsatzkommando (SEK), a special tactical unit of the German state police, were assembling to respond to the base to assist. They'd arrive within 90 minutes or less and more than likely assume command and control – including tactical control.

This was welcome news because of the complexity of a possible hostage rescue on the third floor of this apartment building. The SEK or the federal Grenzschutzgruppe 9 (Border Protection Group 9, or

---

* This wouldn't be the first time a group like the RAF would attempt a kidnapping of a U.S. general. In December 1981 in Verona, Italy, the Italian Red Brigade (a Marxist-Leninist militant group aligned with RAF ideology) kidnapped U.S. Army Brigadier General James Dozier. Forty-two days later, he was rescued by an Italian counterterrorism unit. These events and others led to many security changes throughout military installations overseas, especially in Germany, but it also raised the risk of other similar kidnappings.

GSG9) – Germany's version of the U.S. Army Special Forces or Navy SEALs, who both specialize in counterterrorism operations – would be the best chance to end this without any hostages being killed. We would gladly relinquish the potential assault to these teams, as their training, equipment and experience would make them a much better option for success.

Just a few months earlier, our EST had received several weeks of specialized training from the SEK. This was the first time the SEK and their governing ministers had ever authorized any level of training to any U.S. military unit, and it is when I first met and formed a lifelong bond and friendship with Horst Mehlinger, Director of Training for the Rheinland-Pfalz branch of the SEK. Our EST would continue to benefit from various training courses from the SEK, and it was the start of a lasting professional relationship between our two special units that would continue for many years to come.

But today, until SEK or GSG9 could arrive, we had to continue to plan as if we would be given the green light to make the rescue attempt. As such, we continued to go over the plans of the building looking for any advantages we could gain. We brought over a few members from the Army Corps of Engineers and building maintenance on site to help us better understand its construction – specifically the general's apartment or the adjacent units. We were quite interested in the crawl space above this unit and the potential access it could give us to the general's apartment.

Our team was also very interested in the thickness of the walls separating the general's apartment and the apartment next door. One thing Germans do well is construction; the interior walls in most German buildings are more than 12 inches of block, concrete and plaster. This meant the chance of hearing anything without drilling a small hole to insert a listening device was probably slim, but we needed all the intelligence we could gather. We would have to leave the decision to drill the hole to SEK once they arrived.

The layout of this building was very similar to a building on our air base that was empty and undergoing a total renovation. We generally conducted various types of assaults on these sorts of buildings before they gutted them, training with door rams and explosives, rappelling the sides, breaching through windows, and rehearsing both stealth and dynamic hostage rescue assaults.

Approximately 20 minutes had passed since we established communications with Tango 1 over the phone. His first demands through the CID negotiator didn't include any money. Rather, the terrorists wanted only a large four-door sedan with black tape covering the inside of all the windows except for small two-inch holes in each. Also, they wanted the car parked directly outside the front entrance of the stairwell and the front steps.

Our negotiator said we would begin preparing the vehicle and asked for some "proof of life" that the general, his wife and his daughter were okay. We were anxiously waiting for this, not just for the general's sake but because we'd take any intelligence we could get for our assault plan.

Tango 1 continued running up and down the stairs to the field phone and putting increasing pressure on his demands. Stress was getting high on both sides. We felt we could take this one terrorist out with our sniper or Team 2 in the basement, but we were concerned with what the other suspect with the general and his family would do in desperation.

As our team continued preparing for an assault on the building, Sergeant Higgins walked over to the command post where the negotiator was pacing the floor. When he came back, he said, "The negotiation is not going well – and I'm afraid these guys are not prepared for what these tangos are throwing at them. I hope SEK gets here soon."

One of our EST team members (who would not be part of the assault team) was in the command post listening and taking notes. A runner was taking any new tactical information back to our own makeshift tactical command post just a few yards away. As a rule, our team and most SWAT teams will not normally let any operator (tactical team member) in the room with negotiators. Psychologists will tell you the last thing you want is your operator to overhear any conversation that would put emotions or influence in his head. If an operator has been authorized to assault and potentially shoot a suspect, you don't want even a split second of doubt before pulling the trigger. The operator must maintain neutrality and be prepared to simply follow instructions based on the tactical and threat inputs and rules of engagement.

At this very moment, our spotter and sniper team watching the front door (Casper 1) radioed that Tango 1 and one female were coming down the stairs. When they reached the front door, Tango 1 pushed what appeared to be the daughter – gagged and with her hands tied behind her back – just to the opening of the front door. He yelled from the doorway that we had five minutes to get the taped-up car in front of the building or her blood would be on our hands.

The incident command post and negotiator were at a total loss. Mass confusion was beginning to take place, as the clock was ticking and the vehicle they agreed to provide hadn't arrived yet.

Casper 1 had limited view of Tango 1 and was not sure his .308-caliber round could penetrate the thickness of the wall where he felt the terrorist's body or head would be. Even if it could, there was no guarantee he would have a shot. And if he missed, the girl would probably die as well – not to mention, we couldn't be sure what the other terrorist would do with the general and his wife. We knew based on RAF profiles they would not want to be taken alive and probably wouldn't surrender.*

At this point, Team 2 in the basement hallway was our best chance of saving the daughter. They were approximately 100 feet from the stairwell and were watching via a small tactical mirror which allowed them to remain unseen as they awaited further instructions. They requested permission to advance to the stairwell where Tango 1 and the girl were standing, but the command post and scene commander denied their request, telling them to hold their position.

As the girl stood at the door, Tango 1 held her by a rope. He made one more call to his negotiator and demanded his car. The negotiator hesitated because he didn't have a good answer but assured him we were working on it.

At that moment, we all heard a gunshot.

---

* That being said, other members of their group had been taken alive and imprisoned years before, including two of their founders, Andreas Baader and Ulrike Meinhof. (Before they changed their group's name to the RAF, they were called the Baader-Meinhof Gang.)

The young girl's body fell limp to the front step.

Everyone's heart sank. We knew Team 2 in the basement could have saved her if they had been given permission to move forward. But if they had moved on their own, it would have been without the on-scene commander's approval, and it would have meant a decision to be discussed in detail later during an after-action review.

The advantage now was obviously in the terrorists' hands. We saw the field phone tossed into the street through the crack of the door – it appeared Tango 1 ran back up the stairs to the general's apartment. At one point, our sniper with a possible shot requested permission to fire but was told to stand down. With the general and his wife still hopefully alive in their apartment, our commanders didn't want to take any chances and further incite the terrorists to start killing their hostages in desperation. If they were indeed members of the RAF, the terrorists knew all too well the GSG9 or SEK would already be on their way and their time to get out was shrinking fast. Knowing this, they probably shot the daughter to put immediate pressure on the negotiator to provide their getaway car before the German assault teams could arrive.

Through his scope, Casper 1 advised he saw no movement coming from the girl, but we couldn't be sure she was dead. Now with Team 2 positioned below the steps near the door where the girl's body was, they immediately requested permission to recover her and see if she was still alive by extracting her via the basement to the other end of the building. The problem was, this move could announce Team 2's presence in the staircase. We needed every element of surprise once we were at the door to the apartment if we had any chance of rescuing the general and his wife – *if* they were still alive.

But we also couldn't let the girl bleed out if she were still alive too. Back at the command post, Sergeant Higgins heard Team 2's request. Instead of sending them to get her, he ordered the MP to prepare a vehicle, driver, two MP personnel and a medic to drive to the girl, pull her into the vehicle and go directly to the base medical unit just a few hundred yards away.

With pressure mounting, the on-scene commander asked Sergeant Higgins if he had an assault plan prepared. He replied with a yes. The commander hesitated for a moment and with a big sigh gave a green light – i.e., *command and control are now yours.*

Over the radio, we heard Higgins's voice: "Green light, green light, green light, all teams acknowledge. Sandbox* acknowledge, Team 1 acknowledge, Team 2 acknowledge, Casper 1 acknowledge, Casper 2 acknowledge." This was not a green light to start pulling our plan together – we had already devised and (hastily) rehearsed it. It was a signal to *go*, and we felt we had less than 10 minutes to get to that door before more shots were fired.

Team 2 had already moved down the basement hall to a position just below the steps, cursing the fact they had not moved there sooner. Higgins made the difficult decision to tell Team 2 to hold their position until Team 1 (my team) could reach our pre-assault position, which was the apartment one level down from the general's third-floor apartment and across the hall. We wanted to call the occupants of this apartment and let them know we would be coming in through their bathroom window, but there was one problem: German phones rang very loud and, given the echoing within the block walls of the apartments, it was important we didn't draw the terrorists' attention to the residence we'd be entering. This meant we would have to move in without warning the apartment occupants *or* causing a stir that would attract attention.

Team 1 moved out immediately, running together like a herd of five buffaloes with weapons, one behind the other with me crouched in the front position. At a height of 5'9" I normally took the point position (in front) so my taller team members behind me had a better line of sight over me with their weapons – I just had to keep my head down.

We traveled as light as possible, taking only what we absolutely needed to execute this plan. This included H&K MP5 submachine guns, Beretta 92F pistols, a Remington 870 shotgun, ropes and a 75-pound door ram. The five of us had to get to the south end of the building but not be seen from the windows of the general's apartment, so we ran several hundred yards around the neighborhood to hide our approach.

Our team proceeded with the assumption we would continue until

---

* The command post

we had more information, were ready to conduct our assault, or were advised the German special forces had arrived. In that case, we knew we might be instructed to let them take over, but we kept going anyway.

We had discussed this very type of situation months before with our SEK counterparts: If there were hostages on a U.S. base in Germany, when would the German authorities move in and take over? The baseline thinking was, if an American took American hostages, the U.S. forces would have control and conduct any assault – unless the Americans requested German government support. After all, the Germans did not want to be in a situation to kill an American – or, worse yet, an American military member on an American base who had taken American hostages. The Germans' threshold seemed to be if a German was involved (either the hostage-taker or the hostage), they would insist on command and control and assault.

We had preliminary information indicating the terrorists were possibly German and potentially members of the RAF, so we knew the Germans would take command and control as soon as they arrived. The Germans would especially not want to deal with the fallout from members of the RAF killing a U.S. general and his family on a U.S. military base – and this seemed to be where the situation was heading.

But now with the shooting of the general's daughter, we couldn't wait.

Our sniper scouts had identified all open or closed windows already, so we knew the second-floor window had been slightly open at the south end of the building – we just hoped it still was. As the five of us only had ropes (no ladders) we readied to create a "human ladder" to scale the wall and access the window.

Fortunately for us, we had just practiced this technique months before during training with the SEK at the French Military Commando School. Built in the early 1900s, this school contained some of the most unique structures and obstacles we had ever seen. The school had set up several small mock European villages to practice assaults – including scaling walls, shimmying up and down water pipes, crossing cables or telephone wires from building to building, and climbing down chimneys.

One of the most taxing challenges was working as a team to navigate through a completely dark "pill-box" – basically a 100-yard tunnel through a mountain big enough for an individual to walk, crawl or climb inside. The tunnel included ramps, water, rats, and other unique and unrecognizable obstacles to maneuver through in total darkness.

In this exercise, five of us would stack into a room the size of a coat closet. At the bottom of the small room was a three-foot hole that led into a tunnel. One at a time, we would bend down and force our way into the small tube while only feeling our way through. There was absolutely no light. In addition, we were all searched before entering to make sure we had nothing on us to aid our escape. It would take almost an hour for teams to come out the other side of the mountain – always soaking wet from water or sweat and with eyes as big as those of owls.

At one point in the tunnel (reached after about 30 minutes in the dark), the only way out was through a small hole at the bottom of the wall. This hole included a channel with water running through it. You could reach as far as you could, but you couldn't feel the other side. After searching every inch of the wall by hand in this small passage, the choice was either to turn around and head back the way we came, or press on through the water with the hope the other side was the end.

Generally, I was the shortest guy and became the point man on the team, so I was the first one to explore the water tunnel. Even before this spot, there were plenty of places where one might feel the need to back out, but this obstacle in particular presented an even bigger challenge because the claustrophobia was (almost) unbearable. Looking back, I don't think I would do it again today (given a choice), but it was a great test of mental strength.

Back at the general's building, our team made the human ladder up to the second-floor window. I quickly climbed up my team members' knees, hips, shoulders and heads until I reached the bottom of the sill. Once inside, I quietly shut the bathroom door and pulled the next man up. We lowered a rope with knots every few feet to aid in the climb, and quickly pulled the other team members up one by one until we had all five in the bathroom. This room was barely big enough for two adults, but we squeezed five guys and our door ram in there.

By our watches, our run to the building and climb up the wall had taken less than six minutes, which meant we had three minutes to get to the general's door and prepare to breach. There was still no word of the SEK's arrival, so our team got into position to move out.

According to our information, we were about to enter an apartment belonging to another general, his young daughter and her child. With two guys standing in the bathtub and three stacked at the door, I slowly opened it. As I did, I glanced through at a crib – and was astonished to see a baby there. Before I could say anything, I saw a woman walking into the bedroom. I had no choice – I quickly holstered my Beretta 9mm and pulled my black balaclava mask up to the top of my head, exposing my face while opening the door to grab the woman and tell her we were the good guys.

Her eyes were huge with a terrified expression – all she saw was five guys in black uniforms coming in with firearms and balaclava masks showing only their eyes. And all she knew was her baby was in the room and there was a lot of frightening commotion outside. She started to scream, but it was more of a sharp inhale. I grabbed her and covered her mouth. Her father quickly figured out what was going on, came up behind her and reassured her it was all right: "These are the good guys – here to take care of the situation outside. Everything is going to be okay."

Being the professional enlisted types (even in a crisis situation), we quickly moved past them, each of us whispering "sorry," "excuse me," "sorry," "pardon me…" We asked them to lock themselves and their baby in the bathroom and not to come out until they had been told by us or the MP that it was safe.

The five of us now stacked up at the front door to the hallway. I was able to look through the peephole as our team leader Ziggy radioed everyone we were at our pre-assault position (across the hall and one floor down from our target's apartment) and preparing to move into the stairwell. He advised from this point forward we were to adhere to radio silence unless Team 2 or one of the Casper units had a mission-critical message or update. We had reached the point of no return, regardless of whether or not SEK, GSG9 or even a platoon of U.S. Marines arrived on scene.

The command post, Casper 1 and 2, and Team 2 copied. Higgins was standing by with the MP vehicle to collect the daughter on the street as soon as we initiated our assault. Everyone was waiting for us to begin. The plan was, once we were in place outside the general's door, we would give a signal to initiate two distractions on each side of the building with loud sirens from nearby fire trucks on standby. This would hopefully draw the attention of the terrorists to the windows for at least a second while we breached the front door.

But before I could open this door, Tango 1 ran downstairs – right in front of the peephole. I made the decision to let him pass but whispered to Team 2 over the radio they had a tango coming to them now. I told my team to prepare to move, using only hand signals.

Seconds later, we heard shots from downstairs. We simultaneously opened the door and started moving out to the stairs leading up to the general's apartment. At the same time, we heard over our radio ear-pieces from Team 2: "One tango down." We only had two confirmed terrorists present, but there could be others. With at least one taken care of downstairs, we believed one was still in the general's apartment.

Three of us started across the landing and turned to head upstairs to the third-floor door. Our fourth team member covered downstairs and our fifth team member braced in back, aiming his weapon forward and up the stairs at the target's door. Still on point position, I moved across the landing with two team members, including Ziggy.

When we were halfway across the landing, the general's door opened. Ziggy couldn't get over in time, so he stopped and took aim at the door. My cover man and I were able to reach the wall leading up the stairs – out of sight of the doorway.

A man appeared in the entrance whom we immediately believed to be the general. He had wiring wrapped around him and what appeared to be a claymore mine strapped to his stomach. He was being held by another man whose feet were all I could see from my position below. Almost at the same time, we heard two gunshots downstairs, with a follow-on radio call of "Second tango down."

Where did he come from?

Apparently, there was a terrorist in the basement hallway all this time holed up in a small storage room just past the staircase where Team 2 held their position. After Team 2 shot Tango 1, this man (Tango 3) stepped out of the room into the hall thinking he would surprise our team on the stairs – but the fifth man on Team 2 was providing rear cover and quickly engaged him as he popped out. That fifth guy probably saved most of his team from being shot in the back.

Immediately, the terrorist (Tango 2) who was holding the general began yelling at us in German and English as Ziggy held his position behind the stair railing and our fifth team member held his position aiming at the door. Tango 2 was moving back and forth too much for Ziggy to take a shot; we also didn't know exactly how the device was rigged on the general's chest or where his wife was at that moment. Nor did we know whether or not there were more tangos.

Suddenly, Tango 2 said, "You have five seconds to put your guns down and get out of this building or I'm going to blow him up and kill us all."

Well at least we have a shot clock to work with now.

During this yelling between Tango 2 and Ziggy, I had been able to take two more steps upward, hugging the wall as tightly and as quietly as I possibly could. I was now less than two feet from the edge of the target door's opening. I could see the general in the doorway, but I didn't think he saw me with the commotion of Tango 2 holding him tight in front of him as a human shield. I remember I could actually smell Tango 2's sweat and body odor – and I could see the spit coming from his mouth as he was screaming at Ziggy to drop his weapon and get out.

We could *not* let him close this door. As he started to count "one," I gave Ziggy a quick glance and nod. He knew what I was getting ready to do, but I didn't want to surprise him if *he* was going to take the shot – only for me to step into his path and have his bullet impact the back of my head. (That's what we would call a bad day at work.)

Which reminds me – a few months earlier on a U.S. Army training base in southern Germany, we were having a live-fire weapons exercise regarding attacks on principals. In these exercises, we would drive up with our (role-played) principals to a predetermined arrival or departure point, exit our vehicles and walk toward a building. Depending on the scenario being conducted, Horst Mehlinger from the SEK would toss a flashbang or fire off a weapon, simulating an explosion or live gunfire as our team would enter or depart the building or vehicle with our principal.

This would initiate a surprise attack. Our team would draw weapons and respond to the threat. A number of targets would pop up representing attackers for the team to engage as the team member closest to the "principal" would cover and rush him to the vehicle, building or another covered position depending on where the attack originated.

On one of these exercises, I was riding in the front right seat ("shift leader" position) of the follow car as we pulled up to an office building. I exited my vehicle and stood at the rear of the principal's car facing out and across the street. The team member riding in the front right seat of the principal's car (the "hot seat") exited and prepared to open the door for the principal. Once all team members were in place and we were sure the area was safe, the hot seat team member opened the principal's door and he exited.

As our advance agent began leading them toward the front door of the building, I was turning to bring up the rear when gunshots rang out. I looked over and across the principal's vehicle and saw several gunman targets pop up. I dropped to the front area of the principal's vehicle (the closest cover) behind the engine block, and immediately began returning *live fire* at the targets. The hot seat agent, advance agent and one other team member covered the principal and took him into the building.

One other team member and I continued to actively engage the popup targets. Once a target had successfully been hit, it would fall. As I was firing at the targets, Horst stepped up behind me, tapped me on the shoulder and said, "Holster your weapon and lay on the ground, you've been hit and you're out of play, you cannot speak."

Horst backed up to where he could see and evaluate our actions. I laid there for less than a minute while my team member finished engaging the other standing targets. Once all the targets seemed to be down, my partner yelled out, "Trott is down!"

One of the team members from the building, Eric, responded with, "I'll get Trott – cover me – coming out."

He came out with his Beretta 92F in his right hand, pointing it over the vehicles as he approached my location. Eric was probably our biggest team member – well over six feet and very strong. As he got closer to me, I was on my back. I rolled my head over slightly toward Eric coming at me.

It was like a slow-motion movie as I recall it now. He was less than 10 feet away and still running in a low squat to my location. As he got closer to me, I noticed he was still gripping his Beretta in his right hand, and his left hand was reaching out in order to scoop me up. When he got within a few feet, I saw his handgun was *now pointing toward my head.*

Suddenly I heard a CRACK and saw a flash from the barrel of his gun. Dirt and gravel flew in my face from near my head. I froze, as I wasn't actually sure if I had been hit or not – I was waiting for the pain, blood, or some sign I had a new hole in my head.

Horst saw this happen, immediately blew his whistle and yelled "TERMINATE TERMINATE TERMINATE THE EXERCISE!!" and ran over to Eric and me. Eric dropped to one knee in front of me and put away his Beretta, as I thought, *NOW you holster your weapon.*

Horst came up, put his hand on Eric's back and, with what I felt was hesitation, looked at my face. Everything froze for a moment, as only Horst, Eric and I knew what had just happened. After they knew I was okay, they were incredibly relieved – and so was I.

We reviewed the details of the exercise later. It was evident that, as Eric reached down with one hand to pick me up while his Beretta was in his other hand, his trigger finger was not where it was supposed to be – off-trigger and straight. His hand tensed and caused him to accidentally squeeze off a shot just inches from my head.

Over the years, there have been countless special operators, soldiers and police officers accidentally shot and killed during live-fire exercises. I came too close to being one of those statistics that day.

Back on the staircase, Ziggy gave a slight head nod as I heard the tango count "two." Without hesitation, I pushed past the doorframe with my pistol in my right hand, exactly where I thought Tango 2's head would be. I was only inches from his head when I pulled the trigger (without ammo) and said, "You're dead."

The next thing we heard was "TERMINATE TERMINATE TERMINATE THE EXERCISE!!" from one of the Army evaluators who had been in the stairwell observing our assault from one flight down. We later found out the evaluators weren't aware of our exact location until the last couple minutes, as they hadn't realized we had gone through the second-floor bathroom window to enter the building.

After "pulling" the trigger, I began detaching the inert claymore from the general as the rest of our team continued to clear the apartment; even though the exercise was over, our training and instinct taught us to continue until the mission was complete.

We holstered and slung our weapons and had a quick chat as we continued to untangle the general from the claymore. I don't recall this general's name, but we were impressed he and his family were willing to be part of this *extremely* realistic exercise. Higgins gave the orders to rally back to our tactical command post, where we met with the rest of our EST team as well as the MP officers, negotiators, on-scene commander, CID agents and others who were part of this exercise. We made a quick stop at the other apartment on the second floor and apologized to the traumatized family. This general's daughter was still shaking.

This was strictly an Army CID negotiations exercise for the base MP and local CID office. As an Air Force tactical team, our EST group had never been part of this type of joint exercise before, especially on an Army base. Our field supervisor had been contacted the day prior and was asked if we could respond and be part of the negotiation exercise. The Army said we might help set up a perimeter if they needed more support, but it was really just a matter of checking the box for ensuring all the right players were there. They said we would not be used as an assault team – "negotiation exercise only."

It was only during the exercise it appeared to the team of Inspector General evaluators the process of negotiations was not going well. They were reaching such a level of frustration one of the Army evaluators said, as a slight joke, "Let's send in the 'Wing Nuts'" (an affectionate term our Army brethren will often use to refer to their Air Force counterparts).

Higgins had prearranged with the armory no live ammunition would be issued – only Higgins had a loaded firearm to secure our weapons while traveling off base. We had been through many realistic exercises over the years, but this was as real as it got before weapons "simunition" (non-lethal training paint pellets) and other useful equipment replaced first-generation laser engagement equipment.

For security forces, special operators, police officers, and EP agents and teams, these types of exercises or tactical rehearsals (including attacks on principals) are critical to overall success and reaction time to a threat – whether in a vehicle, office, residence, hotel, yacht or open venue. Not all threats involve hostage rescue, taking on a terrorist, firing a weapon or laying your hands on someone. There are times when situations present an overzealous fan or a not-so-friendly person at a public event getting in your principal's personal space. In all cases imaginable, you must have a plan and, at the very least, discuss your response options.

We assembled back at our tactical command post to collect our gear and equipment and head back to the base for a few cold German beers, grilled bratwurst and, yes, some high-fives and gloating over our successful assault – even if it was only an exercise. All those who have served in the military will understand the unbridled joy you feel when you've been successful in the presence of other military service units. *Esprit de corps* is very real, especially where inter-service rivalry is concerned.

That being said, we're all one team – and it's a great feeling I can still miss today.

On our way out, the primary Army evaluator who said to send in the "Wing Nuts" met us at our vehicles as we were loading up. "Okay, where are you boys from and where did you receive your training?" This Sergeant Major was a former member of the U.S. Army's elite counterterrorism unit and was now serving with the Army Inspector General, evaluating various Army resources and facilities around the world regarding anti-terrorism preparedness.

He went on to say this had been one of the most impressive training assaults he had ever seen. Notably, he felt the daughter "being shot" was unacceptable and he realized we were in a position to rescue her; he knew we asked for permission but were denied it by their chief negotiator. He did acknowledge the timing could have led to the killing of the general and his wife, since we weren't in the position to conduct multiple assaults on two floors simultaneously.

In addition, he knew the situation was slow to unfold and created uncertainty. He commented that we kept it simple and didn't over-complicate the mission, yet had all areas covered with less than 16 team members. And we were also able to pull off the best element of an assault – surprise.

"Well done," he said, then joked, "Again, really, what Army unit trained you guys?"

The best compliment came two weeks later, when the major general who agreed to roleplay in the hostage exercise was having a change of command ceremony and requested our tactical presence there. A change of command ceremony is a very important part of military history, where one senior commanding officer passes the torch to his or her replacement. Most change of command ceremonies are held outdoors or in large aircraft hangars; they are large events attended by many high-ranking military and government officials. Before the fall of the Berlin Wall and demise of the RAF, these events in Germany were still considered high-risk for potential attacks.

We were honored to participate. It wasn't the last Army or Air Force change of command we were requested to support – not to mention many other high-profile events and unique missions after this exercise and demonstration of our team's capabilities.

Short caveat: This story was not about how good we were or to embellish our roles or capabilities. The late '70s and '80s were very important initial training and development years for most new special military units and counterterrorism teams. These new roles and responsibilities resulted from a very active decade of terrorist attacks, airplane hijackings and kidnappings all over the world.

Our small 16-man team, with an average age of 25, was underequipped and underfunded compared with any German special tactical unit or most U.S. military special operations teams. However, on that day, we earned the respect of the military community (and gained a new respect for ourselves). We proved that realistic training, proper mindset and fitness, along with can-do attitudes can overcome seemingly insurmountable odds, even with our disadvantages. We were able to adapt and develop an impressive capability as a young but motivated team.

A few months later, I was promoted to EST Field Supervisor and assumed the role Higgins and Ziggy had occupied before me. Taking advantage of the success of this exercise and other real-world deployments, I drafted a white paper requesting full-time EST status for our team. This request ran through our EST unit commander, the security forces group commander and eventually our vice base commander. It was ultimately approved, and we were relieved of our normal duties and assigned 24/7 alert status. To my knowledge, this might have been a first for the U.S. Air Force EST.

Vice Base Commander Colonel Cassius A. ("Cash") Harris IV was on loan from the Defense Intelligence Agency (DIA) and would provide us all the top cover we needed to successfully operate and gave approval for our EST's full-time status. He was an important mentor in my military life and later regarding my CIA recruitment and decision. I often referred to him as my Air Force father. He and his lovely wife Beverly also opened their home and guest bedroom for me years later when I first entered the CIA and needed a place to land in the D.C. area.

The first real EP training I ever received in my military career was in 1988 and included instructors who were former members of the original counterterrorism SEAL team under Richard ("Dick") Marcinko, a larger-than-life and sometimes controversial member of the SEAL community, best-selling author and TV commentator. Dick and Cash had a long professional and personal history going back to their days in Vietnam together. They coordinated my first defensive (counterterrorism) driver training and tactical shooting course back in the U.S., which is where I met and spent several days with Frank, another founding member of the same special SEAL team, and Lee, a former Army Special Forces counterterrorism team commander. Both gentlemen left an indelible impression on me, a young airman who was just getting started in his career.

On more than one occasion in the early '90s, I was instructed by Cash to meet with Dick to discuss certain professional decisions in my life. I am not sure these discussions produced anything tangible but spending a few hours with Dick was always interesting and, as anyone who knows him would probably agree, very entertaining.

While catching up with a group of former Air Force colleagues/ friends not long ago in Texas, one of them reminded me of the time awhile back when he was going through a very rough patch in his career and life. Dick had gone through a similar experience so, at that time, I asked if he would call my friend and provide him some much-needed encouragement, which I felt only Dick could. For no personal gain or recognition, Dick didn't hesitate to help another veteran in need and surprised him with a call. My friend had a hard time believing Dick was actually calling – and he kept saying to him, "Who the fuck is this really??" Finally, he got past his doubt and they began to connect on a level that most could not. For that call, both he and I were extremely appreciative.

Our EST commander at the time was Captain Clifford ("Skip") Day, who provided us with all the group support we needed to be relieved of normal duties in order to train and travel as needed. Skip went on to become one of the most senior and decorated colonels in the USAF Security Forces (and the Air Force as a whole) and served in several commands. He also received a Bronze Star in Operation Just Cause during the incursion in Panama.

Many of our team members during this time went on to have very successful careers within the USAF Security Forces, Office of Special Investigations, special units and other organizations during and after their enlistments.

Team leader Garth ("Ziggy") Freund continued up the ranks in the USAF Security Forces, achieving the highest enlisted grade of chief master sergeant before retiring after 30 years of service. Garth was also highly respected and decorated, known for being one of the best Air Force competitive shooters and an extremely resourceful leader in the field while taking care of his troops in various theaters of operation around the world.

EST member William Calvin ("Will" or "Charlie Mike," his military call sign) Markham eventually cross-trained to be a part of the Air Force Combat Control Teams. In the weeks after 9/11, Will was requested by name to join the U.S. Army's 5th Special Forces Group Operational Detachment Alpha (ODA) 555 that linked up with CIA Counterterrorism Center (CTC) operators under the direction of Cofer Black, Gary Schroen, Hank Crumpton and others.

I would eventually come to know both Hank and Cofer, and at times both of them would fall under our protective umbrella while traveling with Director Tenet. The 5th Special Forces ODA detachments were the first military teams on the ground in Afghanistan in the U.S. manhunt for Osama bin Laden. Will was attached as the link between the ground team and the Air Force support; he directed numerous GPS-guided Joint Direct Attack Munitions (JDAMs) during the initial response to what would become Operation Enduring Freedom.

Will went on to serve as a three-time command chief with the 352nd Special Operations Wing at RAF Mildenhall in the U.K., the Combined Joint Special Operations Air Component in Afghanistan, and the Special Operations Air Warfare Center at Hurlburt Field in

Florida. I was fortunate to be able to attend his retirement ceremony along with Skip and other friends from our former military days.

In the mid-1990s, I was recruited by the CIA after serving 10 years on military active duty. A few years later, I helped pave the path to the Agency for two former EST members and good friends from our days in Europe. I bumped into one of these team members at the White House after I had been a special agent serving on the Director's protection detail for a couple years. Todd was a Secret Service tactical team member assigned to the White House, but I hadn't seen him in almost six years. Months later, I was able to assist in Todd's transition to the CIA, where our paths would cross a little more often as Todd would eventually assume a senior and important role in the Agency's global close protection capabilities.

Jim ("Z-man") was another EST team member and close friend during those days. After serving more than 20 years and honorably retiring from the Air Force Security Forces, we were able to bring Z-man into the CIA as well, with most of his time dedicated to overseas protective operations. Many other team members went on to serve in other unique roles and positions, both in the military and as civilians and dedicating their lives and work to our nation's security. Twenty-five years ago, those of us who trained hard and belonged to a little "ragtag" special tactics team in Europe had no idea what was in our futures – or that we then belonged to a unique "career incubator" which fed our desire for more out of our lives and service to our country.

In retrospect, I have enormous gratitude for the direction I received from my superiors. I also made lifelong friends, as we were all committed to the same objective: protecting others.

Flugtag Air Show Disaster – A Defining Experience

On August 28, 1988, the roadways, autobahns, hotels and *gasthausen* (guest houses) around Ramstein, Germany, were packed with enthusiastic crowds in anticipation of the annual Ramstein Air Base air show called "Flugtag" (German for "air display").

Flugtag had its humble beginnings in the late 1950s and continued through three subsequent decades. The annual turnout continued to grow from thousands to hundreds of thousands. In 1988, the crowd had grown to over 300,000 – an enormous number of people to manage for one day only on an overseas U.S. air base normally closed to all non-authorized civilians.

In the 1980s, criticism of the air show was increasing among the "peace" and anti-military activist movements. Criticism was also voiced by other groups with a more aggressive position of opposition: Seven years prior in 1981, the German terrorist group known as the Red Army Faction slipped onto the base and detonated a car bomb at the USAFE headquarters.

Nevertheless, Flugtag was always an overwhelmingly spectacular annual event which united the local German and American communities as they hosted thousands of other European visitors to an air show full of thrills, drinks, food, souvenirs, cameras and smiles. But, in a matter of seconds that day, smiles and laughter were replaced with screams that turned to disbelief, nausea and shock.

No one could have anticipated the tragedy that unfolded during the very last event of the day, changing thousands of lives forever.

During this time, I was serving as a ground combat instructor and a member of the Air Force Emergency Service Team (EST), which consisted of 15 operators, a field supervisor and a team commander. As mentioned previously, EST was the Air Force equivalent of SWAT blended with anti-terrorism and counterterrorism training and responsibilities. On this day, in addition to the hundreds of Air Force security forces and other assigned security personnel, the SEK German special police and our EST had rehearsed and were prepared for bilateral counterterrorism measures in the event of an attack. Our EST members were dressed in our black "sterilized" tactical uniforms, meaning they had no names or patches other than the American flag on the upper-left shoulder.

Our preparations were extensive: We had strategic teams in place for surveillance from building tops and helicopters, and others who wore civilian clothes to blend in with the crowds. We had multiple teams ready for deployment to counter an attack in key areas of the base to protect vital operational resources. One team provided a buffer zone across the runway positioned in front of our base weapons storage area – a large and very significant armament depository being used at that time as a major deterrent during the Cold War.

At about 3:30 pm, 10 Aermacchi MB-339 jets from the Italian Frecce Tricolori team took off for what was supposed to be the most exciting performance of the day – and the show's grand finale. First, two groups of jets would create a vertical heart shape with smoke trails over the audience and along the runway. To complete the lower tip of the heart, the two groups would pass each other parallel to the runway. At the same time and location, the heart would be "pierced" in the direction of the spectators by a single aircraft. This extremely close crossing of aircraft at a single point would take place at the center of the runway less than 500 feet above the ground.

This spectacular aeronautical maneuver had been performed hundreds of times flawlessly to the excitement and amazement of audiences throughout Europe. Unfortunately, on this sunny German afternoon, disaster struck.

At 3:44 pm, three of the aircraft collided at the point of the pierced heart. Lt. Colonel Ivo Nutarelli, the pilot of the solo aircraft, was flying too low and fast at the end of his maneuver. Just seconds before the crash, it was reported he lowered his landing gear in a possible attempt to slow his speed. He was unable to adjust before striking the tail section of one of the crossing jets at roughly 300 miles per hour.

The second jet lost control and struck a third jet, which crashed into a U.S. Army UH-60 Black Hawk medevac helicopter sitting off the runway, standing ready for use in an emergency. The third jet crashed and disintegrated in the collision; parts were spread all over the runway. The pilot ejected but died after hitting the ground when his parachute didn't open in time. A few of the seven remaining Aermacchi jets sustained damage but all were able to land at nearby Sembach Air Base.

The solo jet's trajectory after the mid-air collision could not have been worse; it took a path like an unguided missile straight to the ground toward the spectators and exploded in a massive fireball of jet fuel. The aircraft tumbled and rolled off the runway, exploding over the top of a German police vehicle, killing the officer and his working dog. The wreckage continued tumbling and picking up razor-sharp concertina wire that had been placed along the runway to keep spectators from wandering onto it during the show.

What was left of the solo jet eventually came to rest against a refrigerated trailer being used to provide ice cream and ice to various food booths during the air show – but not before the jet, fuel, fire, razor wire, debris and exploding shrapnel had left a path of death and destruction in its wake. Tragically, this path went through thousands of international spectators. Most were German civilians from all over the country, including air show enthusiasts. Others included our U.S. servicemen and women, their families and friends.

Approximately 40 people died instantly at the crash site, including the three Italian pilots. At least another 30 died hours and days later from their injuries. Some suspect the final number to be higher, since the official count was made a few months after the crash while many surviving victims were still hospitalized and being treated for their injuries. Nearly 1,000 people needed emergency medical treatment following the crash, and many had to endure painful skin graft surgeries on their burns for years to come.

At the time of the crash, I was with Technical Sergeant Garth Freund (Team Leader), two other members of our EST team and Horst Mehlinger from SEK. We happened to be walking toward the area near the runway* – and were only about 100 yards away when the mid-air collision occurred. The three of us watched with horror and disbelief as the large fireball rose high in the air. We quickly sprinted to the crash site without hesitation – but had no idea what we were running toward.

Like everyone that day, we were not prepared for what we saw. I can still vividly recall the horrific images that would consume us for the

---

* At that very location, members of the 7002 Combat Engineers Group (Red Horse) had set up a food booth (as many units often did to make a little extra money).

next several days – and affect many for the rest of their lives. Many of these images are too graphic to describe, but it's said a badly burned body is one of the worst sights and smells a human can take in – and I will agree. It is especially terrible when the injured person is still alive and begging for help but is missing body parts or has no identifiable features.

Our second EST was positioned near the weapons storage area, very close to the UH-60 Black Hawk helicopter impacted by the third plane. Several members of our team ran to the helicopter to help, but they couldn't reach the pilot, 1st Lt. Kim Strader, who was pinned inside the aircraft because of the flames. They did their best but couldn't pull him from the fire until after the fire trucks arrived and extinguished the blaze. Lt. Strader was eventually flown to Brooke Army Medical Center in Texas to receive treatment for the burns covering most of his body. While at the Burn Center, the Army promoted him to the rank of captain. The newly promoted captain and father of five died that same evening.

Soon, I ran into Sergeants Mike Maloney and Tony Weatherholt, two good friends and fellow combat instructors, who partnered with me to provide any assistance we could to the injured. All first responders realized a triage area needed to be established quickly to try to distinguish those who required immediate help from those who needed only minor first aid – or those who had already perished from their injuries.

Immediately, it became evident we were not prepared or equipped for such a mass casualty event. We used makeshift stretchers and litters to load the injured into buses and other vehicles now used as ambulances, and we quickly ran out of the medical supplies most victims needed, including IV fluids.

Military personnel and civilians alike pulled together to provide aid to the injured and assist those searching for lost family members and friends – many of whom were separated by the crash and some of whom had literally vanished from where they were last standing. I remember one man I was helping to find his wife saying, "It was as if she just evaporated in front of me – where did she go…?"

Mike and I ran to more than 10 individuals lying on the ground with significant injuries and trauma, most of whom died as we tried to provide some level of first aid or just an assurance they would be okay – even when we could tell they would not survive. I remember one woman who had a large piece of aircraft shrapnel lodged in her chest with most of her intestines exposed. Amazingly, she was still alive and begging for us to help her, but as we tried to keep the shrapnel stable and assess what we could do, it was not enough. I'll never forget the helpless look in her eyes, and I'm sure we probably had the same look in ours.

As events unfolded around us at Ramstein, a couple members of our team knew their wives were near this location. That meant while we were helping others, we were also looking for their loved ones. When we would find a badly injured or deceased woman who was difficult to identify due to her injuries, it was with painful trepidation we would look at her face in fear it would be one of our team members' wives. Hours later, we were able to confirm all were accounted for.

Our EST duty had started at 5:00 am, and most of us didn't turn our weapons in and return home until nearly 40 hours later. Through those long hours, we continued to do our best to help the injured, and assisted our security forces with the effort of ensuring over 300,000 spectators were escorted from our secure base. We established a temporary morgue at the south gym and an incident scene command post, and we secured the crash scene corridor.

We helped to direct scores of individuals and families to a nearby base's movie theater, which had been established as a rallying point for those still looking for friends and family members. Many would remain at the theater for days, waiting to receive information about their loved ones, as the injured were sent to more than 20 different local and regional hospitals (many were found without identification and were unconscious long after).

A couple hours after the crash and by pure happenstance, a frantic woman approached me looking for help to find someone she knew. It was apparent very quickly she was the wife of the solo pilot, Lt. Colonel Nutarelli. My heart sank as I had seen his body earlier at the crash scene – he died instantly at the point of impact with the other aircraft.

I couldn't be the one to tell her, so I gently escorted her to another location for delivery of the devastating news.

Perhaps Roland Fuchs, who had been seriously burned over 65 percent of his body, summed it up best when he said:

> I cannot forget Ramstein. But I learnt to live with it. When someone says, "But it's so many years ago now, why do you still have to talk about it? Why do you still think about it?" I say that my dear ones will not come alive again even after so many years – and that even after so many years, my skin still has not grown back.[62]

It was only later that week after the events slowed down around me that I was able to process the crash. Fortunately, my wife and 18-month-old son had returned to the United States a few days before the air show to visit family. I was shaken by the thought that if they had been at the air show, they would likely have been at the same spot as they were the year prior. We had talked about how it was the perfect location from which to watch the show – and it was the exact location where the jet had now crashed into the spectators.

Shortly before completing the last edits to this book, my wife Cheryl and I made a trip to Germany to attend the yearly Flugtag disaster memorial service. Over the past 30 years, a memorial has been held in both the town of Ramstein, Germany, and on Ramstein Air Base, including at the actual crash site.[63] Though I had visited and traveled through Ramstein while at the CIA, I never had the opportunity to attend this event – and unfortunately had no knowledge of the fates of those I had tried to assist that day.

On this day, approximately 200 people (survivors and the families of those who perished) gathered at the city hall of Ramstein, where local German officials spoke before everyone was given an opportunity for about an hour of coffee and conversation. Afterward, we proceeded next door to St. Nikolaus Parish Church for a candlelit memorial service.[64]

As Cheryl and I first entered the municipal hall, many long tables were already full. We took seats at one of the only tables available, and a German gentleman and his wife sat down across from us. Almost immediately, and in our initial brief conversation before the speeches, he passed his cell phone across to me, where Cheryl and I began reading his (English) narrative of his experiences that day and the months after.[65] This man, Roland Fuchs, had been burned over 65 percent of his body and had been airlifted to a hospital, having no idea of the fate of his family until many weeks later, as he had to be put into an induced coma. Sadly, it was only then that he learned his beloved wife, Carmen, died at the crash site and their five-year-old daughter, Nadine, died several days later.

We also spoke with Sybille Jatzko, a trauma therapist, and her husband, Hartmut Jatzko, a former internal medicine physician and doctor of psychiatry. Since 1989, their work in providing free counseling to victims and survivors of Flugtag has been of immense importance. They have also been highly involved in organizing the memorial services over the past many years. In addition, they have volunteered their services by rendering post-disaster counseling to victims of major tragedies in other parts of the world, such as the 2000 Kaprun glacier railway fire in Austria and the 2004 earthquake and tsunami in South Asia, to name only a few. Through their aftercare foundation, they want to continue to provide long-term support to the many victims and survivors of tragedies around the world.

Though we couldn't speak German fluently, we nevertheless had very emotional connections with several others who suffered devastating injuries and/ or lost so many friends and family members at Flugtag. Marc-David Jung was only four years old when he attended the air show with his mother and father. His father died at the crash immediately; his mother was able to pull Marc-David from the jet-fueled flames, but not before he sustained burns over large portions of his body, including on much of his face. Today, he is an energetic testament to what the human spirit can endure – even after more than 30 operations, he takes his great smile and positive personality and inspires others at a foundation that champions care for victims after such tragedies.

As it happened, most of the victims were German, but an American couple came for the first time as well – Kirt and Laurie Shaffer. I somewhat recalled Kirt's face from those long-ago days at Ramstein: He was a member of the Air Force Explosive Ordnance Disposal (EOD) team, and our EST and EOD had worked together back then. Laurie and Kirt were newlyweds and Laurie had arrived in Germany just four days before the air show. Kirt sustained minor injuries, but Laurie had second- and third-degree burns over a quarter of her body and endured many months of treatments.

I also met Giancarlo Nutarelli, the brother of the Italian solo pilot whose miscalculations were believed to have caused the catastrophe. Giancarlo has honorably (and no doubt painfully) represented his brother and the Italian Air Force in their shared sorrow for what happened on that day. He has spoken at many of the annual memorials and met many of the survivors and family members of the victims – perhaps to give voice to his brother's perpetual request for forgiveness.

(L to R) Giancarlo Nutarelli (pilot Ivo Nutarelli's brother) and his wife, Laura Cecchini; Roland and Elisabeth Fuchs; Kirt and Laurie Shaffer; and me.

Later in the evening as I reflected on this very emotional day, I felt a sense of familiarity with Roland, a person I had only just met. I kept thinking: *How would I have known him?* I reread what I had included in the book about Flugtag – it turned out, some time ago I had read some articles and saw a quote by Roland when a reporter asked why he kept coming to the memorial services. When I first put down my reflections of that terrible day, I knew I wanted to use his profound quote. It still gives me chills to know he was the first person I happened to meet and speak with at this memorial, 30 years later.

In one tragic afternoon, so many lives were altered forever. And, like for so many others that day, for me, it was only the result of a few small details in timing that prevented me and my family from being yet another part of their shared tragedy. I believe Roland sums it up well when he says, "I cannot forget Ramstein."

The memorial honoring those who died at the Flugtag Air Show that has been created on the Ramstein Air Base, Kaiserslautern, Germany.

My time and experiences at Ramstein were amazingly diverse. I would even say they were life-changing and became part of the most formative years of my life. I watched my son grow up through his fifth birthday, made many lifelong friends, trained hard and developed skills I have utilized throughout my career, and experienced events which would shape my future perspective on life.

Undercover Narcotics – Basic Training for a Solo Practitioner

Until 1990, I had mostly worked in teams. I was in for a rude awakening that year when I was requested to go undercover. In many ways, those experiences have remained with me today – especially when I've needed to operate alone.

I spent the last 18 months of my assignment in Germany as an undercover narcotics agent on a trilateral Joint Drug Enforcement Team (JDET). This team consisted of members of the Air Force Office of Special Investigators and Security Forces, criminal investigators from Army Criminal Investigation Command (CID) and the German Police narcotics division (better known as K5) from nearby Kaiserslautern.

Our primary directive was to investigate any military members or attached civilians (family members, contractors or civil service employees) using, selling or facilitating the use of illegal narcotics – as well as anyone distributing to these groups or having a negative impact on U.S. military operations within Germany and USAFE.

Our team became very successful because of the flexibility we had as a trilateral unit. For example, we would sometimes need to allow a dealer to take money in a small drug purchase that we felt might lead to a bigger deal or arrest. If the Air Force wouldn't supply the cash, our Army counterparts might be in a better position to do so via their judge advocate.* And if they couldn't for some reason, our German counterparts might provide it themselves.

Similarly, if we couldn't get a search warrant on an American living off base, we would ask our German partners who could secure it in most cases. The Germans made use of our team too; for instance, if

---

* All branches of military service have their own judge advocate office, "legal offices" and military attorneys who represent our Uniform Code of Military Justice (UCMJ).

they couldn't get a military source in a club, they would ask us or our CID partners for assistance.

After my initial investigations and undercover training, I spent my remaining time in Germany recruiting and managing human sources regarding illegal narcotics use, possession and distribution. This was a 180-degree turn from my military role as a special weapons and tactics operator, instructor and close protection driver – and a particular turn I really didn't see coming in my military career.

One of the first things that often happened working in undercover narcotics – especially in Europe during the early '90s – is that you had to grow out your hair and try not to look like you're a soldier or an investigator. For someone like me, who had a clean-cut look for the prior seven years, it took some getting used to, as well as time to let it all grow out. Today, many of our special operators and contractors serving in various locations around the world look like desert Bedouins or Sons of Anarchy and do not shave for months, if not years. Even today, the military has a very strict code regarding hygiene and hair length, so I had to receive an AFR35-10 (USAF military dress code regulation) waiver since I was no longer compliant. Many of my superiors didn't like this, but it came with the job requirements.

At the time, I had no real idea where my professional career would take me or how working as an undercover narcotics investigator would benefit me after Germany or the Air Force. As I found out, it gave me invaluable new skills, especially when it comes to working alone, staying calm under pressure, and the crucial requirement to pay particular attention to many details at once. In many instances, my life and the well-being of a source depended on these abilities.

Working alone as an undercover agent is like walking a tightwire without a net. When you are part of a team, you train and operate together – and you know someone has your back. Even if you get injured, someone will grab you and pull you to safety. But as an undercover agent buying or orchestrating the purchase of drugs from dealers in the streets, if it goes wrong and you're solo, it's all on you. This is similar to being a single EP agent and, even though it's not recommended, sometimes it comes with the position.

I had to learn many of the required skills very quickly out of necessity – and they still resonate with me today. Often, I'll find myself in situations where certain flashbacks have occurred that have given me a subtle reminder to pay particular attention to a situation or person – or acknowledge a gut feeling.

There are many books and business leaders providing advice and techniques to help a person master quick decision-making. Malcolm Gladwell refers to it as "thin-slicing" in his book *Blink: The Art of Thinking Without Thinking*.[66] Whatever you call it and wherever you learn it, it is a required skill in undercover narcotics, and I have found that it transfers well to close protection.

Drug Bust Gone Wrong

In one mission, the Air Force undercover narcotics team was working with the German narcotics division to target a dealer who was reportedly selling drugs to American military members. The plan included using a German undercover officer to attempt a "buy bust" where the dealer often conducted his transactions. The purchase was being conducted in a German low-income housing community.

On this warm July day, I and two other German agents were positioned in the back of a large truck that had small holes out of which we could observe and take photographs of the transaction(s).

After waiting longer than we expected in the back of this truck – with no ventilation and now soaking wet after three hours – our undercover officer made contact: He was making the purchase as planned, just three hours late. (Drug dealers are never on time.)

After the officer made the purchase, he immediately advised the dealer he was under arrest. The dealer looked defeated, as if he wasn't going to resist – when suddenly he took a swing at the officer and took off running. Our team had two vehicles on opposite ends of the main road, but they were far enough away they couldn't see or be seen by the dealer. We were closer – less than 75 feet away in the truck. We saw the signal for the deal, but before we could open the truck door, he was already making a run for it. As we all took off on foot pursuit, the officer who made the buy yelled out, "He has a gun!"

The dealer was fast, but I was 26 years old and probably in the best shape of my life – I was on his heels. Two German officers were behind me, but one officer detoured through a small alleyway to head him off if he turned at the next corner, which he did. As we approached, I was only a few steps behind him; I took the corner wide in case he stopped and was waiting for me to come around.

As I cleared the corner, I saw him jump, slide over the hood of a vehicle and pull out a handgun. I yelled, "GUN!" and shouted his position to the other officers, who now stopped at the corner. I was now at the front of another vehicle adjacent to the one he had jumped behind. I positioned myself behind the engine block, assuming he might rise up over his vehicle and begin shooting. By now, I had pulled my weapon and was aiming where I saw him go over the hood.

At that point, he slowly rose above the hood. His pistol came up first – not pointing my way or at the other officers, but up in the air. This was not the first time someone had pointed a weapon at me or in my direction, yet it struck me as odd. Certain movements and details can seem like they play out in slow motion and you focus on the smallest of elements. What I remember most was a distinctive small red tip at the end of his barrel – after over 25 years I can still see it. I drew aim at what I thought would be his head following his weapon and yelled something like, "Drop your weapon or I WILL shoot you."

I couldn't be positive, but I felt the gun was possibly a pellet or BB pistol. *But was it?* In Germany at that time, carrying a handgun was very rare for anyone. Even most criminals didn't carry a weapon because of the strong gun laws and lack of tolerance for firearms – especially if someone carried a weapon in conjunction with a drug deal.

I continued to verbally challenge him with my weapon drawn and aimed toward a small portion of his exposed head. My finger was on the trigger, and I waited for a movement that would allow me to shoot based on the situation and my training. He needed to display the reasons for deadly force, which consisted of *opportunity, capability* and *intent to shoot* at me, the other officers or bystanders. He was getting dangerously close, but he had not committed a violent crime *yet* or, more importantly, clearly presented justification for deadly force.

Then he dropped behind the vehicle again and went out of view. I continued to verbally challenge him when, suddenly, a handgun flew up in the air. It landed on the hood of the car and he took off running again.

I ran after him once more and yelled to the German officers behind me to grab the gun. We ran for another block; I was just a few feet from him and reached to grab his neck as we cleared another corner – but this time the officer who broke off earlier to enter the alley stepped out and clotheslined the dealer as he ran past at full speed. This guy literally came off his feet, flew through the air and landed hard on his head against the cobblestone street.

The pursuit was officially over. As it turned out, the gun was a CO_2 pellet pistol, and the end of the barrel was in fact red. The dealer will never know just how close he came to being shot in the head but, after hitting the hard cobblestone street, he probably felt like he had been.

Narcotics Team: 1 – Drug Dealers: 0

The A-Team

Three months later, this local drug gang got us back when we were conducting a similar operation. We were in an old, beat-up 1983 GMC van with blacked-out windows in the middle of a small German village where they were conducting "rolling" drug deals.

Their scheme worked like this: A car would turn onto a known dealer street and drive slowly. A runner (young kid) would jog up to the car, take the buyer's order and their money. He would run back into one of several apartment buildings and exit near the end of the street, then run back to the same car which was still driving slowly. He'd toss the drugs through the window and then run away.

As we drove down the street, the driver of our GMC van would toggle a custom switch that would stop fuel from getting to the carburetor, and we would pull over as if the van were out of gas. He would try to restart the van a few times; everyone watching could hear the engine turning but not starting. The driver would exit the van kicking and swearing and walk off.

In the meantime, I and another agent would be in the back of the van with a telescoping camera lens inside a pop-up roof vent on top of the vehicle. Our job was simply to observe the activity on the street, take pictures and capture license plates. We would radio in the make, plate and description of each driver and confirm the drug deal. The buying vehicle would drive out of the neighborhood and undercover German police officers would pull them over after they had cleared the area.

We had done this before and it was like shooting fish in a barrel – it seemed almost unfair. On this particular day, we had a lot of success in the morning. But as the day went on, the back of this van could get very warm. We had to be very quiet and ensure our movements didn't rock the vehicle, but after a few hours we were down to shorts and a shoulder holster with no shirts. As the day progressed, one young runner walked down to us and actually leaned against the side of the van waiting for his next customer. He was so close, we couldn't even see him from the telescoping camera on top of our vehicle.

This went on for some time and we had to be as still as possible. He stepped away and my partner (Army CID agent) slowly moved his stool to reposition where he was sitting. As he was getting ready to sit back down, the runner leaned against our vehicle again. My partner fell back ever so slightly and rocked the van. *Shit.*

We both froze – maybe the runner didn't notice. But he stepped away from the van, looking like a dog who had just heard a high-pitched whistle, and yelled to his buddies, "Jemand ist im van!" (Translation: "Someone is in the van!") *Shit.*

We radioed our support officers, but they were a mile down the road. Our driver was having lunch somewhere – probably smoking a cigarette and having a beer as he waited for the call to come back to our location (where he was to pretend to add fuel to the van, and drive off).

In the meantime, the young runner ran off and we thought: *Well this is a wrap, no more deals today.*

Minutes later, we saw him and a few others walk out of one of the apartments toward our van. Even though we couldn't see exactly what they were doing at first, we knew at once when we saw the flame of a Molotov cocktail coming toward us. We heard it hit the street in front of the van and slide underneath us – and had to admit, it was a good throw.

At this point, we had reasonably concluded they were sure someone was in the van.

Our radio communication was now a little more animated. Within seconds, we could smell smoke and see flames coming from under us. As trained investigators, this is what we call a "clue" and we decided at this point it might be a good time to exit the van. We flung the side doors open and leaped out wearing nothing but shorts and tennis shoes with guns drawn; it felt like an episode of *The A-Team*.

The dealers took off and our support team rolled in. Everyone was concerned for a few seconds but, as only a bunch of narcotics officers could do, they immediately started laughing and busting on my partner and me.

Narcotics Team: 1 – Drug Dealers: 1

Deep Undercover Assignment

By this time, I had bought, facilitated and investigated the purchase of narcotics for nearly 18 months. I had followed or, in some cases, led a bilateral German-American assault team through many doors of suspected dealers' homes or businesses.

On one occasion, I accepted a 60-day deep undercover assignment out of my normal area of operation. At a military base in central Europe, it had been reported a group of civil service contractors performing maintenance support for Air Force F-15 fighter jets were heavily using and distributing various types of narcotics.

An American source caught trafficking narcotics across the German-Dutch border was now cooperating with German and American authorities to reduce the sentence hanging over his head.

(We call this a "hammer.") I was to use him as an introduction into this group and as a way to urgently investigate the reports of the narcotics used by these contractors – which included acid, hashish, cocaine and other substances.

I had a support agent who was with AFOSI and was my investigation lifeline if I needed anything. Other than that, I was on my own to investigate and collect as much information as possible on this group's illegal and potentially dangerous activity – including doing whatever it took legally to gain access to this group and confirm the use, sale and distribution of drugs. This mission was especially important because their activity could lead to the crash of a $30 million F-15 fighter jet and the possible deaths of a pilot and/or those on the ground.

My cover story was deep: I had recently arrived in Germany and was living in a hotel waiting for my active-duty Air Force wife to return from an assignment in Turkey. I would be joining her as we moved into base housing, which we were waiting to become available. I had met my source in a bar and we both had knowledge of living in Arizona (true). Our conversations had at some point turned to drugs. I wanted access to large quantities to smuggle back to the U.S. via military aircraft. Since I was new to Germany and the area, my source had supposedly offered to hook me up with some small personal-use drugs and introduce me to some of his new friends. My goal was to get him to help identify any active-duty military members using or distributing narcotics throughout the investigation.

It wasn't long before he introduced me to the group with whom he had been partying, which led me straight into the den of a very warped group of civilians who spent most of their time drunk, high and hallucinating – and, did I mention, *worked on F-15 fighter jets.*

My support agent had secured a small covert office for me in an industrial park in the back of an empty warehouse, where I would go late at night to work on documents, record statements and secure evidence in a safe. I also had a small bed and TV there for times when I just needed a place to get away and crash for a while, which came in handy after long nights.

Because this case included investigating foreign nationals in addition to potential active-duty military members, military dependents and civil service employees, my investigation and documentation process was extensive. As any deep undercover agent can tell you, keeping up with all the moving parts of your own story is hard enough, but keeping up with everyone else's story and the evidence trail are the essential elements that would eventually lead to a successful conclusion (prosecution) after thousands of hours of work and personal sacrifice.

The one major difference between undercover and normal investigations is you don't have an "off" switch – you're on stage performing until the director yells, "It's a wrap!" For some agents, this can be weeks or months; for some, it's years. Some even die while remaining undercover. True undercover performance for long periods of time takes incredibly unique people who are able to put their real lives on hold throughout the time they must assume their new roles. Very few people can do it and, after my 18 months, I realized it was all becoming too much of a sacrifice for me and my family.

Straining me further, I rarely got to speak with my wife or son over the phone during this one 60-day assignment. We didn't have FaceTime or Skype during those days, nor did the average person even have a cell phone. Any separation from your family and children can be very difficult, but during this undercover operation, it was imperative my cover story was never compromised. I was instructed not to contact my family unless absolutely necessary, but not seeing or talking to my four-year-old son for those months might have been the hardest part of this operation.

My efforts, introductions and "confidence" purchases or gifts (drugs) from my new friends had taken me all over central Germany and across the borders to several other countries. During the final meeting, where I had arranged for a large purchase of hashish and negotiated for kilos of cocaine, we met at a location familiar to the dealers – a small private dining room in a restaurant owned by one of them. My German investigator counterparts didn't like the meeting location because it made it difficult for them to conduct surveillance or respond to me if I was in trouble. I didn't disagree, but the dealers were insistent, and I consented to their location so as not to spook them.

After several hours of conversation, food and liquor, they did what many dealers usually do: They wanted to see us (the buyers) use drugs as well. Without going into details, there are ways to simulate the actual use of certain narcotics. I was able to excuse my way out of using a *heavy* narcotic that night, but my main contact rolled a joint the size of a Churchill cigar to be shared at the table. With what I felt were all eyes on me, I will admit, my "simulation" this time was not as "simulating" as other times.

Over the weeks leading up to this night – and especially that night at the table – we had discussed a lot of information which allowed me into their criminal world, and my source and I were not walking out of there without a deal. After all, I wasn't going to give them any reason to suspect I wasn't a real dealer myself. With any criminal element, when you have been invited behind closed doors and given insight to their operations (e.g., names, locations, methods, etc.), you have just become a liability – and some will not think twice about eliminating a liability when they feel it's necessary, especially if their freedom is on the line.

I've always been able to control my simulated drug or alcohol use to be able to maintain my composure (and more importantly, my cognitive thought process to keep me alive). But my source was losing his mind and control over shots of vodka – in addition to the hashish he had used without my knowledge. I felt I was now losing command over the situation and didn't like where this could go. He was beginning to ramble about sensitive subjects and conversations, and it was becoming a major concern for our cover. After kicking him several times under the table, I knew I had to move the deal forward quickly before he said the wrong thing and created a situation where it was the two of us against the eight of them – not the kind of odds I like, especially since I was unarmed and he wasn't able to stand up straight.

It was after midnight by now. The restaurant was closed and only we "dealers" were inside. As we concluded the deal, it was time to show the money, but I had to see what I was buying first. They took me out the back door into the alley. After confirming the presence and the grade of the narcotics, I told them the money was in the glove box of my car outside. One of them escorted me back through the restaurant to the front, where my car was parked across the street and under a streetlight.

The signal for the German police and assault team was me coming out to my car. If I had seen the narcotics and the deal was in fact going down, I would enter the passenger side to get the money. If I hadn't seen the drugs yet and they just wanted to see the money first, I would enter the driver's side. If I needed help right now, I would tap the brake lights when I got the money out of the glove box. Otherwise, five minutes after returning to the restaurant, the assault team would descend on the building – so I had to wrap it up fast and get my source in a safe position. I'd worked with the German assault teams before, and when they hit a target, it was all business.

As we went back inside, the guy who had escorted me locked the front entryway by sliding three deadbolts on a solid-core door. After being inside for more than three hours, my main concern was: Did the German team see me come out and enter the car (i.e., give the signal)? The best-case scenario was leaving the restaurant with a large amount of narcotics and the team pouncing on the restaurant, arresting anyone still there, seizing the money and drugs, and calling it a night.

The worst-case scenario was they would take my money (supplied by the German police), not give me my drugs and escape out to the back alley – after beating the shit out of me and my drunk and extremely high source. I had a few other scenarios racing through my mind, too – none of them good.

Fortunately, before any of the worst cases played out, we heard a loud bang and crash in the front of the restaurant. Like clockwork, the assault team arrived, making mincemeat of the heavy secure door and a large plate glass window. Within seconds, the German assault team was tossing us around like rag dolls with guns in our faces as they apprehended everyone in the restaurant. I pulled a "Marion Barry" and accused my new friends of setting me up as they threatened to kill me. After we all exchanged a series of vulgar "pleasantries," we were all handcuffed and hauled away to the German police department.

Naturally, I was part of the arrest in order to preserve my cover. But realistically, once the team assaulted the location, the jig was up and all eyes were on me. Fortunately, I had been able to cultivate all the required intelligence and evidence for a major buy-bust that culminated on that very night. This 60-day buy-bust investigation included a group of Italian dealers that were smuggling large quantities of narcotics across the German and Italian borders.

While the operation resulted in numerous arrests and the largest seizure of narcotics since our JDET's inception, unfortunately, it didn't even scratch the surface. The arrests made big news within the German military community, and the best news was that all the contractors were removed from their positions as F-15 maintenance workers.

A few weeks later, I was presented with a Commendation Medal for my undercover investigation and efforts. After being in Germany for nearly six years, it all now came to an end, as the general consensus was there could be retaliation against me after the arrests. A few months later, my family and I were headed back to the United States, where I served the next two years as an instructor for the Air Force Security Forces Academy – and where my career path made the transition from the Air Force to the CIA.

Returning to the Academy

When my undercover narcotics agent days ended, I accepted a special duty assignment as an instructor at the 343rd Training Squadron Security Forces Academy at Lackland Air Force Base in San Antonio, Texas. After leaving the academy nearly eight years prior, I didn't expect to be back as an instructor, but it was a rewarding assignment for which I'm very thankful now.

I spent the years from 1992 to 1995 back at the Academy. During this time, we taught a variety of courses to thousands of students, including in field, tactical and weapons training, basic first aid, self-defense skills, nuclear weapons and convoy security, along with many other academic and field topics.

The responsibility of training another person is an important skill and can be inspiring as you see the individual grow in knowledge and confidence. In many cases, you can watch the transformation right in front of your eyes – and it's a source of pride that stays with you for life.

During those 30 months, my fellow instructors and I helped prepare young men and women who had entered the Air Force Security Forces career field and, after graduation, would be sent to all parts of the world to protect Air Force people, assets and operations. Many airmen go on to receive other advanced training and are assigned to unique military operations around the world.

Even a few years after I had left the U.S. Air Force, there were times I didn't feel I had strayed too far from the service, as I would often find myself on USAF aircraft again. On one particular trip to a high-threat area overseas, an airman came up to me and said, "Are you Sergeant Trott and were you a Team Four instructor at the Security Forces Academy?"

I replied, "Yes." He said, "You were my instructor." Once we caught up a little on life after the Academy, he told me what he took from my conversations with him and the other students: to remain motivated and not settle for routine assignments if there was something else you wanted to do with your career. Shortly after his graduation, he looked for greater responsibilities and sought out special duty assignments. "And here I am," he said. He was a member of the Air Force Ravens, a specially trained security team assigned to protect USAF aircraft and airfields in high-risk areas. We chatted awhile about all the extra stress we instructors would put on students as he recalled some of his most memorable moments at the Academy.

There would be other times where I would bump into other military personnel around the world, sometimes when I needed them the most. This continued to instill in me the importance of maintaining the network we build as part of the *other* "one-percent club" – those serving or who have served in the U.S. armed forces.

My Time at the CIA

Being a special agent for the CIA was an honor, privilege and sometimes just simply cool. These were perhaps my best professional years. It was a lot like being in the military, with patriotism, camaraderie, extensive travel, mission and success all wrapped up together in various degrees of adventure and risk – and I was being paid on top of it all.

It was an incredible privilege to work with so many distinguished and talented colleagues who also became my friends while serving on the Director's security staff. I'm sure every organization can talk about the talent and skills within their group, but there was a good reason the Director's security staff was known as a talent pool for other groups within the Office of Security and other Agency directorates, especially the Directorate of Operations. Because of the diversity of skills, backgrounds, education, language, experience, training, commitment and amount of global travel most agents had under their belts after a few years on the staff, they all were a much-sought-after commodity within the Agency.

I know government jobs and employees can be the butt of jokes, but I can tell you firsthand I've never seen an organization work harder, be more determined and exhibit an all-consuming dedication to performance than the men and women of the CIA. For the purposes of this book, I don't wish to debate or defend the Agency's work, break down its successes or failures, or discuss politics and decisions made. I'm simply saying it was a time in my career where I belonged to a cadre of true professionals. I am very proud to have been a part of it, and to this day I still call them family. Like any family, we too have found ways to stay connected and support one another through the years, even after we've left "home."

However, I do consider many of the years at the Agency as my "lost" years regarding my actual family, which was also true for many other Agency employees. The tempo of the work of the CIA was all-consuming and often caused us to sacrifice birthdays, anniversaries and many holidays. Working for the 24/7 protective detail for the Director of Central Intelligence with an exhausting travel schedule and long hours of overtime didn't leave much time for family. My first wife (Angie) was also a government employee; she was very good at her job and often sought after because she was so competent and dedicated.

Regrettably, after 9/11, my travels and Agency commitments along with our grueling schedules caused our son to become a "latchkey" child during periods of his early teens. The many years of stress, long hours and work separation between the military and CIA led to what happens to so many couples at both institutions, and unfortunately our marriage ended after 21 years.

Thank God, I was given a second chance a few years later with a wonderful woman who has spent most of her career working for high-profile and UHNW individuals – including the late Teddy Forstmann, co-founder of Forstmann, Little & Co. and former Chairman of Gulfstream Aerospace. Cheryl's familiarity with and understanding of CEOs and executives, as well as the responsibilities, commitments and absences from home that often accompany executive protection, have all been much appreciated and endearing to me in my life and career. So, too, have been her uncompromising efforts in assisting with the editing of this book. Without her, it would not have been written. I have been blessed.

It's not possible to talk about my tenure and work at the Agency without including my primary principal, George Tenet. Almost all protectees, especially government officials, are given call signs; George was given "Iceman" by one of our agents.

In March 1997, I was assigned to the protective staff of the Director of Central Intelligence (i.e., the CIA's director). At the time, Tenet was the CIA's deputy director and serving as acting director following the resignation of John Deutch in December 1996.

When President Clinton's nominee to replace Deutch withdrew from consideration, George Tenet was the next natural choice. Clinton needed someone who could do the job and truly understand the Agency he would lead – and, of course, get through the nomination process. This was especially important after Deutch's very short stint as director. In July 1997, Tenet was confirmed by a unanimous vote in the Senate as the 18th Director of Central Intelligence.

George served as the CIA's director for seven years under two presidential administrations, one Democrat and one Republican, and was the second-longest-serving director behind Allen Dulles. I was assigned to his protective detail for five of those seven years as a senior agent and assistant team leader.

It's often said if you want to know about a person of power or position, just ask their security detail about them. Again, this book is not about politics, nor am I trying to debate the history regarding the Agency or George Tenet as the CIA's director. But you will not find a special agent who was assigned to protect George to ever have a negative word about him as a man, principal or leader. Maybe it was the Agency, maybe the nature of the mission and maybe the excitement of our travels. But it also had to do with the way he treated and showed respect for his protective detail and the Agency. In turn, the men and women who had this assignment would have given their lives to ensure the safety of the Director and his family, and I can't think of a better principal to have had the privilege to protect than George Tenet.

I have all the respect in the world for all protective details, but one of the most dynamic and fast-paced careers or assignments you'll ever have is that of a CIA special agent serving on the Director's protective detail or for the CIA's special overseas security. I recall a poster in our office above our weapons safe room that read, "Sit down, shut up and hang on." Those words couldn't have been more accurate.

Americans – and most of the rest of the world – will never forget exactly where they were when the news coverage of the attacks of 9/11 began and the shock and disbelief that followed. Working for the CIA during this time felt like we were experiencing an undeclared war on our nation's intelligence community and capabilities, and for that reason it seemed personal to many of us.

On that morning, I was attending an off-road driving course located a couple hours outside of Washington, D.C., with a dozen other special agents and members of CIA overseas security. One of our instructors called us into a small trailer near the track that had a TV. We all sat in this small room, glued to the screen like millions of others, with a moment of shock but also with a bad gut feeling this wasn't just an accident. We contacted our offices in Langley for any direct updates and instructions. Then the second plane hit the towers, and, without conversation, we all ran to our vehicles and drove as fast as we could back to CIA headquarters.

Meanwhile, Director Tenet was having breakfast with ex-Senator David Boren at the St. Regis Washington, D.C., when Agent Tim Ward informed him a plane had flown into the World Trade Center's South Tower. As Tenet would later write in his book,[67] before the second plane hit the towers, Tenet knew this had to be the work of Al-Qaeda. He and his security detail immediately headed back to Langley headquarters.

As our team drove northbound on I-395, we approached the Pentagon – smoke was still billowing from the northwest side of the iconic building where hijacked American Airlines Flight 77 had been flown into it. We had emergency lights and sirens to expedite our drive but, for a brief moment, we pulled to the side of the road and tried to wrap our heads around this coordinated attack and loss of life. We had no idea if there would be further attacks – *was this only the beginning?*

But we also knew we had an important mission: protecting Director Tenet and Agency leadership during this attack on our country. This was the beginning of a "tour of duty" no one could have seen coming.

Not long after arriving back at headquarters, a decision had been made to move the Director and certain members of his executive team out of the main building to another location. Previous intel reports indicated Al-Qaeda had discussed flying a plane into the CIA headquarters and, given that there were planes still in the air with unconfirmed status, senior leadership just couldn't take that chance. The Counterterrorism Center (CTC), led by Cofer Black, hunkered down in their offices and immediately went into overdrive, essentially pulling out all of the CIA/CTC Al-Qaeda playbooks – the CTC had been sounding the alarm for some time.

Stephanie and George Tenet were friends with a couple named Michele and Tom Heidenberger, as their sons were also friends and schoolmates. Michele was a flight attendant for American Airlines and scheduled to fly that morning, but Tom had not heard from her. George was able to review the flight manifest and knew Michele was on Flight 77 from Dulles bound for Los Angeles – the hijacked plane that hit the Pentagon. A few days later, Tom asked George if he could see the Pentagon and the site where his wife and the others had died.

I was the shift leader that day as we took the Director, Stephanie and Tom to the Pentagon. With our credentials and by coordinating with our counterparts there, we were able to drive up very close. We got out of the vehicles and stood near the site of impact – still reeling with disbelief.

George recalls a moment in his book when he was home on his first day off after a couple months following the attacks and had a brief moment of personal reflection. He had been running on pure adrenaline and was under an incredible amount of stress ever since the planes hit the towers. He recalled how on this day, he went outside his home, sat in an Adirondack chair in the yard and "just lost it."

Any CIA director suffers enormous stress on a regular basis, but the weight of the attacks of 9/11 and leading the Agency's response to it was, understandably, overwhelming. I and another agent were at the Director's home that day in a vehicle across the yard from where he was sitting in that Adirondack chair. It was a poignant moment for us – we could now see the evidence of the cumulative strain and pressure he had silently carried over the past two months. Stephanie came out and sat with him – if she hadn't, we would have.

Of course, after 9/11, everyone's pace changed dramatically throughout all levels of the federal and state governments – e.g., first responders, military, police, contractors, investigators and supporting organizations. As I reflect back, the pace we had during this time was unsustainable. I recall sometimes only days or fast-paced weeks between foreign trips or other assignments.

A day in the life of a special agent can vary tremendously within hours – let alone a week, a month or a year. There was a reason we all had "go-bags" in the trunks of our vehicles. On more than one occasion, I would receive a call from headquarters directing me straight to the airport or an air base – sometimes with only a few minutes to swing by the house to repack a few things and tell my family I would be gone again. To see the heart-wrenching look and disappointment in my son's eyes during these short-notice trips as I rushed out the door was always like a punch in the gut. I always hated those moments and struggled each time I had to go so abruptly, leaving my young son when he needed Dad at home.

I was on a flight to Pakistan just days after 9/11 to prepare for an urgent meeting between the CIA's deputy director and Pakistani intelligence regarding certain cooperation requests the White House and the Agency had made regarding our efforts against Al-Qaeda. Given how recently we had been attacked, the prominence of our principal and our destination, this was not a normal advance. Tensions were high and so was our sense of street awareness – which you might have described as a "reasonable degree of paranoia."

Nine days later (and less than 48 hours after returning to CIA headquarters from Pakistan), I was back with the security detail and Director Tenet at Camp David (the presidential retreat compound and a location President Bush used for many meetings and planning sessions).

I'll never forget this particular Camp David trip. At this time, the administration was in full "plan-of-attack" mode and everyone was present: President George W. Bush, Vice President Dick Cheney, National Security Advisor Condoleezza Rice, Secretary of Defense Donald Rumsfeld, most of the rest of the cabinet and many members of the Joint Chiefs of Staff.

It was evening and the group was entering the dining room when I was contacted by the CIA Operations Center saying an urgent message was being sent through secure fax to be passed to the Director for immediate response. I was the shift leader, so I immediately took off on foot across the parking lot and down the hill to the Camp David communications office, where the message was being sent.

When I arrived at the communications office, I was handed an envelope marked "Director Eyes Only" and "Top Secret." As I was leaving the communications building, I received another call from the Ops Center asking me if I had the message. I said, "In hand ... I'm on the way to the Director." The caller responded, "We need an answer back in less than 10 minutes with a 'go' or 'no-go' or we lose a critical window."

I took off in a full sprint back up the hill to the main building where dinner was being served. I ran past our Secret Service colleagues at the front door and found our detail leader. As I reached out to give him the message to give to the Director, he pointed to the dining room and said with a smirk, "You give it to him." *Thanks.*

Out of breath, I looked at my watch, which I'd marked when I had the initial call with the Ops Center. Four minutes had passed. I peered through the door to the dining room to see where the Director was sitting. With only a couple exceptions, the entire cabinet of the President of the United States was gathered and getting ready to have dinner. Then I noticed the Director, sitting about as far as he could from the door. *Thanks again.*

I cracked the door open enough to hopefully get his attention. And I did get his attention – as well as the attention of the President, Vice President and everyone else sitting at the long dining table. I held up the envelope to the Director, hoping he would excuse himself and come out of the dining room to read it. He didn't. Instead, he waved for me to come to him. *I just couldn't catch a break.*

I looked at the Secret Service agent at the door and he looked at me as if to say: *Better you than me.* I entered the room and quickly took notice of everyone and their significance regarding our response to the attacks on our country that had taken place so recently. I paused slightly as I absorbed the magnitude of the group assembled there. I could feel my feet become heavy as anvils – it was almost as if everything was happening in slow motion as I walked across the room and looked at the faces present in this significant moment in time and history. It has been etched in my memory forever.

In those slow-motion seconds, the recent past flashed through my mind: I had just returned from South Asia less than 48 hours before, with aroma from the streets of Islamabad and the mountain air of northern Pakistan still fresh. Just a few months prior, I was supporting a mission in North Africa.

Now I was handing over a "Director Eyes Only" message with a critical time constraint of less than three minutes for response to a window of opportunity that was urgent to someone in the field waiting with major anticipation and the hope I was able to reach the Director in time.

I handed the Director the message, squatted near his seat and whispered, "The Ops Center needs a 'go, no-go' in less than three minutes." He quickly read it and said, "Go." As I was walking out of the room, I was already hitting the Ops Center speed dial on my cell phone.

I didn't know exactly what the message was requesting or if I actually had one hour or truly one minute to respond. I did know the answer the next morning after arriving back at Langley, which again reminded me of the incredibly dynamic and diverse responsibility of a special agent protecting and serving the CIA's director. From the repetitive and mundane to the ridiculously dangerous or precarious (and many classified moments in history), these experiences for me will never be forgotten – or exceeded.

As the previous example demonstrates, a unique privilege but extraordinary responsibility we had as CIA special agents was the exposure to highly sensitive and classified information – similar to what I passed to the Director that day. At times, this access could challenge your ability to maintain optimism regarding our nation's and the world's safety and security. Other times, it might be the very reason *for* optimism, but I must admit, not as frequently. Often, I would be in the presence of the Director when he was receiving the President's Daily Briefing (PDB) from our CIA briefer, most times in the vehicle and very early in the morning on our way to the White House to report to the President.

This exclusive and sensitive material is also known as the "President's

Book of Secrets." Since the days of President Kennedy, it has been prepared and delivered nearly 365 days a year by a dedicated team of CIA analysts to ensure the President and his closest national security and military advisors have the most up-to-date information regarding threats against our country or our national interests.

When George W. Bush became the Republican presidential nominee in 2000, I traveled to his ranch in Crawford, Texas, in advance of John McLaughlin (the CIA's deputy director), who would be part of Mr. Bush's intelligence briefing. Along with our technical team, I arrived to make sure the space was physically and technically secure for the soon-to-be 43rd president as he received his first major intelligence briefing, courtesy of the CIA.

After a quick check-in with the local Secret Service agent assigned to the nominee at that time, I knocked on the door of the small ranch house just down the road from where he would eventually build his new home (which became his "Crawford White House" and a place to which we would often return over the following years). To my surprise, Mr. Bush answered the door, welcomed me inside and kindly offered me a cup of coffee as we waited for McLaughlin and his team. I recall the comfortable and simple ranch home with stained concrete floors and a large picture that hung over the stone fireplace of "41" and "43" fishing from their bass boat, a favorite family activity.

George W. Bush would be a avid consumer of the CIA's PDB or "Book of Secrets" and often wanted the Director himself in the room during his briefings, a rare request among presidents. The major impact this had on Director Tenet and our protective detail was the day always started very, very early in the morning. The agents may have had a shift change at the 8th, 12th or 16th hours, but the Director didn't have that luxury – these were long days for him.

After my departure from the Agency, I still occasionally meet with former Director Tenet or see him at events we're both attending – sometimes even when I've been with a new protectee. At these levels, the circles get smaller and, in most cases, there is only one degree of separation between different protectees.

These small degrees of separation have continued throughout my career after leaving the Agency. I served four years (2004–2008) as Senior EP Security Advisor for a technology manufacturing company, its founder and their family. At one point, I was asked by another company if I would consider taking a position as an embedded security advisor for one of our Middle East allies. This project was managed by a Washington, D.C., consulting company led by Richard Clarke, former National Coordinator for Counterterrorism in the Clinton administration and Special Advisor for Cyberspace Security under former President Bush (43).

It's no secret Dick and George had opposing views on various subjects, including Iraq and Afghanistan. They didn't always see eye to eye, but I believe they do respect one another's work on behalf of our nation's intelligence efforts. George was kind enough to make a call on my behalf and deliver a personal reference for this job that intrigued me and I wanted to pursue. After that, my wife Cheryl and I spent the next two years living in the United Arab Emirates, where we forged many new friendships in this amazing and exciting country.

Comedy in Errors

To make mistakes is human, to stumble is commonplace;
to be able to laugh at yourself is maturity.

– William Arthur Ward

EP professionals are not perfect. Because we spend so much time and energy providing protection to our principals, it goes without saying sometimes we get it wrong or make very human mistakes. Some may be dangerously close calls or missteps. They're often embarrassing when they happen – but let's face it, they are just part of being human.

After the fact, and assuming no one was hurt and no resources were damaged (other than egos), these instances can be extremely humorous. Anyone who has been in this profession for any length of time has their own funny stories to tell – or not to tell. The following are just a couple of mine.

"Is this really my car?"

Late one evening as we were taking Director Tenet home from head-quarters, he asked to stop at a grocery store near his house. As the security detail for someone like him, our protection was 24/7 – i.e., at all places and all times.

On this day, I was the shift leader and riding in the "follow car" behind Tenet's black armored Suburban. As we approached the parking lot of the grocery store, the follow car dropped back to allow Tenet's vehicle to unassumingly drop him and his accompanying agent off at a spot near the front entrance. We always tried to avoid drawing unnecessary attention to Tenet or his protective detail while in public, and we knew three agents jumping out of two black Suburbans would stick out like a sore thumb here at the grocery store.

Mike (another Mike), the Director's accompanying agent on that day, notified us he would be taking his radio earpiece out to avoid drawing attention. Seeing guys in suits is not unusual in the Washington, D.C., area, but it is a telltale sign someone important is around when you see a man in a suit with an earpiece and wire dangling from his ear.

Initially, Tenet's vehicle remained parked where he and Mike had gotten out. We positioned our follow car a couple of lanes over in the parking lot, facing the vehicle and the store's entrance. We waited for Mike's notification they would be coming out of the store. As time passed, the parking lot and entrance became congested with lots of people stopping by on their way home from work, picking up other family members and wheeling their grocery carts around.

At this moment, we watched as Tenet's driver pulled away from his prime spot in front of the store, circled the parking lot, and repositioned himself approximately 60 feet from his previous location.

As we continued to wait, another black suburban pulled up and stopped in the same spot where Tenet's vehicle had initially been parked. Anyone who has been in the Washington, D.C., area can tell you seeing a black Suburban is as common as seeing a Toyota Prius in the San Francisco Bay Area. A man in his late 60s was driving this car and obviously waiting for someone.

As we watched the scene unfold, those of us in the follow car saw exactly where this was heading. Suddenly, Mike and Tenet walked out of the store and headed directly for the black suburban parked exactly where they had exited their vehicle before.

I quickly radioed Mike to tell him this vehicle was not his car, but Mike still had his radio earpiece out. He and Tenet walked to the waiting Suburban, Mike opened the rear passenger door, Tenet got in and Mike shut the door. Mike's first clue should have been how light the door was – Tenet's car was an armored vehicle with very heavy doors. Mike didn't notice this change and he opened his door and jumped in the front seat.

By this time, Tenet's actual car had pulled up behind the black Suburban, and I had jumped out of the follow car and was walking quickly toward the random Suburban which now contained the Director of Central Intelligence.

Of course, you can imagine what the startled driver of the Suburban was thinking. By now, the Director was looking around the back of the suburban with his bag of groceries and thinking to himself: *Where is my briefcase?* and *This is not my tan rain coat!* Mike was getting comfortable in the front seat and, looking straight ahead, told the driver: "Let's go."

An instant later, Mike and the driver looked at each other with complete shock and confusion. The Director, sitting in the back, began to have the same thought that now raced through Mike's head: *Who the hell are you and what have you done with our driver?*

After a moment of feeling caught in what I am sure felt like a great car switch scene from *Mission Impossible*, both Mike and Tenet realized they had gotten into the wrong car. They quickly apologized to the now-traumatized man waiting for his wife to come out of the grocery store. As quickly as they had gotten into the car, they were out and hurried toward *their* Suburban – right behind them.

As serious as this could have been, we knew there was no real risk involved. The reality of what had happened was so incredibly funny we could barely keep from laughing uncontrollably. Once we got back, we all laughed for days – make that weeks – about this *Three Stooges* moment. After this, when Mike was with Tenet and putting him in a vehicle (anywhere in the world), the Director never missed the opportunity to pause before getting in and say, "Mike – is this really my car?"

"This is the White House – is the Director home?"

In the fall of 1999, Director Tenet spent a lot of his time at the White House meeting with President Clinton and his national security team on pressing issues. I recall Tenet wasn't particularly happy during this particular period with the (now) late National Security Advisor Sandy Berger.

We had a security command post in the basement of Tenet's home staffed around the clock. Late one evening, a call came in from the White House Communications Room; the caller stated they had Mr. Berger on the line. At this time, we had a push-to-talk intercom speaker system hooked up to a couple rooms in the upstairs area of Tenet's home.

It was late in the evening, so our (new) agent set the phone receiver on the desk and buzzed the Director's bedroom, announcing he had Mr. Berger on the line. While I don't know the subject of the call, I am sure the Director was not in the mood to talk to Berger as he was getting ready for bed. Irritated, he said to the agent, "You can tell him I'm not home … or just not available for his call."

Suddenly, the agent's eyes were as big as golf balls as he realized he hadn't put Berger's call on hold and the person on the other end had probably heard the Director's less-than-accurate response. Hesitantly, the agent picked up the handset, which was less than five inches from the intercom speaker box. With some trepidation, he said, "I'm sorry, the Director is not available."

By this time, the White House communications operator had already transferred the call to Berger, who was waiting for Tenet. Berger slowly told the agent, "I know George is home – tell him to pick up the phone." The agent had to have thought: *Oh crap – now I have to call the Director again on the intercom and tell him what just happened.*

The agent placed the call on hold – for real, this time – and again called Tenet on his bedroom intercom, confessed what he had done, and said Mr. Berger heard him and still wanted to speak to him.

Less than a minute later, the Director made his way downstairs to the command post in his boxers and T-shirt, where this "green" agent was waiting, no doubt anticipating the worst. Our command post was positioned in the basement of the Director's modest home in Maryland – and you could hear his footsteps from the bedroom to the staircase. I'm sure the agent listened to every single footstep like it was coming from an approaching executioner. Tenet reached the door of the command post, where he walked in with a look that only the Director could give you.

The next day, we had a slight change in our intercom procedures and moved the intercom to a new location within the command post. We also had great fun with our new agent. Welcome to the team.

Other Indelible Memories

Fields of Blackbirds and a Little Girl's Notebook

As in any war where civilians remain in the area affected by the conflict, innocents will always become casualties at some point – whether accidental, part of "collateral damage" or, in some cases, actually targeted by ruthless regimes.

Just weeks after the 1999 NATO coalition air campaign in Kosovo ended, our first team in the country established an initial base of post-war operations. I was on the second team, arriving on site a month later to provide relief and rotation for the first. Most Kosovar homes were damaged or destroyed after the opposing military passed through, leaving a path of utter destruction in their wake. The nearby power station had been damaged during the bombing campaign, so electricity and water at our base house could be hit or miss. At night, we would often be awakened by small arms fire and the occasional grenade being tossed at a nearby restaurant, home or mosque where the local opposing religious and ethnic factions were still going at each other.

A few weeks earlier, a NATO airstrike had accidentally hit a civilian bus in the town of Luzane, killing at least 34 people. The bus was split in half by the missile strike, one half still on the bridge and the other half laying approximately 35 meters below. Locals reported seeing several critically injured and many lifeless bodies lying all around, a number of them badly burned.

Tragically, the injured or dead included 15 children, though locals reported the numbers being much higher. When we arrived at the site, most of the debris had been removed, and what remained of the bus had been pushed off the bridge, where it now became part of the Kosovo landscape. There were no signs of casualties except parts of clothing scattered around and other small personal items that obviously belonged to the passengers. The acrid smell of burnt flesh and death still lingered. My mind quickly took me back to 1988 and the air show crash at Ramstein.

Operating in the open and with the growing level of unwanted attention we were getting around the small capital town, we knew it was probably just a matter of time before we wouldn't be safe anymore. Occasionally, we traveled to a part of town we affectionately named "Hogan's Alley" (after the FBI's tactical training facility, designed to provide a realistic urban setting for agents to use in live-fire tactical "shoot/don't shoot" scenarios).

This area was a street which had been bombed, burned and looted – but one small café had been left partially intact. Only a few local patrons and perhaps various spies and agents working in the area would dine at this outdoor spot, yet this little café was *the* place to meet in the evenings for a simple margarita pizza, Coke and/or a cappuccino, which were the only items on the menu. It was always surreal to be sitting amongst the burned-out buildings, vehicles and storefronts at small white plastic tables and chairs, heavily armed and watching all the "usual suspects" come out at night. Here, we would try to find a moment of normalcy in a time of confusion, death, chaos and rebuilding as this little country was trying to find its new identity.

The Kosovo War, which had just ended, was one of the final conflicts in the breakup of the former Yugoslavia. Throughout the 1990s, the republics comprising the Serb-dominated country had broken off one by one.

From 1992 to 1995, the Bosnian War resulted in over 100,000 deaths, NATO intervention against Yugoslavia and the reemergence of genocide in Europe. The Kosovo War between Yugoslavia and Kosovar Albanian separatists began in 1998; NATO intervened against Yugoslavia once more in 1999 after allegations of ethnic persecution against the local Albanians.

Ethnic conflict in this region wasn't just a product of the breakup of Yugoslavia in the 1990s. As far back as the 14th century, another major battle was fought in Kosovo: "Kosovo Polje" (or "Field of Blackbirds" as it's now known there). On June 15, 1389, the Ottoman Turkish army (led by Sultan Murad I) and Serbian army (led by Prince Lazar) met in a battle that resulted in the near-total destruction of both forces. Both commanders were killed, but the Ottomans came out on top, leading to the beginning of the end of Serbia's independence. The Balkans continued to be a center of violence and instability in the centuries that followed.

Over 600 years after the Field of Blackbirds, I found myself walking the grounds where these wars were fought, across the places locals quote as "running red with blood" shed over this land for centuries.

Our missions went as far north as Mitrovica, one of my favorite parts of Kosovo, as it reminded me of some of the picturesque Bosnian landscapes where I had operated before. The southern end of our operations went as far as Skopje, Macedonia, where we would need to go on occasion for meetings and resupply – and for the only McDonald's. While McDonald's is not part of my normal diet, I must admit when you're in a war-torn environment living on nuts and a few energy bars, a Big Mac and fries can taste really good.

Our travels would normally take us past the refugee camps near the Macedonian border, where Kosovars and others waited to return to their war-ravaged homes to see what was left.

During one of our area familiarization drives to determine our best routes for safe travel, we came across a large towering monument called "Gazimestan" just northwest of Pristina. Gazimestan commemorated the 1389 Battle of Kosovo and was built in 1953 by the Federal People's Republic of Yugoslavia. In 1989, Serbian leader Slobodan Milosevic marked the 600th anniversary of that battle by delivering a controversial speech at the monument – which of course only continued to increase the ethnic tensions in this land and the eventual breakup of Yugoslavia.

During the NATO-led air campaign and the Serbian raid on the Kosovar city of Pristina, Serbian snipers would use the high ground of the Gazimestan tower to shoot Kosovar forces and civilians trying to flee. We found many shell casings at the top of the tower; you could just imagine the advantage this position would give a sniper against the roadways nearby.

For protective agents or anyone operating in a hostile foreign environment, area familiarization or "FAM" drives are essential and, in some cases, can be when we face our most dangerous exposure. In 2011, an American security contractor was arrested in Pakistan and accused of killing two attackers during a FAM drive through the streets of Lahore. He was eventually released through intense negotiations a few months later. This incident exemplifies the inherent level of risk some of these operations can have – they're not your normal EP missions.

Back in Luzane, we walked down under the bridge where the bus was hit by the missile. As we did, I noticed a small paper notebook with handwritten notes in English. I realized the person to whom this little notebook belonged was practicing her English writing and translations. I surmised the little girl might have been fifteen years old, and I believed her name might have been Angela. She wrote of her time in school with her friends, who were Albanian, Serbian and Turkish.

In one part of the notebook, she was practicing a letter to a pen pal somewhere in the United States describing her life in Kosovo. She wrote she had a family of six, and several brothers who weren't in school yet. Her father worked in an office and her mother was a housewife. She described how she loved pop music and wanted to know what her pen pal's favorite group was.

As I read, I couldn't help but visualize this little girl riding the bus on this particular morning, maybe with a brother or sister or even her parents. She might have even been writing in this very book, unaware she only had a few seconds longer to live as a missile was inbound for her bus and would take her life and others on that morning.

I brought her notebook home with me and, several weeks later, I sat with my son (who was 12 years old at the time) and told him about where I found this book and what probably happened to this little girl.

I read a few pages to him and explained how this young girl was forced to attend classes at night mostly underground due to the fact she was a Kosovar and under Serbian control.

I had him keep this little girl's book and would ask him to read it now and then to remind him how fortunate he was to freely attend school and learn openly without the fear of being attacked by a missile on the way there. I was never really sure how much he understood at that time, but for me it was important to keep this little girl's memory alive. I always tried to bring back a small piece of the world with me to give my son a global perspective, so he would realize how good his life was in our country.

You're never really sure how much your child understands during those teaching years. My son has since spent many years himself in war-torn countries and witnessed similar events; he was fortunate to achieve a greater perspective after spending some time with locals who were trying to survive under unimaginable conditions. After returning home, he would say, "Dad, they just want the same thing we want – to be safe, have food, training and opportunities to provide for their families and friends." According to Maslow's Hierarchy of Needs, it's what we're all seeking. I know he gets it now, and I'm sure one day when the time is right he will convey his new perspective to his beautiful daughters.

Shaking the Hand of a Terrorist?

As an instructor at the 343rd Training Squadron Security Forces Academy in San Antonio, one particular course I appreciated teaching was on global terrorism. This particular curriculum explored terrorist group ideologies over the decades, reviewed past attacks and examined modern-day terror methodologies. As the instructor, I would often highlight various leadership and organizational profiles and how they allowed some organizations to gain outsized levels of recognition and funding – especially when key leaders had bigger personas than the groups they sometimes led.

Yasser Arafat's name would always surface during these courses and conversations. Arafat's association with and leadership of organizations like Fatah, the Palestine Liberation Organization (PLO) and

Black September generated many interesting debates over whether he was a terrorist, freedom fighter or leader of a country.

I believe most saw him as a "reformed terrorist" – i.e., a former terrorist you could have coffee with.* In a 1988 speech to the United Nations, he renounced terrorism and acknowledged Israel's right to exist. Most amazingly, he was presented with the Nobel Peace Prize in 1994 alongside Israeli leaders Shimon Peres and Yitzhak Rabin after the signing of the Oslo Accords – and, of course, there was his famous handshake photo with Rabin and President Clinton.

(AP Photo/Ron Edmonds)

Prime Minister Yitzhak Rabin, President Clinton, and Chairman Yasser Arafat.

But in the view of some in the intelligence business, including many Israelis with whom I have unofficially spoken, he was, at his core, an opportunistic and manipulative former terrorist. And as long as many in the Palestinian territories clung to him as their leader, no one was

---

* After all, he and his wife spent a lot of time in Paris – and, many would argue, thoroughly enjoyed spending the money he received for "fighting for the cause."

willing to arrest him or put a bullet in his head. Without a doubt, he was a complicated world figure.

Whatever you call him, Arafat was a controversial man with a lot of blood on his hands in his early years. He may not have been the person to pull the trigger in most cases, but the groups he led and financed were definitely murderers.

In 1998, President Clinton and many others requested Director Tenet be involved with the Wye River negotiations, which ultimately resulted in a short-lived peace memorandum between Israel and the Palestinian Authority.

During, before and after the negotiations, we made several trips with the Director, Deputy Director and senior Agency officials to Israel and the Palestinian territories for high-level talks. Our trips into the Palestinian territories (to Arafat's compound or elsewhere) were always tense for security reasons. I have no issues with the Palestinian people, and I've had many good conversations with Palestinians inside and outside of the region. But taking the Director across the border late at night into Palestinian-controlled territory always felt like entering a lion's cage without a trainer. We had no choice but to trust Arafat's intelligence and security forces to round up any members of Hamas or any other group who might want to disrupt peace efforts by attacking the Director.

Over the years on various interagency cross-border visits and operations, there have been several close calls – i.e., edgy confrontations with both sides, or being on the receiving end of hostile fire. On one occasion during a period of intense conflict, we were about to take the Director across the border to Arafat's compound when he received an urgent call from his Israeli counterpart. The caller advised him to turn around immediately and not to enter the Palestinian territories. Shortly after this call, the Israeli military launched a major missile strike on Arafat's compound.

When we did travel to Arafat's compound for meetings, it would normally be late at night. After navigating the border and enduring long travel by motorcade, we would be greeted by the Palestinian security forces protecting Arafat – always with professional (but anxious) attitudes. Arafat's compound and offices in Ramallah were small, so the Palestinians would normally only allow a couple of our agents to accompany the Director. We had to leave the rest of our agents at strategic locations outside and in vehicles for what sometimes seemed like an eternity. This was something we didn't like, but it was their country and their rules, so compromises had to be made.

On one trip in particular, tensions between the Israelis and Palestinians were so high they were palpable. Shortly after we arrived at the compound, we heard gunshots in the distance and excited radio traffic coming over the Palestinians' security radios. We postured up and our fingers inched closer to the triggers on our weapons. A couple of Palestinian vehicles rushed off as if responding to an incident; a few minutes later, one of their SUVs returned and parked across the compound at another building adjacent to our location and within our view. A couple Palestinian officers pulled a black body bag from the back of the SUV and dropped it on the ground.

We assumed this was all for show – there might have been only rocks and sand in that bag. Later, as we were getting ready to leave, we learned something that made us think otherwise.

After we had initially arrived at the compound, a couple of our counterassault team members had secretly made their way through a nearby warehouse to obtain a high-ground position while the Director was in the building. If needed, they would be able to provide our detail with key visual and weapons coverage.

On their way out, they noticed something they hadn't seen on the way in. As they passed through the warehouse this time, they stepped over an iron grate – and stopped in their tracks when they saw several men in a cage under the floor. Again, we knew some Palestinians opposed any negotiations with the U.S. or the Israelis and might try to derail progress by attacking someone like the Director. We believed our team had stumbled across a roundup of certain members of Hamas or other known opposition.

On one of our last trips to the Palestinian territories, I was to ride "hot seat" (front right seat) in the Director's vehicle on our way out. As the Director and Arafat exited the Ramallah compound, our team was quickly getting all the U.S. officials loaded up in the other convoy vehicles and ready to roll.

Every time I would see Arafat dressed in his green uniform and trademark black-and-white *keffiyeh*, I couldn't help but see the resemblance to Fidel Castro, Che Guevara, Muammar Gaddafi and other controversial figures who considered themselves freedom fighters. What I came to realize through all those encounters with men like Yasser Arafat was the relevance of the quote: "Keep your friends close but your enemies closer." In other words, you sometimes have to sit at the table with your adversaries to maintain security in the world of politics and diplomacy.

After the Director said goodbye and got into his vehicle, I closed the door and secured him inside. I stepped forward to open my door in front but was suddenly facing Arafat. He reached out, grabbed my shoulder and extended his right hand, saying "Take good care of the Director – he is a good man."

My immediate reaction was one of reluctance because of my opinions of this man and his bloody past. Now facing this strange diplomatic position in which security professionals sometimes find themselves, I reached out with a slight hesitation but shook his hand firmly, saying "Yes, I know he is" before getting in the vehicle and shutting my door.

I may have crossed my own professional line by letting my personal feelings surface, but it's another moment I will not forget.

Our motorcades in and out of the Palestinian territories were always equally interesting and tense. As we departed in the midst of a power blackout (fairly routine for the area), I found myself questioning whether or not I had just shaken the hand of a reformed terrorist or freedom fighter. *How much American blood did he have on his hands?*

By the time we reached the Israeli border, I had decided what my answer was.

The Kidnapping of Daniel Pearl

Everyone has the capacity for courage. We don't need to face extreme circumstances to become admirable people.

– Mariane Pearl

In February 2002, I was in Islamabad, Pakistan, again, advancing the region for Director Tenet's official visits to East Asia and the Middle East. On these types of trips, we would often choose random hotels, only occasionally staying at those we had used on previous trips. Cities in places like Pakistan often only have one hotel used regularly by foreign expats and contractors visiting the city. In some cases, such a location might be monitored and controlled by local intelligence, security services and others, so we try to avoid them at times.*

I had been to Islamabad many times, but this trip would be much different. My colleague and I were at the U.S. embassy on a weekend finalizing certain logistical and security requirements before the Director's arrival. We were working in a small office that we had commandeered, when a counterpart who was assigned to the embassy entered the office and sat down.

His face told us something was seriously wrong; he just sat for a few seconds, speechless, and shook his head. On the desk, there was a small TV with a built-in VHS player – something to be used for reviewing investigative tapes, or maybe to watch a movie while working in the office during the weekends. In places like Pakistan and for those assigned to these embassy posts, offices would often become second homes and personal sanctuaries.

He inserted the videotape he brought in with him and said the embassy had just received it from a courier. He told us we would be among the first to view it, and also added that we needed to brace ourselves. Our counterpart felt we ought to be aware of its contents, as the Director would be arriving soon and we should be prepared for anything that could affect his meetings in Islamabad and our security in the region.

With that setup, I really did not know what to expect or what I might see on the videotape. He hit play – and what I watched remains with me today. When recalled, it evokes nauseating disgust and hatred of those responsible.

---

* Notably, a few years after my 2002 visit, the hotel we had used previously was nearly destroyed by a dump truck filled with explosives, killing more than 50 people and seriously injuring hundreds more – which might have included a good friend if he hadn't left the hotel minutes before.

The three of us viewed the brutal and savage beheading of Daniel Pearl. A few weeks earlier, Danny had been kidnapped in a small village restaurant in Karachi. A journalist based in Mumbai, India, he was the South Asia bureau chief of the *Wall Street Journal* and was investigating the relationship between "shoe bomber" Richard Reid and Al-Qaeda. What Danny didn't know at the time was that Ahmed Omar Saeed Sheikh (a terrorist with links to Islamist militant organizations) and others were plotting to kidnap him. Sheikh and some associates related to the kidnapping were arrested but not before Danny had disappeared.

Danny was born in Princeton, New Jersey, but spent his youth in Los Angeles. He was a very respected and well-traveled journalist and an accomplished violinist. At this time, his wife Mariane (also a journalist) was carrying their son, Adam Daniel Pearl. Adam would be born four months after his father's death.[68]

I was aware of Danny's kidnapping before I departed the U.S. for Pakistan and had further conversation after arriving with our CIA chief of station and other embassy officials. As a CIA agent, I was also aware of efforts on the part of the U.S. and Pakistan to locate him, coordinated with the assistance of the State Department and led by Regional Security Officer (RSO) Randall Bennett, who was assigned to the U.S. Consulate General in Karachi.

Some of the intel reports indicated he might be a prisoner for long time if not found and rescued soon. We all expected he might be used in some sort of prisoner exchange. When it became known his captors were linked to Al-Qaeda and the demand for his release was the release of all Muslim prisoners in Guantanamo Bay, I knew Danny Pearl's life was in serious jeopardy if his whereabouts could not be determined quickly.

If the U.S. or any of our allies knew the exact location where Danny was being held hostage, an operation to rescue him would have been launched immediately. But everyone involved also knew time was not on their side. For Agent Bennett, Danny's kidnapping was also personal: He met him just days prior when Danny came into the consulate and he had provided him with a local security briefing.

The day before we saw the video, Agent Bennett had received the tape in Karachi. With trusted members of the Pakistani police, a few individuals from the *Journal* and the Consul General, they sat in Bennett's home and watched the horrifying and devastating video together – which was even more terrible given the extensive efforts that had been underway to find him.

Danny was a journalist. He was not a combatant or a spy, and he did not deserve what happened to him.

Daniel Pearl

As for Agent Bennett and many of us with this type of knowledge and exposure, we are always going to be influenced by these experiences. At times, we can perhaps be a little overcautious when our principals want to travel to areas of the world where we have knowledge of the inherent dangers. At the same time, we must be rational ourselves and be able to balance the actual risks or threats without projecting the same "fear factor" to our principals when not appropriate.

When we think of events and locations that have left a mark on us, our hands might sweat a little, our pulse rates might increase and we might ask our principals why they need to travel *there* right now. If it is a trip that must be taken, we may insist that principals follow our instructions precisely. In most cases, a well-thought-out plan with certain contingencies and staying under the radar is a preferred manner of travel. But when the principal's profile, reasons for travel and personal exposure in a high-risk area are prominent enough, a higher level of personal protection must be considered.

For Danny's family, Special Agent Bennett and many others, this story ended with a small measure of retribution when Khalid Sheikh Mohammed (KSM) was captured 13 months later. I recall exactly where I was one morning soon after his capture, when I bumped into a colleague who was also a former military team member from my days in Germany. He had just returned from Pakistan and, with a smile on his face, he said, "We got that fucker."

KSM had been identified as one of the primary architects of the 9/11 attacks, was arguably ranked as number three within Al-Qaeda, and had various roles in numerous other attacks associated with the terrorist group – including the first attempt to blow up the World Trade Center in 1993. In prison, he admitted to murdering Danny Pearl and when the FBI later examined the video of Danny's killer, they used vein-matching technology to compare KSM's hands to the hooded man on the video and determined with a high degree of certainty that the hands were the same.

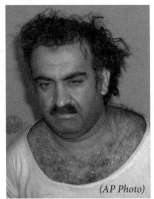

(AP Photo)

Khalid Sheikh Mohammed after his capture

Many of KSM's confessions have been controversial due to the nature of his interrogations, but no one will disagree based on years of other strong evidence that KSM is a very dangerous man. He continues to be held at Guantanamo Bay (one of the last prisoners) on charges of mass murder.

In late 2003, Bennett was honored by Robert Mueller, then director of the FBI, for his contributions to the investigations of Danny's kidnapping and murder. Mariane Pearl was also present during this presentation.

From Russia with "Love"

On August 8, 2000, during the evening rush hour, a loud explosion erupted and a plume of dark black smoke could be seen billowing from the Metro underpass at Pushkinskaya station in the center of Moscow. An improvised explosive device equivalent to almost a kilogram of TNT took the lives of 12 and injured 150 others.

This attack still remains unsolved. The Russian government blamed Chechen separatists hailing from a mostly Muslim ethnic group that has resisted Russian rule in the Caucasus for centuries. Many local Russians I've since spoken with seem skeptical of the claim, feeling it was something the government did to boost popular support for taking down Chechen terrorist groups. I tend to believe the official story, but the negative sentiment represented the widespread lack of trust in the Russian government.

Coincidentally, the Director was due to arrive in Moscow for meetings and, less than 24 hours after the attack, I landed in the city with another agent to conduct our advance. Our hotel happened to be just two blocks away from the site of the blast. The agent and I went down to get a firsthand look at what had occurred, as we wanted to find out how this might affect the Director and his group. The area had already been sprayed with high-pressure water hoses and the blood was wiped cleaned with mops, but the smell of the explosion and death still lingered.

The ironic thing about this specific blast location is that, over the next three days performing our advance, we must have walked the same route a half-dozen times; it was a major underground area for pedestrians to cross in central Moscow and a short walk away from the famed Red Square.

I hate to think what would have happened if we'd arrived a day earlier. This event exemplifies what has played out too many times recently around the world with individuals finding themselves at the "wrong place at the wrong time." If you or I took the time to calculate time or distance, it would probably be shocking to see how often we've come within days, hours, seconds and even inches of such an event.

This advance turned out to be one of the most interesting I have ever conducted. Our security counterparts were the FSB (formerly and notoriously known as the KGB). But what was remarkable was not so much the organization as it was the location they chose to conduct our first meeting: none other than the famed Lubyanka building.

In 2014, Dmitriy Romendik and Georgy Manaev wrote: "For Russians, the word Lubyanka has a menacing sound to it – similar to the word Gulag. Home first to the Soviet and then the Russian security agencies, Lubyanka Square became synonymous with execution, violence and torture."[69]

It was not unusual for us to meet with other countries' intelligence organizations to support and facilitate the Director's official meetings, missions, dinners and other events. In fact, just like spies do sometimes, these are often interesting opportunities to work alongside other intelligence and special security services – e.g., the U.K.'s MI6, Jordan's GID, Germany's BND, Israel's Mossad and many others around the world.

(AP Photo/Pavel Golovkin)

Lubyanka, former KGB headquarters in Moscow, where we met with Russian security services for the advance arrival of Director Tenet.

We met our host from the FSB in a large conference room just off a side entrance of the building. The interior walls were lined with oil paintings of various chiefs of the KGB and now FSB secret police. This is the same building where they took Gary Powers, the CIA U2 pilot who was shot down over Russia in May of 1960. Powers was taken to Lubyanka and kept in a prison cell for months before being convicted of espionage by the Russians. He was eventually transferred to a prison camp outside of Moscow where he remained until early 1962, when he was part of an American and Russian spy swap on a bridge in Berlin.

We left what I would describe as a rather intense but cooperative meeting with the FSB. A senior colleague that was part of our meetings and familiar with Russian history stated that (other than Powers) we might just be part of a very small group of Americans to ever enter Lubyanka and come back out alive. Needless to say, it was a quiet ride back to the office as we considered what he said.

As in many foreign advances for the CIA, we were never alone. A team of burly Russians would conspicuously follow us throughout our days and nights in Moscow. Our new "friends" would, on occasion, send beautiful women to see if we needed anything during our stay, enhancing the meaning of "From Russia with Love."

In many countries, we always assumed our hotel rooms were bugged and included complimentary video recording. It was always fun to step out of the shower and see the bathroom mirror covered with steam – except for a two-inch "un-steamed" circle in the middle of the mirror. In some cases like this one, I played the *I know you're listening* game and said aloud standing in front of the in-room beverage cooler, "I wish this hotel had Diet Dr. Pepper." The next day, after returning to my room, a couple of cans of Diet Dr. Pepper miraculously made their way into my refrigerator.

Depending on the country or your specific mission, you would not want to play these fun little "spy games." The last thing you'd want would be for hostile surveillance to actually become hostile during your trip or your protective mission.

This was not my last experience with the former KGB. A few months later, I spent a few days and nights with former KGB agents advancing Astana and Almaty in Kazakhstan, where the temperatures went well below zero and a few shots of vodka kept us warm during our long dinner conversations.

My Father and the "Bridge of No Return"

My dad was the youngest of seven brothers and sisters. His father, James, fought in World War I, where he survived a mustard gas attack by the German Army. Mustard gas actually killed very few during the war, but the gas had a terrible effect on the health of many soldiers for years afterward; my dad's father suffered from heart and lung problems for the rest of his life. One afternoon, my dad and his father went to a movie. After they got home, his father laid down on the couch for a nap, but never got up. He suffered a massive heart attack and died in his sleep. My dad was only 10 years old.

In 1950, my father enlisted in the Army at 17 and went through basic training at Fort Knox, Kentucky. Two years later, he shipped out to South Korea along with his new buddies, bound for the land of rice and *kimchi*.

This was the cold and bloody conflict that history often refers to as the Korean War. Neither President Truman nor President Eisenhower – nor the U.S. Congress – ever *technically* declared it as such, but my father and the thousands of other soldiers would tell you the unvarnished truth: They served in a war.

Starting in April of 1953, after the success of Operation Little Switch (a trial run for prisoner swaps during the Korean War), Operation Big Switch began with a general exchange of prisoners at the banks of the Sachong River in Panmunjom, Korea. Consenting prisoners would be taken to a bridge crossing the Sachong River, which divided North and South Korea. Once they crossed the bridge, there was no turning back.

My dad's memories were always very vivid regarding his time in Korea and, on occasion, he would reflect and tell us a little about it. Until the war, my dad had rarely ever left his small hometown in south Knoxville, Tennessee – which was not uncommon for most of the military men and women who answered the call to service. He would sometimes speak of the friends he made serving in Korea, some of whom never made it home.

My father in Korea – winter of 1952.

When I was growing up, the series *M*A*S*H* was my dad's favorite show on television and we watched it religiously for many years. I can recall looking at him from the corner of my eye and feeling that each episode he watched took him right back to those days. I never felt like he told us all the stories he had inside; I didn't understand why then, but I do now.

By the time he was only 73 years old, my dad's health had started to dramatically decline, as he had been diagnosed with leukemia less than two years earlier. At the time, my son Jonathan was still going through basic training at Fort Knox, Kentucky, the same place where my father was more than 50 years before him. When they talked on the phone during that time, my dad reminisced about running Misery Hill, a long steep road on base that was part of the training for platoons of recruits. Now it was paved, but Dad recalled it being dirt and gravel during his time. He joked with my son, "You boys got it easy now."

My wife and I lived in Austin, Texas, and I was a senior security advisor and EP agent for the CEO and founder of a large global electronics/technology company. As often as possible, we would make trips to Phoenix to see Mom and Dad. In late October, I received a call from my brother in Phoenix telling me the doctors wanted to meet with him and the family. I didn't need to hear more to know what that was about. We flew out the next day and began the sad process of engaging the services of hospice care.

After we arrived in Phoenix, the family discussed asking the Army to allow Jonathan to come to Arizona to see his grandfather before he passed – a very difficult conversation. My dad caught wind of the discussion and told us not to let him leave basic training; my dad was very proud of Jonathan's new direction in life and knew he could be held back and possibly sent to another platoon to finish or repeat portions. He knew the importance of *finishing with the platoon you started with* and made us promise not to let him come home – as if we needed something else to be sad about.

My son had the closest relationship with my dad of all the grandkids because of the time they had together over the previous 19 years and their similar personalities. Four days before my father passed, he received a handwritten letter from Jonathan describing his experience in basic and connecting in a way only they could because of these shared days at Fort Knox. This was one of the few letters my son had written at that time. He couldn't have written a more appropriate letter, and it arrived at the most important moment. Just a few hours later, my dad would not have been able to read it nor, I believe, understand the significance. In many ways, that letter was precious closure for them both.

My dad and mom had been married for 54 years. They wed when she was 18 and he had just turned 19 – and it wasn't long before he shipped out to Korea. When he left, my mom was carrying my oldest brother (their first child). With the exception of this time and only a few other very rare occasions over their years, they were never apart.

During those days of medical treatments and setbacks, my dad spent many weeks and then sometimes months in hospitals between Phoenix and Tennessee. Even during this time, my mom (all of her 5'1") would curl up in a chair or sometimes in the bed with him and stay the night. At times, it would take an army to convince her she should go home and get a good night's sleep. She put heart and soul to the song "Stand by Your Man."

I remember just a couple days before he passed, a man came to the front door, which had a screen allowing the cooler autumn Arizona breezes to pass through. We were all sitting quietly with him in the living room when this deliveryman from the oxygen company knocked and said: "Vernon Trott?" We all quickly looked at Dad because he was sleeping and we didn't want to startle him. But even with his eyes closed, in a loud, confident voice – without missing a beat – he answered in a way only my dad could: "YIP, that's me!"

We all laughed and for the moment thought, *he's still with us*. But the night before he passed, you could tell he was rapidly losing the fight. My brothers and their families had come to visit as they did every day in the final days. We would try to carry on the best we could as a family – playing cards, laughing, making dinner and watching movies with Dad sitting in a comfortable chair and fading in and out of sleep. That night I sat slightly away from the family and wrote his obituary – perhaps the single most difficult thing I've ever done in my life.

As my brothers were getting ready to leave for the night, I'm not sure it had really sunk in with everyone he was actually dying. For obvious reasons, I think we didn't want to admit defeat or allow my mom to realize she was days or hours from losing the love of her life. I knew in my gut this would be his last night.

After moving my dad to bed, my mom gave him a goodnight kiss and he faded fast to sleep or unconsciousness. I sat in a chair beside his bed and turned down the lights. Holding his hand, I could barely control the flood of thoughts, emotions and memories going through my mind. At some point around 4:00 am, while I was alone with my dad, his spirit left this earth after 73 too-short years to what I trust was a sweet reunion with his mother, father, family and friends.

On that early October morning, my dad crossed his "bridge of no return" as he took his last breath. He was laid to rest in the National Memorial Cemetery of Arizona in Phoenix, a place he had chosen weeks prior to passing and where my mother's only sibling, Robert, was buried more than 30 years before.*

Six years before my dad passed, I advanced Director Tenet's visit to South Korea. It was part of an Asia tour with key intelligence meetings in the region. Along with my good friend and colleague, Special Agent Michael Chang, we advanced South Korea, including a rare tour of the DMZ. (The benefit of being the advance agent is you get to spend a little more time at the destination.) We had a lot of work to do before the Director's arrival, but the ability to explore and ask more questions was an unexpected privilege. This advance was especially important to both Agent Chang and me. Chang was Korean-American and his father actually had extended family still living in North Korea; he had many stories from his family's past regarding the war and separation between the two countries.

I'll never forget arriving at the Seoul airport. Agent Chang had arrived a day prior and told me he would meet me with our expeditor after I cleared customs. I walked through the immigration doors to a sea of Korean faces and hesitated for a moment to get my bearings. I began

---

* His full name was Robert Hollingsworth, and he was a veteran of the U.S. Army who served in Europe.

walking past local family members and friends looking for their loved ones, as well as taxi drivers and other Koreans looking to get their grips on an unassuming tourist.

Suddenly, I heard someone yell, "Mike!"

I stopped and looked all around but didn't see anyone I knew, nor was anyone waving or making themselves known to me. Maybe I was just hearing things. I started to walk away but this time I heard, "Trott!"

I turned again, trying to identify who was calling my name. I looked left, right and all around – then I heard a frustrated voice coming from right in front of me saying, "Trott." It was my colleague Agent Chang standing directly in front of me, and it wasn't until that moment I realized just how Korean he really looked.

He quickly realized my pathetic confusion in not being able to pick him out in a crowd of his countrymen. His only comment: "Asshole."

The Korean schedule was packed. We had meetings with our Agency staff, Korean counterparts, the President of South Korea and the U.S. ambassador, and a quick UH-60 Black Hawk helicopter trip up to the DMZ, courtesy of the U.S. Army.

The U.S. Army and the South Korean military get very nervous when any high-profile officials visit the DMZ. History has shown that, even though the North Korean military assigned to the DMZ are very loyal to North Korea and their beloved leader, there have been occasions when someone wanting to defect will take the opportunity during a high-profile visit. Defectors like this rely on all the extra South Korean and U.S. Army presence and preparedness for an unexpected event – sometimes taking the opportunity to risk their lives running across the border in hopes the South will protect the crossing before the North can shoot the defector in the back. (Though not during an official visit, a North Korean soldier successfully defected at Panmunjom on November 13, 2017. As he crossed, he was shot by North Korean troops but was picked up by South Korean soldiers and survived the escape.[70])

Tensions were (and are still) high during these times. Because of the DMZ agreements, no visiting groups are allowed to have weapons. All of our agents were required to surrender their weapons to the U.S. Army as we came off the helicopters.

Our protective detail leader was very uncomfortable with having no weapons in the event of a bad situation, so we decided to adopt a plan that would allow us to have at least one pistol within our group by observing a weakness in the process a day prior during our advance. We meant no disrespect and understood the potential ramifications of not following the rules, but putting the sitting Director of Central Intelligence on the DMZ within 20 yards of armed North Korean soldiers was something we just didn't feel comfortable doing.

In the event of an incident or attack, the U.S. Army and South Korean military would address the attackers; we would cover and get the Director to one of several prepositioned safe areas until we reached the helicopters or secondary armored vehicles for evacuation.

We moved as a group to the Military Armistice Commission conference building – better known as the "blue hut" that straddles the 38th parallel or "Demilitarized Zone" (DMZ) between North and South Korea. Even today, this is still considered one of the most dangerous borders in the world. We stood in the plywood structure with windows on all sides, one door entering from North Korea and another entering from South Korea. Director Tenet, his wife Stephanie, Deputy Director John McLaughlin and others slowly walked around the room and table where the armistice was signed that brought an end to the war (or "conflict"). You could feel the history all around you as you stepped over the DMZ and into North Korea – all within the hut.

At the "Bridge of No Return" along the Korean DMZ, where my father's unit assisted in one of the first prisoner exchanges.

A visit and tour to the DMZ is well coordinated and choreographed – no deviations are allowed. Maybe it was the knowledge that my father was near this same spot nearly 47 years before, but this was one of the most memorable moments from my extensive travels with the Director.

The day before during our advance, I had lunch in a Korean War–era Quonset hut at Panmunjom Army Base, where my dad was stationed in 1953. The base commander also took me out to the "Bridge of No Return" where my dad and his unit assisted with Operation Little Switch. I stood near the bridge and walked around the area I imagined my dad may have stood while protecting the North Koreans who didn't want to remain in their homeland, as well as our U.S. soldiers walking across the same bridge to finally return home.

My dad's vivid stories of his time in Korea and my own experiences now had a connection and association that would have never been possible if it hadn't been for my advance to Korea. I am very grateful to have had this unique opportunity to not only advance such a unique site as the Korean DMZ for the Director, but also to walk the same historic grounds as my father when he served our nation during one of the many dark periods in our history.

Before leaving Korea, I collected some military DMZ mementos. Through some Air Force connections, I was able to have a U.S. flag flown high over North Korea on a routine U.S. reconnaissance mission. This flag, mementos, and my dad's military awards and decorations were placed in a shadow box and presented to him on his and my mom's 50th wedding anniversary. It now hangs in my son's home.

Over the years, I have spent a great deal of time in our nation's capital. On many occasions, I've taken a long stroll through the Vietnam, Korean and World War II memorial sites, often after midnight and when there is not a soul around. I also always feel it is such an honor to visit Arlington National Cemetery. Walking these hallowed grounds among the garden of stones is always a humbling and emotional experience, where the pace of life slows and you have the time to consider what is really important.

At many airports, I am always excited and even emotional to see a group of World War II veterans either departing or arriving on an "honor flight"* to tour the WWII memorial in Washington, D.C. I can see my uncles in the faces of those in wheelchairs, using canes or being assisted, many wearing their military pins, uniforms and caps.

---

* The Honor Flight Network is a nonprofit that brings veterans to see the national memorial monuments to the wars in which they served – at no charge.

One late fall evening just a few weeks after Dad passed away, I was in Washington, D.C., advancing another trip for my principal. It was after midnight and I couldn't sleep, so I put on my sneakers and walked from my hotel on M and 23rd Streets. I don't recall intentionally walking in that direction, but I soon found myself in the area of the Lincoln Memorial and strolling toward the Korean War Memorial.

There was a heavy fog in the cold November night air after a light snow earlier. The sidewalk led to the memorial where 19 stainless steel soldiers stood, all over seven feet tall and frozen in time patrolling in a V formation, wearing their cold-weather ponchos – which were very appropriate for this particular night, but also a true representation of the harsh weather they had to endure at times in Korea.

I was the only one there. Slowly, I walked the path as if I were a part of the patrol, stopping occasionally until I reached the front of the formation. As I looked at the large granite wall that surrounded the memorial with images immortalizing actual soldiers, I could see my father's face in them, and I recalled the black-and-white pictures of him in uniform and in Korea.

Korean War Memorial, Washington, D.C.

Standing at the front of the formation, I looked back at the soldiers and the fog hovering around them. With the rain now dripping down my face as I looked into their cold, haunting and expressionless features, I did that night what I had needed to do but had not yet allowed myself to – I cried uncontrollably and told my Dad goodbye.

CIA Overseas Security – Operating at a Higher Price

Military or government organizations operating overseas have always been exposed to a higher level of operational risk. While there have been numerous attacks on our government and military installations in recent years that have captured our attention (including the 2012 raid on the compound in Benghazi where four Americans were killed), there have been many other devastating attacks that highlight the risks and sacrifices inherent in this service.

These hostile assaults have occurred in places like Manila, Tehran, Beirut, Islamabad, Syria, Dar es Salaam and Nairobi. Attacks in Iraq and Afghanistan have almost become a daily occurrence. All of these locations have brave staff serving under high-risk conditions and all have a dedicated security team providing constant protection for these individuals and their missions.

As we do for the men and women serving in our military, we must express our utmost respect for these seldom-mentioned civilian heroes who also spend months and years away from their homes and families – all the while putting their lives on the line to protect our nation's interests and missions under conditions most people could not endure for even 24 hours. It takes a specific breed of person who is willing and able to serve as a full-time agent, officer, contractor or any CIA employee serving overseas. Unfortunately, on too many occasions, they have paid the ultimate price.

I supported the CIA's overseas security teams on several missions and deployments, but this was not my full-time position; my permanent position was almost exclusively as a special agent assigned to the protective detail of the CIA's director.

Without a doubt, overseas security training over the past two decades has become much more intense. After the attacks of 9/11, the CIA was tasked with hunting down Osama bin Laden and other high-value CIA and military targets. Everyone's tempo increased significantly, including that of the overseas security deployments. Today, the skills and tradecraft have become even more advanced since my initial training through the Protective Operations Cadre (POC) course, in order to keep up with the many new environments and threats the Agency faces.

With that said, there is nothing like deploying with a band of colleagues who are cut from similar operational cloth. Regardless of backgrounds, military units of origin, specific skills or language abilities, these teams find a way to weave it all together to do the job. Being from different units, service branches and backgrounds (including former police officers with significant advanced training) fosters a healthy level of cooperation and amusing banter between team members to release the stress of long days, weeks and months living together. For groups like this, there is nothing better than a little innocent ragging on each other to pass the time, along with many books, decks of cards and useless trivia games.

But make no mistake, these professionals can make the mindset switch before you can blink an eye and say "WTF."

The following events highlight inherently dangerous environments and situations that have resulted in the "ultimate sacrifice" by some CIA compatriots. Regardless of their titles and roles under the Agency or our government, their sacrifice and heroism will always be acknowledged and remembered.

In December 2009, the CIA suffered one of its most devastating blows when a Jordanian triple agent blew himself up in the presence of his Jordanian handler and several Agency employees (including three security agents) at Forward Operating Base Chapman, commonly known as "Khost."

The Jordanian had ostensibly infiltrated Al-Qaeda at the highest level. Most promising was his potential access to Osama bin Laden. But instead of loyalty to his handler or the Americans he would be meeting, he had pledged his allegiance to the terror group – and was on a course of dual national subversion and death.

Shortly after arriving at the U.S. camp near the Afghan city of Khost for his debrief by his Jordanian handler (cousin to King Abdullah II of Jordan) and CIA officers, triple agent Humam Khalil Abu-Mulal al-Balawi stepped out of the passenger side of the car.

Almost immediately, security agents suspected something was wrong. Before they could even isolate him from the site where the others were gathered to meet him, al-Balawi mumbled "Allahu Akbar" and detonated a suicide vest that killed him, his Jordanian handler, CIA officers Jennifer Matthews, Darren LaBonte and Harold Brown, Jr., CIA analyst Elizabeth Hanson, and CIA security agents Scott Roberson (former police detective and security professional), Dane Paresi (former Army Special Forces soldier) and Jeremy Wise (former Navy SEAL). A local Afghan security officer was also killed, and several others were injured from the suicide attack.[71]

The 2012 attack on the American diplomatic compound in Benghazi brought attention to the U.S. government's mission in Libya as well as to the CIA and their mission support at a nearby annex location. During the attack, several frantic requests were made by the compound for support; shortly after these requests, a small security response force launched from the annex to the diplomatic compound.

This team consisted of Tyrone Woods and other security officers. While their response was credited with saving others, unfortunately they could not save Ambassador Christopher Stevens and U.S. diplomat Sean Smith. After some time, Woods, the combined teams and others made their way back to the CIA annex while still being pursued by the attackers.

Four hundred miles away, security contractor Glen Doherty and a small team in Tripoli were extremely aware of the significance and urgency to get to Benghazi to support the cut-off annex team. The Tripoli team flew to the Benghazi airport, where they mounted up in vehicles and made their way to the annex to assist their friends and colleagues against further attacks. Through the night, Woods and the other officers at the annex continued to hold off additional attacks. Sometime after 4:00 am, Doherty and the others arrived to provide much-needed support and morale to the annex under siege.

Not long after Doherty and his team arrived, he made his way to the rooftop to check in with Woods, his longtime friend and former Navy SEAL teammate. Minutes later, around dawn, the annex was hit by a brutal round of mortar attacks. Several security officers sustained severe injuries; tragically, Doherty and Woods were both killed by the mortar attacks while still on the roof.

Other overseas close protection officers have been killed or injured in action, but their stories did not make the news. Two of my closest friends and colleagues have both served in leadership positions on these overseas security teams and will tell you their most difficult days – without fail – have been making that unannounced knock on the door of a fallen colleague's home to tell them their loved one would not be returning.

If it weren't for these dedicated security teams, one could confidently argue there certainly would be more stars on the white granite memorial wall at the CIA headquarters.[72]

Just as we do when serving our military, we may not always agree with the political decisions that launch us into harm's way, but when I joined the CIA, I took the same oath as I did in the armed forces – to support and defend the Constitution of the United States against all enemies, foreign and domestic.

For most of us – and those who paid the ultimate price – it was about the mission and the protected.

Coming Full Circle

Life is a full circle, widening until it joins the circle motions of the infinite.

– Anaïs Nin

In 2013, the CIA Officers Memorial Foundation honored George Tenet with the Helms Award. Richard Helms was the CIA's director from 1966–1973 and began his career with the CIA's forerunner: the Office of Strategic Services (OSS). These annual dinners honor a former director or someone who played a significant role in our nation's intelligence efforts. More importantly, they are large fundraising events that provide support to the family members and survivors of Agency employees and contractors who have died in service of our country. They also create opportunities for families to come together again and honor the memories of their loved ones.

There were many spouses and children of some of the most recent fallen officers and operators at this particular dinner. I saw several family members of the seven Agency officers and contractors who were killed in the line of duty at Khost, Afghanistan, in 2009.

I also saw Shannon Spann, the wife of the late Captain Johnny Micheal ("Mike") Spann. Mike was the first American killed in combat during the U.S. invasion of Afghanistan, where the 32-year-old former Marine was serving as an operations officer with the Agency's Special Activities Division. He died in a brutal close-quarters battle after a prison outbreak occurred at the Qala-i-Jangi fortress where he was interviewing Taliban prisoners. On that fateful day, Mike was caught with no way out. But being a former Marine and special operator with the CIA Special Activities Division, Captain Spann fought bravely and didn't fall without taking a few attackers down first.

Seeing Shannon Spann again brought back even more memories for me. In November 2001, I was an advance agent in Pakistan preparing for the arrival of Director Tenet and others for meetings with President Pervez Musharraf regarding new intelligence of additional impending Al-Qaeda attacks.*

On November 25, 2001, before the Director departed for Pakistan, we received news about a prison outbreak near Mazar-i-Sharif, Afghanistan, and the early reports were that Mike Spann was missing. Tragically, it was later reported Mike had died in the attack. His body was recovered and being flown to Landstuhl, Germany (near Ramstein Air Base) in preparation to repatriate him to his family in the United States.

---

* Some of the details are listed in George Tenet's book, *At the Center of the Storm*, published by HarperCollins in 2007.

We received word Director Tenet was considering changing his travel plans and diverting to Ramstein; he wanted to personally pick up Mike and bring him back home. Since I had been stationed at Ramstein for several years and had been to Landstuhl many times, I was tasked with going to Germany to meet with some of Mike's team members, as well as CIA and Air Force officials, as we coordinated his return.

By the time I reached Ramstein, it was already determined the Director was coming to Germany himself. I conducted all the advance security preparations for his arrival and coordinated with Mike's team and the Air Force Air Mobility Command (AMC) as we planned and rehearsed respectfully loading the coffin carrying Mike's body onto the Director's aircraft.

On this particular occasion, the Director was flying on an Air Force Boeing C-32 (which is equivalent to a commercial Boeing 757). This plane could be used by the vice president with call sign "Air Force Two" or, at times, by senior cabinet-level officials for "special air missions." No option was considered other than that Mike would fly topside with his Agency family – seats were removed in the main cabin and the crew utilized the same type of brackets used to secure President Kennedy's coffin on Air Force One when his body was flown back from Dallas.

After Mike was on board the Director's plane, we all stood on the tarmac in a misty November rain in a moment of silence and prayer. Then in complete quiet and with not a dry eye among us, the Director, members of Mike's team and our protective detail reverently boarded the plane for the long flight back to Andrews Air Force Base in Maryland – and to his waiting heavy-hearted friends and devastated family, including three young children. His youngest was just a few months old. A few days later, Mike was given full military honors and laid to rest in Arlington National Cemetery.

Back at the Foundation Dinner, in addition to the family members, you could look around the large hotel ballroom and literally see CIA history. Near my table sat Tony Mendez, the real CIA officer behind the movie *Argo* (where he was played by Ben Affleck). The CIA and our country lost another true legend after his passing on January 19, 2019.

I spoke to Cofer Black, who would travel with the Director at times and often fell under our protective umbrella. During Cofer's 30-year career at the Agency, he was responsible for leading the hunt and eventual capture and arrest of the elusive terrorist Ilich Ramírez Sánchez, also known as "Carlos the Jackal." He was also instrumental in our initial war against Al-Qaeda after 9/11 and was an early advocate of arming Predator drones when serving as Director of the CIA's Counterterrorism Center (CTC).

Jack Devine was sitting nearby as well. Jack is another legend within the Agency with accomplishments that included working in Afghanistan with the *mujahedeen* in their efforts to drive the Russians out. (Jack replaced CIA officer Gust Avrakotos, who was portrayed by the late Philip Seymour Hoffman in *Charlie Wilson's War*). Jack also assisted in the efforts to capture Pablo Escobar when he led the Agency's Counternarcotics Center.

Then there was Henry Kissinger, who needs no introduction.

The room was full of patriots, legends of past and present, many friends, protectees and former colleagues. This particular year, George and his wife sponsored a few tables for former and current special agents of his protective detail, allowing them to attend this wonderful event for an excellent cause – yet another example of his sincere appreciation for his protective staff, the CIA and the Foundation. At this time, I was the president of a new security and intelligence company and we sponsored a table for many of our staff, along with my son and a few friends from my military and Agency days.

It was like a class reunion where we all had aged a little but not enough that we didn't recognize one another. It was great catching up and reminiscing with many friends, former colleagues and even other principals I had protected during my tenure. There wasn't enough time in the evening to reconnect with everyone – deputy directors, executive directors, chiefs of station, base chiefs, case officers, staff members and others.

This list also included three major figures in the recent history of the CIA: former Director John Brennan, former Deputy and Acting Director Michael Morell, and former Deputy Director John McLaughlin (who was also one of my favorite principals). The event was co-hosted by Brennan and McLaughlin, who roasted George with a brilliant balance of respect and humor that had the room laughing out loud for more than an hour.

What I remember most, though, was how that night brought me full circle. Having my son there gave me more to reflect on as well. He was only ten years old when I joined the Agency and now he was sitting at the table with me after serving his country honorably over more than four years in Germany, Iraq and Afghanistan.

George concluded the evening with his own reflections of seven years at the Agency. There were too many stories and too many memories to put into a few minutes, but he did it in the way that only George Tenet could do: with style, wit, humility and sincerity. He recalled many stories about his protective detail and commented that, while his son John Michael was an only child, he was never really alone as he had dozens of older brothers and sisters (special agents) who helped protect and, in some ways, raise him. We mostly kept him out of trouble, but sometimes got him *in* trouble with his mom – sorry, Stephanie!

The evening could not have ended in a more appropriate and nostalgic manner, as many of us made our way down to the hotel lounge. More than a hundred former and current staff congregated there, catching up with old friends and remembering days and years past. I was with a small group of friends and former colleagues gathered near the crackling fireplace with our favorite spirits in hand, when John McDermott, the popular Scottish folk singer who had sung the National Anthem at the start of the event, joined us at the bar.

Mr. McDermott then stood on a bar stool and, in a voice only a Scot has, sang "Danny Boy" in a cappella. I'm sure I wasn't the only one with many personal reflections running through my head and mist in my eyes for those who were no longer with us. We raised our glasses in a toast to the Director, and perhaps to us all, as the evening and that era formally came to a close – and full circle.

MAY WE NEVER FORGET

Close personal protection comes with an inherent level of personal risk and danger. I would like to take a moment to pay tribute to those brave individuals from around the world who have made the ultimate sacrifice protecting their principals and others.

These individuals and their combined sacrifices over the years have been enormous. Let us never forget them and perhaps take some comfort from the words of John 15:13:

> *Greater love hath no one than this:*
> *to lay down one's life for one's friends.*

There will be those who may read this book who have the ability to make financial contributions to the *many* worthwhile nonprofit foundations established to assist the family members of our fallen heroes killed in the line of duty. I encourage you to take a moment to consider a donation to the organization(s) closest to your heart in their honor. One that is of special importance to me and my former Agency colleagues is the CIA Officers Memorial Foundation (www.ciamemorialfoundation.org):

> *The CIA Officers Memorial Foundation provides educational support and emergency financial assistance to the families of CIA officers who die while on active duty or who are severely wounded or disabled serving in a war zone.* [73]
> *The CIA Officers Memorial Foundation's unique mission has supported the CIA community since 2001.*

Its role has been validated repeatedly by CIA leader-ship as well as legislatively by the Warner Amendment, which affirmed the Foundation's preeminent responsi-bility to the families of deceased CIA personnel. The Foundation was established in 2001 to honor Johnny Micheal Spann, the first CIA officer killed in the line of duty in Afghanistan following the September 11, 2001 terrorist attacks. Today, we serve all CIA officers who gave their last full measure of devotion to their country.[74]

Appendix

Glossary of Acronyms

Below is a list of some of the acronyms/terms used throughout the book:

ABGD	Air Base Ground Defense
AFOSI	U.S. Air Force Office of Special Investigations (also OSI)
AOP	Attack on Principal
CIA	Central Intelligence Agency
DCI	Director, Central Intelligence
DDCI	Deputy Director, Central Intelligence
EP	Executive Protection
IP	Intellectual Property
OSAC	Overseas Security Advisory Council
POI	Person of Interest
PSO	Protective Service Operation
RSO	Regional Security Officer
SME	Subject-Matter Expert
TVRA	Threat, Vulnerability and Risk Assessment
UHNW	Ultra High Net Worth
USAF	United States Air Force
USAFE	U.S. Air Forces in Europe (headquartered at Ramstein Air Base, Germany)

General Essential Requirements for an EP Program Manager

- Bachelor's or associate's degree
- Ten or more years of specific executive protection experience
  - Former military, government or corporate private-sector security management/leadership experience combined with ten-plus years of executive protection experience (or a combination of equivalent education and experience)
- Completion of an accredited or internationally recognized executive protection course or school in the private, government or military sectors
- First aid training preferred (i.e., First Responder or Medic certifications).
  - At a minimum, certification in all basic life support skills (CPR, AED, etc.)
- Advanced weapons training and experience
- Solid understanding of use of force policies and how they apply to rules of engagement
- Basic competency in self-defense techniques, but preferably advanced certification or experience
- Experience with conducting Threat, Vulnerability and Risk Assessments (TVRAs) related to executive and personal security
- Ability to identify, analyze and implement solutions for operational and management problems (from routine to moderately complex) with respect to EP, TVRAs, safeguarding of personnel and information, foreign travel and other special project areas as required
- Solid understanding and operational knowledge of obtaining institutional and open-source information for protective intelligence in order to plan and staff operations appropriately
- Strong understanding and previous experience with various types of security technology resources
- Comfort with and capacity for professional client interaction on the executive level
- Proven track record of planning, organizing and executing all levels of EP, inclusive of high-risk situations and travel to high-threat regions as required

- Ability to establish and maintain professional relationships with counterparts in related industries/disciplines to obtain common understanding of similar problems and sharing of any known solutions
- Ability and willingness to be available 24/7 and travel as needed

This person would also manage, develop key components for, and serve as an internal subject-matter expert to other program-related areas, which may include:

- Threat, Vulnerability and Risk Assessments (TVRAs)
- Protective intelligence
- Security driver programs
- Residential security design
- Manned 24/7 residential security
- Executive mail screening program
- Employee foreign travel safety and security
- Surveillance detection/countersurveillance
- Managing international third-party close protection specialist(s)
- Secure international ground transportation
- Private investigative services related to executive threats and persons of interest
- Security awareness training
- Specific skill training
- First responder and advanced medical training
- Background criminal checks and investigations relating to EP and persons of interest
- Special event security and security management relating to EP support
- Technical security countermeasures (TSCMs)
- Emergency preparedness planning
- Private aviation assessment and security
- Professional liaison and coordination efforts with local and federal law enforcement agencies
- Kidnap, ransom and recovery efforts based on profile of principal(s)

Endnotes

1   Ali Jaber. "Lebanon's President Killed as Bomb Rips His Motorcade; Peace Efforts Are Set Back." *The New York Times.* November 23, 1989. https://www.nytimes.com/1989/11/23/world/lebanon-s-president-killed-as-bomb-rips-his-motorcade-peace-efforts-are-set-back.html

2   Luisa Kroll and Kerry Dolan (editors). "Meet The Members Of The Three-Comma Club." Forbes. March 6, 2018. https://www.forbes.com/billionaires/#54f02136251c

3   Sam Meredith. "One billionaire created every two days in Asia, study says." CNBC. October 26, 2017. https://www.cnbc.com/2017/10/26/one-billionaire-created-every-two-days-in-asia-study-says.html

4   MarketsandMarkets. *Physical Security Market by Type (System (Access Control, Video Surveillance, PSIM, Perimeter Intrusion Detection & Prevention, Security Scanning, Imaging & Metal Detection, Fire & Life Safety), & Service), Vertical, and Region - Global Forecast to 2021.* March 2017. http://www.marketsandmarkets.com/Market-Reports/physical-security-market-1014.html

5   Steve Morgan. "Cybersecurity Industry Outlook: 2017 to 2021." CSO. October 20, 2016. http://www.csoonline.com/article/3132722/security/cybersecurity-industry-outlook-2017-to-2021.html

6   Jefferson Graham. "Are embedded microchips dangerous? Ask the Swedes — and pets." *USA Today.* July 25, 2017. https://www.usatoday.com/story/tech/talkingtech/2017/07/25/do-microchip-implants-pose-health-risks-ask-swedes-and-pets/507408001/

7   Aarti Shahani. "Getting 'Physical' And Emotional In Virtual Reality." NPR | All Tech Considered: Tech, Culture and Connection. June 1, 2015. http://www.npr.org/sections/alltechconsidered/2015/06/01/411233592/getting-physical-and-emotional-in-virtual-reality

8   World Economic Forum. *The Global Risks Report 12th Edition.* January 11, 2017. http://www3.weforum.org/docs/GRR17_Report_web.pdf

9   David C. Rapoport. "The Four Waves of Modern Terrorism" in *Attacking Terrorism: Elements of a Grand Strategy* (pp. 46–73), edited by Audrey Kurth Cronin and James M. Ludes. Georgetown University Press. Washington, D.C., 2004.

10   Jeffrey Simon. "Technological and Lone Operator Terrorism: Prospects for a Fifth Wave of Global Terrorism" in *Terrorism, Identity and Legitimacy: The Four Waves Theory and Political Violence* (pp. 44–65), edited by Jean Rosenfeld. Routledge. Oxford and New York. 2010.

11   Joshua Sinai. "Terrorism Future 2030: Identifying Analytic Methodologies to Forecast the Next Phase in the Terrorism Historical Wave" in *Security in 2025* (pp. 1–7), edited by Lawrence J. Fennelly, Mark Beaudry, PhD, CPP, and Marianna A. Perry. ASIS International. Alexandria. 2017.

12   Sophia Chen. "Quantum Internet is 13 Years Away. Wait, What's Quantum Internet?" *Wired.* August 15, 2017. https://www.wired.com/story/quantu m-internet-is-13-years-away-wait-whats-quantum-internet/; Don Hayford. "The Future of Security: Zeroing In On Un-Hackable Data With Quantum Key Distribution." *Wired.* September 2014. https://www.wired.com/ insights/2014/09/quantum-key-distribution/

13   Bulletproof Radio interview. March 17, 2015. https://blog.bulletproof.com/ marc-goodman-cyber-security-transhumanism-future-crimes-203/

14   National Safety Council. "2017 Estimates Show Vehicle Fatalities Topped 40,000 for Second Straight Year." Retrieved September 14, 2018. https:// www.nsc.org/road-safety/safety-topics/fatality-estimates

15   Tony Bradley. "Gartner Predicts Information Security Spending To Reach $93 Billion In 2018." Forbes. August 17, 2017. https://www.forbes.com/ sites/tonybradley/2017/08/17/gartner-predicts-information-security-spen ding-to-reach-93-billion-in-2018/

16   Steve Morgan. "Is cybercrime the greatest threat to every company in the world?" CSO. July 26, 2017. https://www.csoonline.com/article/3210912/se curity/is-cybercrime-the-greatest-threat-to-every-company-in-the-world. html

17   Federal Bureau of Investigation. "Incidents of Ransomware on the Rise." April 29, 2016. https://www.fbi.gov/news/stories/incidents-of-ransomware- on-the-rise

18   Jacob Morgan. "A Simple Explanation Of 'The Internet Of Things'." Forbes. May 13, 2014. https://www.forbes.com/sites/jacobmorgan/2014/05/13/simpl e-explanation-internet-things-that-anyone-can-understand/

19   The Institution of Engineering and Technology. *Automotive Cyber Security: An IET/KTN Thought Leadership Review of risk perspectives for connected*

vehicles. Event held in November 2014. https://www.theiet.org/sectors/transport/topics/autonomous-vehicles/articles/auto-cs.cfm

20 David Shepardson. "FBI chief says threats from drones to U.S. 'steadily escalating'." Reuters. October 10, 2018. https://www.reuters.com/article/us-usa-drones-security/fbi-chief-says-threats-from-drones-to-u-s-steadily-escalating-idUSKCN1MK22J

21 National Highway Traffic Safety Administration, U.S. Department of Transportation. *Distracted Driving 2016*. April 2018. https://crashstats.nhtsa.dot.gov/Api/Public/ViewPublication/812517

22 National Safety Council. "Cell phones are involved in an estimated 27 percent of all car crashes, says National Safety Council." June 17, 2015. https://www.nsc.org/in-the-newsroom/cell-phones-are-involved-in-an-estimated-27-percent-of-all-car-crashes-says-national-safety-council

23 James A. Roberts, Luc Honore Petnji Yaya And Chris Manolis. "The invisible addiction: Cell-phone activities and addiction among male and female college students." *Journal of Behavioral Addictions*, December 2014; 3(4): 254–265. https://www.ncbi.nlm.nih.gov/pmc/articles/PMC4291831/

24 Matt Richtel. "Attached to Technology and Paying a Price." *The New York Times*. June 6, 2010. http://www.nytimes.com/2010/06/07/technology/07brain.html

25 Alanna Petroff. "Elon Musk says Mark Zuckerberg's understanding of AI is 'limited'." CNN Tech. July 25, 2017. http://money.cnn.com/2017/07/25/technology/elon-musk-mark-zuckerberg-ai-artificial-intelligence/index.html

26 Arjun Kharpal. "Stephen Hawking says A.I. could be 'worst event in the history of our civilization'." CNBC. November 6, 2017. https://www.cnbc.com/2017/11/06/stephen-hawking-ai-could-be-worst-event-in-civilization.html

27 Osonde A. Osoba and William Welser IV. "The Risks of Artificial Intelligence to Security and the Future of Work." RAND Corporation. Santa Monica, CA. 2017. https://www.rand.org/pubs/perspectives/PE237.html.

28 Centers for Disease Control and Prevention. "QuickStats: Suicide Rates, for Teens Aged 15–19 Years, by Sex — United States 1975–2015." *Morbidity and Mortality Weekly Report*, 66(30);816. August 4, 2017. https://www.cdc.gov/mmwr/volumes/66/wr/mm6630a6.htm

29 The Jason Foundation. "Facts and Stats." Retrieved September 14, 2018. http://jasonfoundation.com/youth-suicide/facts-stats/

30   Cyberbullying Research Center. "New National Bullying and Cyberbullying Data." October 16, 2016. https://cyberbullying.org/new-national-bullying-cyberbullying-data

31   Monica Anderson and Jingjing Jiang. "Teens, Social Media & Technology 2018." Pew Research Center. May 31, 2018. http://www.pewinternet.org/2018/05/31/teens-social-media-technology-2018/

32   Ray Downs. "VA report: Suicide rate down overall, but up among younger vets." United Press International. September 27, 2018. https://www.upi.com/VA-report-Suicide-rate-down-overall-but-up-among-younger-vets/1491538021791/

33   Office of Suicide Prevention, U.S. Department of Veterans Affairs. *Suicide Among Veterans and Other Americans 2001–2014.* August 3, 2016. Updated August 2017. https://www.mentalhealth.va.gov/docs/2016suicidedatareport.pdf

34   U.S. Department of Veterans Affairs. "PTSD and Substance Abuse in Veterans." Retrieved September 14, 2018. https://www.ptsd.va.gov/public/problems/ptsd_substance_abuse_veterans.asp

35   Melody Petersen. "As need grows for painkiller overdose treatment, companies raise prices." Los Angeles Times. July 17, 2016. http://www.latimes.com/business/la-fi-naloxone-sales-20160707-snap-story.html

36   Dominick Dunne. "Death in Monaco." *Vanity Fair.* December 2000. https://www.vanityfair.com/culture/2000/12/dunne200012

37   Jeffrey Toobin. "The Patty Hearst kidnapping? You don't know the half of it." February 8, 2018. https://www.cnn.com/2018/02/07/opinions/patty-hearst-kidnapping-toobin-opinion/index.html See also *American Heiress: The Wild Saga of the Kidnapping, Crimes and Trial of Patty Hearst.* First Anchor Books, a division of Penguin Random House. April 2017.

38   Merriam-Webster.com. "terrorism." Retrieved September 14, 2018. https://www.merriam-webster.com/dictionary/terrorism

39   Bruce Hoffman. *Inside Terrorism,* Revised and Enlarged Edition. Columbia University Press. June 6, 2006.

40   Walter Laqueur. "Terrorism: A Brief History." *Foreign Policy Agenda* (May 2007), v.12 no.5. United States Department of State. https://www.hsdl.org/?view&did=474007

41   Dave Mosher and Skye Gould. "How likely are foreign terrorists to kill Americans? The odds may surprise you." *Business Insider.* January 31, 2017. http://www.businessinsider.com/death-risk-statistics-terrorism-disease-accidents-2017-1

42 Mariam Khan and Luis Martinez. "More than 5,000 Muslims Serving in US Military, Pentagon Says." ABC News. December 8, 2015. http://abcnews.go.com/US/5000-muslims-serving-us-military-pentagon/story?id=35654904

43 See: Jeremy Diamond and Sunlen Serfarty. "White House says more than 30 Americans held hostage abroad." CNN. June 24, 2015. https://www.cnn.com/2015/06/23/politics/hostage-policy-review-changes-white-house/index.html

44 National Center for Missing and Exploited Children. "Key Facts." Retrieved September 14, 2018. http://www.missingkids.com/KeyFacts

45 Robert A. Fein. "Preventing Attacks on Public Figures" in *The Psychology of Stalking: Clinical and Forensic Perspectives* (p. 191), edited by J. Reid Maloy. Academic Press. 2001.

46 John Mecklin (ed.). "It is 2 minutes to midnight." 2018 Doomsday Clock Statement, Science and Security Board, Bulletin of the Atomic Scientists. January 25, 2018. https://thebulletin.org/sites/default/files/2018%20Doomsday%20Clock%20Statement.pdf

47 2018 Doomsday Clock Statement, Science and Security Board, Bulletin of the Atomic Scientists.

48 Rachel Bronson, in: John Mecklin (ed.). "It is 2 minutes to midnight." 2018 Doomsday Clock Statement, Science and Security Board, Bulletin of the Atomic Scientists. January 25, 2018. https://thebulletin.org/sites/default/files/2018%20Doomsday%20Clock%20Statement.pdf

49 Ted Koppel. *Lights Out: A Cyberattack, A Nation Unprepared, Surviving the Aftermath.* Crown Publishers. 2015.

50 Ted Koppel. "A Letter from Ted Koppel." Retrieved September 14, 2018. http://tedkoppellightsout.com/letter

51 Evan Osnos. "Doomsday Prep for the Super Rich." *The New Yorker.* January 30, 2017. https://www.newyorker.com/magazine/2017/01/30/doomsday-prep-for-the-super-rich

52 Christopher A. Preble. "The Most Dangerous World Ever?" *Cato Policy Report.* Cato Institute. September/October 2014. https://www.cato.org/policy-report/septemberoctober-2014/most-dangerous-world-ever

53 Jessica Dillinger. "The Most Dangerous Cities in the World." World Atlas. Last updated April 25, 2018. https://www.worldatlas.com/articles/most-dangerous-cities-in-the-world.html

54 Gavin de Becker. *The Gift of Fear.* Dell Publishing. 1997.

55 Gavin de Becker. *Fear Less.* Little, Brown and Company. 2002.

56 Institute of Risk Management. "Risk appetite and tolerance." September 2011. https://www.theirm.org/knowledge-and-resources/thought-leadership/risk-appetite-and-tolerance/

57 Peter Hermann. "D.C. fire department medical director resigns, delivers scathing exit letter." *Washington Post*. February 9, 2016. https://www.washingtonpost.com/local/public-safety/dc-fire-departments-medical-director-resigns/2016/02/09/e8c8edd0-cf6f-11e5-88cd-753e80cd29ad_story.html

58 Mordechai Guri, Yisroel Mirsky and Yuval Elovici, Ben-Gurion University of the Negev. "Attackers Can Make it Impossible to Dial 911." January 5, 2017. *Government Technology*. http://www.govtech.com/public-safety/Attackers-Can-Make-it-Impossible-to-Dial-911.html

59 Andrew Blake. "iPhone 911-system hack results in felony charges for Arizona teen." *Washington Times*. October 29, 2016. http://www.washingtontimes.com/news/2016/oct/29/iphone-hack-ends-felony-hacking-charges-arizona-te/

60 "Timothy Webster & Kate Warne." Pinkerton Government Services. Archived from the original on October 15, 2006. Retrieved September 14, 2018. https://web.archive.org/web/20061015194719/http://www.pinkertons.com/webster.htm

61 Pinkerton Government Services.

62 *The 20ᵗʰ Anniversary of a Tragedy*. Center for Documentation and Exhibition of the History of US Americans in the Rhineland Palatinate. August 2008, reprint 2011. http://www.dc-ramstein.de/phocadownload/ausstellungen/211211ramstein.pdf

63 "Mit Video: Hinterbliebene und Überlebende des Ramstein-Flugtages gedachten der Opfer." *Austrian Wings*. August 28, 2018. https://www.austrianwings.info/2018/08/ramstein-gedenkfeierlichkeiten-zum-30-jahrestag-des-flugtagungluecks-haben-begonnen/ (viewed with translation)

64 "Ramstein 1988: Death falling from the clear blue sky." *Austrian Wings*. August 28, 2018. https://www.austrianwings.info/2018/08/ramstein-1988-death-falling-from-the-clear-sky/

65 Roland Fuchs. Personal narratives. Ramstein-1988. Accessed December 9, 2018. http://www.ramstein-1988.de/28412.html

66 Malcolm Gladwell. *Blink: The Power of Thinking Without Thinking*. Back Bay Books. 2007.

67 George Tenet with Bill Harlow. *At the Center of the Storm*. HarperCollins. 2007.

68 The Daniel Pearl Foundation. "About Danny." Retrieved September 14, 2018. http://www.danielpearl.org/home/about-us/about-danny/

69   Georgy Manaev, Dmitriy Romendik. "The dark history of Lubyanka." *Russia Beyond*. February 11, 2014. https://www.rbth.com/arts/2014/02/11/the_dark_history_of_lubyanka_32985

70   Hwang Sunghee. "N. Korean soldier shot trying defecting to S. Korea." Yahoo! News. November 13, 2017. https://www.yahoo.com/news/n-korean-soldier-shot-while-defecting-korea-seoul-081507424.html

71   "Khowst – 5 Years Later." Central Intelligence Agency. December 30, 2014. https://www.cia.gov/news-information/featured-story-archive/2014-featured-story-archive/khowst-5-years-later.html

72   "30 Years of Remembrance." Central Intelligence Agency. Posted May 23, 2017. Updated June 12, 2018. https://www.cia.gov/news-information/featured-story-archive/2017-featured-story-archive/30-years-of-remembrance.html

73   CIA Officers Memorial Foundation. "Foundation Fact Sheet." Retrieved September 14, 2018. https://www.ciamemorialfoundation.org/foundation-fact-sheet

74   CIA Officers Memorial Foundation. "About." Retrieved December 9, 2018. https://www.ciamemorialfoundation.org/about/

About the Author

Michael W. Trott is a respected and accomplished international security professional with over 30 years of experience. He has served as a U.S. Air Force Security Specialist and Special Agent with the CIA, worked for Fortune 100 corporations and protected ultra high net worth families. He continues to provide confidential advice and assistance to a diverse group of international clientele on matters of close protection, intelligence and security.